T0247722

United for Independence

Journal of the American Revolution Books highlight the latest research on new or lesser-known topics of the revolutionary era. The *Journal of the American Revolution* is an online resource and annual volume that provides educational, peer-reviewed articles by professional historians and experts in American Revolution studies.

A JOURNAL OF THE AMERICAN REVOLUTION BOOK

UNITED

FOR

INDEPENDENCE

THE REVOLUTIONARY WAR IN THE MIDDLE COLONIES, 1775–1776

MICHAEL CECERE

WESTHOLME
Yardley

Westholme Publishing, LLC
904 Edgewood Road
Yardley, Pennsylvania 19067
Visit our Web site at www.westholmepublishing.com

ISBN: 978-1-59416-402-6
Also available as an eBook.

Printed in the United States of America.

CONTENTS

Maps and Illustrations

L. Huron

N
W   E
S

Fort Detroit

Lake Ontario

Fort Niagara

Lake Erie

NORTHWEST TERRITORY

River

PROCLAMATION LINE OF 1763

1787

River

Indian Territories

Ohio

Fort Pitt

BLUE RIDGE MTS.

Susquehanna

PENNSYLVANIA

York

Philadelph

MARY

Wilmin
New Castle

Baltimore

Potomac River

LAND

Annapolis

Dover

DE

VIRGINIA

James

Lewistown

Ca
Cape
Henlope

River

Roanoke River

Chesapeake Bay

Williamsburg

VA

NC

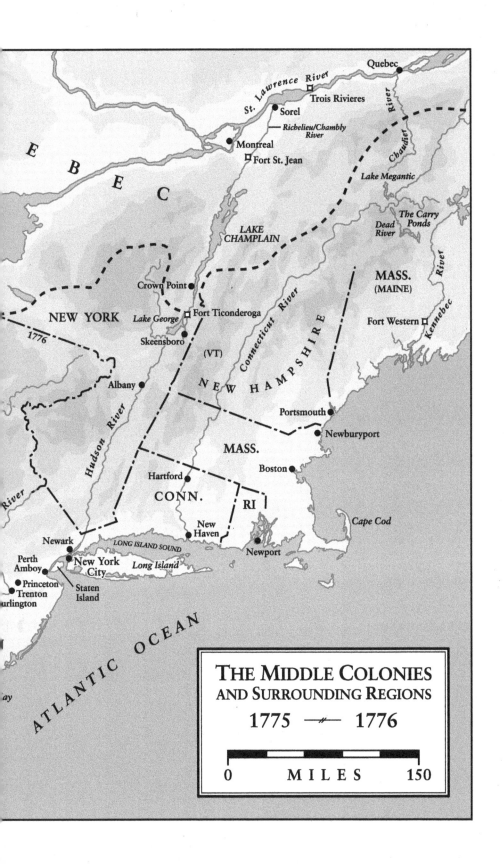

St. Lawrence River

Quebec

Trois Rivieres

Sorel

Richelieu/Chambly River

Montreal

Fort St. Jean

Chaudier River

Lake Megantic

QUEBEC

LAKE CHAMPLAIN

The Carry Ponds

Dead River

MASS. (MAINE)

Crown Point

NEW YORK

Lake George

Fort Ticonderoga

Connecticut River

Fort Western

Kennebec River

1776

Skeensboro

(VT)

NEW HAMPSHIRE

Albany

Hudson River

Portsmouth

Newburyport

MASS.

Boston

Hartford

CONN.

RI

New Haven

Cape Cod

Newark

LONG ISLAND SOUND

Long Island

Newport

Perth Amboy

New York City

Princeton

Staten Island

Trenton

urlington

River

ATLANTIC OCEAN

ay

THE MIDDLE COLONIES
AND SURROUNDING REGIONS
1775 —*— 1776

0   MILES   150

INTRODUCTION

The Middle Colonies on the Eve of the Revolution

IN CLASSROOMS ACROSS AMERICA, THE REVOLUTIONARY WAR IS taught as a conflict between Great Britain and her American colonies over the issues of taxes and independence. Students learn that the war began in the spring of 1775 at Lexington and Concord in Massachusetts. Some also learn about the battle of Bunker Hill near Boston and the creation of the Continental Army with General Washington at its head.

For many students, a great historical leap often occurs that takes them from the summer of 1775 to the summer of 1776 and the Declaration of Independence. After that, a few more battles are discussed (Trenton, Saratoga, Yorktown) and a few key people mentioned. Lessons on the American Revolution typically wrap up with the Treaty of Paris of 1783 and independence for America.

As a former high school history teacher, I am the first to admit that teaching the American Revolution and Revolutionary War under the guidelines of many school districts can be frustrating.

Such an oversimplification of history obscures the fact that a lot of important events occurred in all thirteen colonies during the Revolution that led to the final outcome of independence. For instance, it was not a foregone conclusion that the thirteen colonies would unite to fight against the British. Important events occurred in each colony in 1775 and 1776 to make this happen.

This work explores the key events that occurred in, or involved the inhabitants of, the Middle Colonies (New York, New Jersey, Pennsylvania, Delaware, and Maryland). It focuses on the time period from April 1775 through the summer of 1776. This seventeen-month span, from Lexington and Concord to the fall of New York, was critical to the development of colonial unity, a necessary ingredient for American victory.

Each colony approached the rebellion against Great Britain differently, and each has a unique story to tell. This book seeks to tell some of those stories for the Middle Colonies in the beginning of the Revolutionary War. By exploring these stories, readers should develop a better understanding of the Revolutionary War in the Middle Colonies and a greater appreciation for what occurred there.

New York
Separated geographically from New England by the Hudson River and culturally by its origins as a Dutch colony, the population of New York in 1775 was approximately 185,000 colonists.[1] Inhabitants were concentrated on Manhattan Island and Long Island and along the Hudson River up to Albany. Half of New York's non-native inhabitants were of English descent, nearly one in five were Dutch, and one in ten African, mostly enslaved.[2]

William Tryon was the royal governor of New York in 1775, although he was not present during the first half of that year. A former officer in the British army, he had seen battle in France during the French and Indian War. He also saw battle as governor of North Carolina in 1771 when he led loyal militia against a large number of North Carolina regulators who were upset at what they viewed as government corruption in the colony. Tryon and his smaller force of North Carolina militia crushed the regulators at the Battle of Alamance in May 1771.

Two months after this battle, Tryon assumed the governorship of New York. In late 1773 his home and all its contents were lost in a fire. Several months later he sailed to England to conduct personal affairs, leaving Lieutenant Governor Cadwallader Colden in New York to handle an increasingly tense situation over tea.

Colonists throughout North America waited in the spring of 1774 for Parliament's response to the Boston Tea Party of December 1773. The first reports of Parliament's response arrived in mid-May and sparked widespread concern. Parliament had decided to close Boston Harbor on June 1, occupy the town with thousands of British troops, and suspend the colonial government of Massachusetts, placing General Thomas Gage in charge.

The severity of the measures against Massachusetts prompted a gathering of merchants in New York City to form a Committee of Fifty-One to, "correspond with Our Sister Colonies upon all Matters of Moment."[3] In early July, a large crowd gathered on the edge of the city to denounce the Boston Port Bill, which closed Boston Harbor, and endorse the implementation of a continental wide non-importation association (a boycott of British goods).[4] They also called for a provincial convention to select delegates to a continental congress in Philadelphia and instituted a subscription to raise funds for the relief of Boston.[5]

New York sent nine delegates to the Continental Congress in September 1774 to represent the colony. They were, Isaac Low, John Alsop, James Duane, John Jay, Philip Livingston, William Floyd, Henry Wisner, John Haring, and Simon Boerum. Two months of debate in Philadelphia produced a non-importation and non-exportation agreement known as the Continental Association. It was to remain in effect until Parliament rescinded the Intolerable Acts against Massachusetts.

Although the New York delegation in Philadelphia and the bulk of residents of New York City supported the economic measures adopted by Congress, the more conservative New York colonial legislature, whose members last faced election in 1769, refused by one vote to approve (or even discuss) the proceedings of the Continental Congress.[6] This decision bolstered British hopes of dividing the colonies and disappointed the other American colonies which saw New York, as well as Georgia and East Florida (neither of which sent delegations to the First Continental Congress) as weak links to continental unity.

Lieutenant Governor Colden claimed that the refusal of New York's Assembly to even consider the measures of the Continental Congress reflected the "true sense of a great majority of the people and of men of the best fortunes."[7] Yet, Colden sheepishly acknowledged that the measures adopted by Congress were actually, "rigidly maintained in this place."[8] He lamented to Lord Dartmouth, Secretary of State for the colonies, that "the success . . . which the violent party have had in preventing . . . vessels from landing their cargoes here has given them great spirits and is a strong counterpoise to the conduct of the Assembly."[9] In other words, although the New York legislature had refused to support a boycott of British goods, a large number of New Yorkers had, and commerce with Great Britain was largely halted as a result. Lieutenant Governor Colden described those responsible as, "a set of violent spirits of the lowest rank and desperate fortunes, countenanced by a few of superior condition who lay hold of every occasion to raise mob and excite sedition."[10]

It was concern over the actions of the "violent party," as Colden referred to them, that prompted the lieutenant governor to request reinforcements for the small garrison of approximately one hundred British troops posted in New York City.

He also requested the presence of a large British warship to be available to "put two or three hundred men on shore," if necessary, and to "obstruct the passage of the [Hudson] river."[11] Colden justified his request by citing threats made by some colonies to punish New York for the legislative assembly's refusal to endorse Congress's continental association. The HMS *Kingfisher* (6 guns, 100 men) was anchored in New York Harbor at the time of Colden's request, but with tensions increasing daily, the lieutenant governor was not confident the sloop could adequately protect the King's interests in New York much longer.[12]

Not everyone shared Lieutenant Governor Colden's view that a majority of New Yorkers opposed the Continental Congress. A Committee of Sixty, created in the city in November 1774 to replace the more conservative Committee of Fifty-One and better implement Congress's Continental Association, served as a counterbalance to the more conservative colonial legislature. Despite the legislature's refusal to adopt or endorse the association in January 1775, the Committee of Sixty successfully enforced its measures and in correspondence with other colonies, the committee declared that, "the People [of New York] in general are zealous in the Cause."[13]

The refusal of the New York Assembly to appoint delegates to a Second Continental Congress prompted the Committee of Sixty in March 1775 to call for a Provisional Convention to do so. The convention met on April 20 and the following day appointed thirteen delegates to the Congress, adding Philip Schuyler, George Clinton, Robert Livingston Jr., Lewis Morris, and Francis Lewis to join eight of the nine original delegates. Isaac Law was the only delegate not to return to Congress. The Convention then adjourned, leaving the Committee of Sixty to manage affairs.[14] Shocking news from the north soon arrived to direct the course of those affairs.

NEW JERSEY

New Jersey's population in 1775 was roughly two-thirds the size of New York's with approximately 128,000 colonists, nearly half of whom were English, seventeen percent Dutch, and approximately seven percent African, most of whom were enslaved.[15] The royal governor of New Jersey was William Franklin, son of the most famous American at the time, Benjamin Franklin. With over a decade of service as governor, Franklin was likely the most influential leader in New Jersey. This is perhaps why he pledged to the British Ministry with some confidence upon news of the Intolerable Acts in the spring of 1774 to, "omit nothing in my power to keep this province quiet."[16]

True to his word, Governor Franklin refused to convene the New Jersey Assembly when requested to do so in the wake of reports about Parliament's harsh measures against Boston. Although he could prevent the assembly from meeting, he could do little about the various county committees in New Jersey, so they became the means for the populace to express their opposition to Parliament and their support for Boston. As a result of the county meetings, a provincial convention was convened in New Brunswick on July 21, 1774, to select delegates to the First Continental Congress. Stephen Crane, James Kinsey, Richard Smith Jr., John de Hart, and William Livingston were selected to represent New Jersey.[17] The convention also condemned the Intolerable Acts against Boston and endorsed a non-importation and non-exportation association.

In the fall of 1774 the Continental Congress, with the New Jersey delegation's concurrence, adopted this measure. Governor Franklin tried to persuade the New Jersey Assembly, which met in February 1775, to forsake the Continental Congress the way the New York Assembly had and embrace more moderate measures to oppose British policies. The assembly listened politely to Governor Franklin's appeal and then ignored it, voting overwhelmingly to approve the continental association adopted by the Continental Congress.[18] The assembly did, however, also send its own colonial petition to King George III, risking a possible fracture of unity with the rest of the colonies.

PENNSYLVANIA

Pennsylvania in 1775 was the largest of the mid-Atlantic colonies with a population of approximately 285,000 colonists. The most ethnically diverse of the American colonies, about one-third of the population was English, one-third German, and nearly one-sixth Irish. Approximately 2.5% of Pennsylvania's population was of African origin, most of whom were enslaved.[19] One of the few proprietary colonies remaining, John Penn served as governor of both Pennsylvania and the three lower counties (Delaware). Like Governor Franklin, Governor Penn did nothing to encourage opposition to Parliament and when the news of Parliament's actions against Boston reached Pennsylvania in May 1774, Penn refused several requests to call the Pennsylvania Assembly into session.[20] In response, thousands of colonists met in Philadelphia in June and selected a large committee of correspondence to coordinate their opposition to the Intolerable Acts amongst themselves and the other colonies. The meeting condemned the closure of Boston Harbor, endorsed a continental wide congress, began a subscription for the relief of Boston, and called for a convention to select delegates to the proposed congress.[21]

A crisis on the Pennsylvania and Virginia frontier forced Governor Penn to reluctantly convene the colonial assembly in mid-July 1774, three days after the Pennsylvania Convention convened. The Convention seized the opportunity to solicit the assembly to participate in the process, sending a delegation to the assembly to seek their input on a proposed continental congress. The Pennsylvania assembly agreed that a continental congress was needed and appointed Joseph Galloway, the assembly's conservative speaker, along with Charles Humphreys, Thomas Mifflin, Edward Biddle, John Morton, and George Ross as delegates.[22] John Dickinson, considered by many "the penman of the Revolution" for his series of *Letters from a Pennsylvania Farmer* in the 1760s, which significantly swelled opposition to British colonial policies in the colonies, was added later.

DELAWARE

The colony of Delaware did not actually exist in 1775. Made up of just three counties, New Castle, Kent, and Sussex, the Lower Counties, as they were referred to prior to 1776, were proprietary to the Penn family. As a result, they shared the same governor as Pennsylvania, John Penn, and were closely linked to that colony economically and socially. The Lower Counties did, however, have their own legislative assembly, which provided them with some degree of autonomy from Pennsylvania.

With a population of just 40,000 colonists in 1775, sixty percent of whom were English, ten percent Swedish, and approximately seven percent African, most of whom were enslaved, the Lower Counties did not wield the influence of Massachusetts, New York, Pennsylvania, or Virginia.[23] Yet, when the call went out for delegates to assemble in Philadelphia to meet in a continental congress, Delaware made sure it had a place at the table.

Delaware's decision to send delegates to the Continental Congress in Philadelphia was largely the result of county leaders insisting that steps be taken to support Massachusetts against Parliament's Intolerable Acts. After some grumbling over the location of a provincial convention to select delegates to Congress, it was agreed to hold the meeting in New Castle in early August. Representatives from the three counties gathered and selected Caesar Rodney, George Read, and Thomas McKean as Delaware's delegates.

The Delaware Assembly, which convened in March 1775, approved of the measures adopted by the First Continental Congress and reappointed Rodney, Read and McKean to represent Delaware in the next Congress scheduled for May 1775.[24]

MARYLAND

Maryland's population in 1775 was approximately 225,000 colonists, nearly two-thirds of whom were English and approximately one-third African.[25] The vast majority of the latter were enslaved, most of whom served as field hands to raise tobacco, the chief export of Maryland. There was also a growing German population in the western region of the colony.[26]

Maryland's large slave population and heavy reliance on a cash crop for export was more in keeping with Virginia and the other southern colonies than the mid-Atlantic colonies, but its proximity to Delaware and Pennsylvania drew Maryland into mid-Atlantic affairs as much as southern.

When news of Parliament's measures against Boston reached Maryland in late May 1774, county committees sprang into action, holding meetings throughout the colony that proclaimed their support for Boston. Many called for a non-importation and non-exportation association and subscriptions to send relief to Boston were raised.

Moving faster than most colonies, Maryland held a convention of county delegates in Annapolis on June 22, and selected Matthew Tilghman, Thomas Johnson Jr., Robert Goldsborough, William Paca, and Samuel Chase as Maryland's delegates to the Continental Congress. The convention instructed the delegates to support both a non-importation and a non-exportation measure should the Congress bring them up for consideration.[27] That is, of course, exactly what the Congress approved in the fall of 1774.

Before Congress had completed its work in Philadelphia, an incident occurred in Maryland that demonstrated the colony's determination to resist Parliament's unconstitutional policies. The ship *Peggy Stewart*, a brig, arrived in Annapolis from England on October 15 with over two thousand pounds of tea in its hold.[28] When it was learned that the owner of the vessel paid the duties upon the tea, duties that were universally viewed as unconstitutional by the American colonists, a colony wide meeting in Annapolis was called to consider what was to be done.

Although a majority of those in attendance were willing to accept the ship owner's sincere apology and the destruction of the tea as punishment for his actions, others insisted that his ship be burned as well. The owner, hoping to appease the vocal and violent minority (to prevent his own exposure to tar and feathers) offered to burn his vessel to demonstrate his sincerity and his offer was accepted. The vessel was then beached and torched, sending a clear message that Maryland would embrace extreme measures to oppose Parliament's illegal policies and actions.[29]

That message was reiterated in December when another convention met in Annapolis to endorse the proceedings of the Continental Congress and select delegates to the next congress scheduled for May in Philadelphia. One of the resolutions the Maryland Convention adopted at its December meeting was to recommend to the colony's male inhabitants between the ages of sixteen and fifty, "to form themselves into companies of sixty-eight men . . . use their utmost endeavors to make themselves masters of the military exercise . . . and be in readiness to act on any emergency."[30] Of all of the colonies outside of New England, Maryland adopted the most militaristic response to the Intolerable Acts. The other colonies would soon follow.

Part I
1775

One

Spring

CONTRADICTORY REPORTS FROM GREAT BRITAIN OVER THE winter of 1774-75 of reconciliation efforts in Parliament on the one hand, and new policies to disarm the American colonies and subdue Massachusetts on the other, left most colonists in America uncertain and anxious as spring commenced in 1775. Letters published in the colonial newspapers in the early months of 1775 fostered hope that the continental boycott might persuade Parliament to rescind its harsh measures against Massachusetts. Other reports of gunpowder and arms restrictions upon the colonies and of the King's support for Parliament, however, alarmed the colonists. Their alarm only grew with the advent of spring when reports arrived that additional British troops were bound for Boston. Virginian Patrick Henry captured the view of many colonists in March when he asked at the Second Virginia Convention, "Are fleets and armies necessary . . . [for] reconciliation?"[1]

Henry answered his own question with an emphatic declaration; "Let us not deceive ourselves, sir. These are the implements of war and subjugation!"[2] He was proven correct less than a month later at Lexington and Concord.

New York

Reports began to circulate in New York City on the morning of April 23 of a bloody clash four days earlier in Massachusetts between British troops and Massachusetts militia, but as the first reports contained few details, they were initially discredited.[3] When an express rider from the New Haven Committee of Correspondence arrived in the city around noon with an express confirming the bloodshed in Massachusetts, however, the city erupted in excitement and concern. "This whole city was in a state of alarm," remembered one observer. "Every face appeared animated with resentment."[4] Loyalist Thomas Jones, a justice on New York's Supreme Court, disdainfully described the reaction of the city to the news about Massachusetts.

> Isaac Sears, John Lamb, and Donald Campbell . . . paraded the town with drums beating and colours flying, (attended by a mob of negroes, boys, sailors, and pickpockets) inviting all mankind to take up arms in defence of the "injured rights and liberties of America."[5]

The "mob" described by Jones marched to the docks and forcibly unloaded two ships full of foodstuffs destined for the British army in Boston.[6] They also broke into the public arsenal at City Hall and seized hundreds of muskets, bayonets, and cartridge boxes as well as over a thousand pounds of gunpowder.[7]

Jones recalled that, "the whole city became one continued scene of riot, tumult, and confusion."[8] Captain James Montagu onboard the HMS *Kingfisher* in New York Harbor confirmed Jones's description, reporting that

> The Major part of the People here are almost in a State of Rebellion, they have broke open the City Hall, and distributed the City Arms to the Mob, were it not for the Assistance I have given the Transports, make not the least doubt but they would have burnt them.[9]

Peter Vandervoort's description of events in New York City in the days following the news of Lexington and Concord not only described a state of rebellion in the city, but a preparation for war. "Every day we have had People Marching both day & Night through the Streets with Arms & they are Exercising and Entering into Companies every day."[10] Expecting New York to become a "seat of war in America," Vandervoort, like many, sought to escape the city with his family and valuables.[11] Another account from an unidentified gentleman in New York noted that,

> In the course of the week they formed themselves into companies under Officers of their own chusing, distributed the arms, called a Provincial Congress, demanded the keys of the Customhouse, and shut up the Port, trained their men publically, convened the Citizens by beat of drum, drew the cannon into the interior country, and formed an association of defence in perfect league with the rest of the Continent.[12]

In response to the defiant and illegal actions of the mob in New York, as well as Lieutenant Governor Colden's earlier appeal for a larger warship, Vice Admiral Samuel Graves in Boston ordered the HMS *Asia* (64 guns, 480 men) to New York with instructions to secure whatever cannon, arms, and gunpowder that belonged to the King that had not already been seized by the populace.[13]

With royal authority in New York City largely extinguished by the news of Lexington and Concord, New York's patriot leaders moved to provide some order in the city. On April 26, the Committee of Sixty, which had become the de facto governing body of the city, called for the creation of a larger Committee of One Hundred. They also supported the formation of another Provincial Congress for the colony.[14]

Three days later, a large crowd gathered outside the Merchants' Coffee House and approved a General Association, pledging to

> Adopt and endeavor to carry into execution whatever measures may be recommended by the Continental Congress or . . . our Provincial Convention for the purpose of preserving our Constitution.[15]

On the same day, a much larger crowd of "about six or seven thousand" gathered on the plain just outside the city limits and, "one and all unanimously voted to defend their liberties &ct. at all hazards."[16]

Lieutenant Governor Cadwallader Colden confirmed the near absolute loss of royal authority in early May, writing to Lord Dartmouth in London that upon the news of bloodshed in Massachusetts,

> The people were assembled and that scene of disorder and violence begun which has entirely prostrated the powers of government and produced an association by which this province has solemnly united with the others in resisting the Acts of Parliament.[17]

Support among New Yorkers for the Continental Congress was demonstrated just a few days later when throngs of inhabitants lined the streets to cheer the congressional delegations from Connecticut and Massachusetts that passed through New York on their way to Philadelphia for the Second Continental Congress. Church bells pealed throughout the city to announce their arrival.[18]

While an enormous number of New Yorkers proclaimed their readiness to fight for their rights, 250 miles to the north, colonists from Connecticut, Massachusetts, and the future state of Vermont demonstrated their own readiness by seizing two forts in New York on Lake Champlain, Fort Ticonderoga and Crown Point, from the British.

Fort Ticonderoga was situated on the west bank of Lake Champlain, about thirty miles from the southern end and ninety-five miles from the northern end of the lake. Built by the French in the 1750's to prevent the British from using Lake Champlain as an invasion route to Canada, it fell into British hands in 1759 during the French and Indian War. Although the French withdrawal from Canada after the war reduced the strategic importance of Fort Ticonderoga, it remained a significant, albeit neglected, British post on the New York frontier until 1775.

What made Fort Ticonderoga important to the American rebels in New England was not its location, but rather, the number and size of the cannon and ordnance within the fort, guarded by a tiny garrison of just fifty soldiers. The cannon, shot, and powder stored at Ticonderoga as well as another smaller British fort just twelve miles up the lake at Crown Point, made both forts irresistible targets to those in dire need of both cannon and powder in Massachusetts.

In early May, two separate American detachments, unaware of each other and with no coordination with the Continental Congress, set out to seize Fort Ticonderoga and Crown Point. Colonel Ethan Allen commanded the first detachment, made up mostly of several hundred Green Mountain Boys from the New Hampshire grants (Vermont). Authorized by Connecticut officials to seize the fort as soon as possible, Allen led his men into position on May 9. He was unexpectedly joined by Colonel Benedict Arnold, who was from Connecticut but possessed a commission from the Massachusetts Committee of Safety to seize the fort and send the cannon and ordnance to Massachusetts.

When Arnold discovered Ethan Allen's intention to seize Fort Ticonderoga, he rushed to assume command. As his troops were still being recruited in western Massachusetts and not with him, Arnold's claim of command was ridiculed and ignored. Colonel Allen proceeded across the lake in the early morning hours of May 10 with less than ninety men (and Colonel Arnold, who insisted on accompanying Allen). They charged a lone sentry at the main gate, which was open, and stormed into the fort against no opposition.[19] Allen and Arnold quickly compelled the fort's half-dressed commander, Captain William Delaplace, to surrender the fort and by the end of the day sent the garrison of approximately fifty British prisoners southward to Skenesboro at the southern end of the lake. Two days later Captain Seth Warner with just fifty Green Mountain Boys captured the small British garrison at Crown Point. The two forts held nearly two hundred cannon, three-quarters of which were still serviceable.[20]

The arrival of a schooner captured at Skenesboro allowed Colonel Arnold to take even bolder action a few days later. He sailed up Lake Champlain on the schooner that he named *Liberty*, accompanied by two bateaux with thirty-five men, and raided a small British garrison at St-Jean on the Richelieu River in Canada on May 18. In doing so, he captured a sloop and five additional bateaux, destroying four others to prevent their use by the British.[21]

On the same day that Arnold raided St-Jean, the Continental Congress in Philadelphia reacted to the news of the capture of Fort Ticonderoga by calling for the abandonment of the fort and the movement of the cannon, ordnance, and troops to the southern end of Lake George. Many in Congress still believed the dispute with Great Britain could be peacefully resolved and once it was, the military stores seized in the forts would then be returned.[22]

While Congress maintained hope for reconciliation, it also reacted to growing threats to the colonies, including reports of a large British military force sailing for New York. In response to these reports, Congress recommended that New York's inhabitants act on the defensive and that the one hundred British troops still stationed in New York City "Be permitted to remain in the barracks," so long as they don't build fortifications or interfere with communication with the countryside.[23] If these troops did "commit hostilities or invade private property," asserted Congress, "the inhabitants should defend themselves and their property and repel force by force."[24]

Before the instructions to move the cannon and ordnance from the two forts on Lake Champlain reached Benedict Arnold (who had assumed command of Fort Ticonderoga from Ethan Allen when Allen's force largely dissolved and went home while Arnold's troops finally arrived), Arnold was informed that four hundred British troops, supported by Indians and some French militia, were preparing to move down the lake to attack. Arnold sent several dispatches to Connecticut and Massachusetts calling for reinforcements. When one of the dispatches was forwarded to the Continental Congress at the end of May, Congress reversed itself and ordered Arnold to retain Fort Ticonderoga.[25] It also instructed Connecticut to send a large reinforcement to help hold the fort.

Although New Yorkers played no role in the capture of Fort Ticonderoga in May 1775, many demonstrated their willingness to fight by joining military units formed in the city and colony. One writer to the *New York Mercury* observed in mid-May that,

The Martial Spirit diffused through this Province at this Juncture is almost beyond Conception; many new Companies have been already raised in this City and several more are in Contemplation.[26]

The arrival of the HMS *Asia* on May 26, and continued reports that a large force of British troops were destined for New York, suggested that such a martial spirit was justified.

The day before the *Asia* arrived, the Continental Congress in Philadelphia urged New York's leaders to fortify King's Bridge (on the northern end of Manhattan Island) as well as the Highlands along the Hudson River to obstruct, if necessary, passage of British warships up the river. Congress also urged New York's leaders to put the militia "in Constant readiness to act at a moment's warning," and suggested that up to 3,000 troops, enlisted to serve for the remainder of the year, might be placed under continental establishment. This meant that the Continental Congress might assume responsibility for and ultimately authority over thousands of troops from New York.[27]

New York's Provincial Congress met at the end of May to consider these recommendations and begin the process of governing the colony in place of royal authority.

NEW JERSEY

The news of Lexington and Concord reached New Jersey the same day it reached New York and spread quickly into the interior of the colony. The reaction among the colonists of New Jersey was similar to those in New York. On April 24, the Newark Committee of Safety declared that they were willing to risk their lives and fortunes to support American liberty and recommended to the captains of the local militia to muster and exercise their men at least once a week.[28] The committee in Morris County voted to raise three hundred volunteers to drill once a week and the committee in Woodbridge applauded the bravery of the Massachusetts militia and voted to put themselves in the best posture of defense.[29] Monmouth County's leaders declared that although they wished to remain united with Great Britain, they were determined to oppose Parliament's illegal actions, so they voted to raise funds to purchase gunpowder and shot and recommended that every man capable of bearing arms join volunteer companies to train and prepare to march at a minute's notice.[30] Governor William Franklin was powerless to stop these actions and anxiously described New Jersey's militant response to the events in Massachusetts to Lord Dartmouth in early May.

> The accounts we have from Massachusetts Bay . . . have occasioned such an alarm and excited so much uneasiness among the people throughout this and the other colonies that there is danger of their committing some outrageous violences before the present heats can subside. They are arming themselves, forming into companies and taking uncommon pains to perfect themselves in military discipline. Every day new alarms are spread which make them suspicious, and prevent their paying any attention to the dictates of sober reason and commonsense. . . . All legal authority and government seems to be drawing to an end here and that of congresses, conventions and committees establishing in their place.[31]

Although a number of counties and towns in New Jersey reacted to the news of Lexington and Concord with militant measures intended to bolster their militia in preparation for conflict, this response was not universal throughout the colony, nor were they as militant as what occurred in New York City or in New England.

Rather than look to armed conflict, New Jersey's Committee of Correspondence called for a Provincial Congress to meet to "consider and determine such matters as may then and there come before them."[32] Such an astonishingly vague mandate was nothing short of a call for a replacement of royal authority in New Jersey. The colonial assembly was due to meet in mid-May upon Governor Franklin's summons to consider a reconciliation proposal from the British Ministry, but New Jersey's leaders knew that Franklin had the authority to dismiss the assembly at his pleasure and would likely do so the moment that body took steps to support Massachusetts, steps he would almost certainly disagree with.

In fact, the assembly met in Perth Amboy for only five days. The representatives listened to Governor Franklin's appeal in support of

Britain's reconciliation plan and refused to endorse it, preferring instead to maintain colonial unity by deferring to the Second Continental Congress, which had convened in Philadelphia on May 10. Discouraged by this action and frustrated by the publication of excerpts of letters he had written to the British Ministry months earlier in which he discussed ways to undermine patriot efforts, Governor Franklin prorogued the assembly until late June.[33]

Just three days later, some of the same men who had sat in the assembly joined delegates in Trenton for New Jersey's Provincial Congress. Governor Franklin was powerless to halt the proceedings and those assembled stressed their desire to "make our Provincial measures consistent with that plan which may be devised and recommended by the Continental Congress," in Philadelphia.[34]

Reluctant to get out ahead of the Continental Congress, the New Jersey Provincial Congress was cautious until the end of its session in early June. Declaring their belief that it was "highly necessary that the inhabitants of this Province be forthwith properly armed and disciplined, for defending the cause of American liberty," the delegates passed several resolutions to strengthen the colony's militia.[35] They called on each town and county to,

> Acquaint themselves with the number of male inhabitants in their respective districts from the age of sixteen to fifty who are capable of bearing arms; and thereupon form them into companies of eighty men.[36]

Each company would elect its own officers and then join with other companies to form regiments, selecting the regimental officers from among the company commanders.[37]

To pay the substantial costs of raising such a force, the Provincial Congress, "being persuaded that every inhabitant is willing and desirous to contribute his proportion of money for so important a purpose," directed that £10,000 be raised by the townships and counties.[38] The Provincial Congress then adjourned until August.

PENNSYLVANIA

When the news of Lexington and Concord reached Philadelphia on April 24, many of the inhabitants reacted as they did in New York, proclaiming their determination to resist. One unidentified eyewitness reported that the news was read "to multitudes of people, who were animated almost to madness," and "the whole city was in the greatest ferment." [39] One observer noted in the *Pennsylvania Gazette* in early May that "Mars has established his empire in this populous city; and it is not doubted but we shall have in a few weeks from this date, 4000 men, well equipped, for our own defense or for the assistance of our neighbors."[40] Each ward of the city was to raise at least one company of infantry and there were two troops (detachments) of cavalry, two companies of expert riflemen, and two companies of artillery also forming.[41] Another observer claimed that a number of Quakers, who were pacifists, were even swept up by the military display.

> It is impossible to describe the military ardor which now prevails in this City. A considerable number of Friends [Quakers] have joined in the military Association. There is one Company composed entirely of Gentlemen belonging to that religious denomination of people.[42]

The strict pacifism of Pennsylvania's Quakers, which casts doubt on the observation above, was one reason Pennsylvania did not maintain a formal militia system as its neighboring colonies did. Instead, in times of crisis, Pennsylvania's leaders enacted temporary laws to raise troops.[43]

Those who disagreed with this approach, including Benjamin Franklin, formed volunteer military associations as early as 1747. As volunteer organizations, colonial officials had little control or influence over these Associator units and in truth, there had been little need for them since the end of the French and Indian War in 1763. Most had become dormant.[44]

The news of Lexington and Concord changed this, and communities throughout Pennsylvania formed companies of Associators ready to fight. A resident of Reading, Pennsylvania, noted on April 26 that, "We have raised in this Town two Companies of Foot, under proper Officers: and such is the spirit of the people of this free County, that in three weeks time there is not a Township in it that will not have a Company raised and disciplined, ready to assert at the risk of their lives, the freedom of America."[45]

The Pennsylvania Assembly, which convened on May 2 to consider Parliament's reconciliation plan introduced by Governor Penn, politely refused to endorse it because it did not provide a "reasonable ground for a final accommodation."[46] The Assembly's desire to maintain unity with the other colonies was also a significant reason it dismissed the plan.

The Assembly turned its attention to a petition from a large number of inhabitants of Philadelphia that urged the legislature to prepare for civil war, which, according to the petitioners, "in all probability must, in its course, soon reach Pennsylvania."[47] The petitioners specifically requested that the assembly raise "at least . . . Fifty Thousand Pounds, toward putting this Province into a state of defense."[48] The assembly debated the proposal for over a week and formed a committee of thirteen that included John Dickinson, Thomas Mifflin, Anthony Wayne, and William Thompson, to take measures to provide military stores for the growing number of Associators. The assembly disappointed the petitioners, however, by limiting the funds to pay for the military stores to only five thousand pounds.[49] The body then adjourned until mid-June.

While the Pennsylvania Assembly mildly embraced the notion of armed resistance to Great Britain, local communities throughout the commonwealth energetically prepared to fight, and no community prepared with more enthusiasm than Philadelphia. Richard Caswell, a delegate to the Second Continental Congress from North Carolina, described the military activities he witnessed in Philadelphia upon his arrival on May 7.

Here a Greater Martial Spirit prevails if possible, than I have been describing in Virginia & Maryland. They have 28 Companies Compleat which make near 2000 Men who March out to the

Common & go thro their Exercise twice a Day regularly. Scarce any thing But Warlike Musick is to be heard in the Streets, there are Several Companies of Quakers only, and many of them beside enrolled in Other Companies promiscuously. Tis sayd they will in a few days have 3000 Men under Arms ready to defend their Liberties.[50]

Fellow North Carolina delegate Joseph Hewes commented on the amazing change that had gripped the inhabitants of Philadelphia since he was last in town in late 1774 for the First Continental Congress.

It is impossible to describe the Spirit of these people and the alteration they have undergone since I left them in December last. All the Quakers except a few of the old Rigid ones have taken up arms, there is not one Company without several of these people in it.[51]

Hewes confirmed Richard Caswell's observation that "Nothing is heard but the sound of Drums & Fifes, all Ranks & Degrees of men are in Arms learning the Manual Exercise Evolution & the management of Artillery."[52]

Southern delegates to Congress were not the only ones impressed by Pennsylvania's military spirit. Silas Deane, a delegate from Connecticut, declared to his wife upon his arrival in Philadelphia that "You think Your Spirit is high, believe Me it is as much warmer here as the Climate and every kind of preparation goes on rapidly; and I seriously believe Pennsylvania will in one Month, have more than Twenty Thousand well disciplined Troops ready to take the Field."[53]

DELAWARE

The news of fighting in Massachusetts reached Delaware only hours after it reached Philadelphia. Thomas Rodney recalled that when word reached the town of Dover, in Kent County, "The Inhabitants of the Town and its Neighborhood assembled at the Court House, unanimously appointed me their Captain and formed themselves into a Military Company for the defence of their rights."[54] Similar activity occurred in the other two Delaware counties.

Captain Rodney informed his brother Caesar in early May that "There is Ten Companies already inroll'd and we expect all the rest will be inrolled this week . . . . The people go so fully into it that I expect we shall form Twenty Companies."[55]

Caesar Rodney observed similar enthusiasm in the inhabitants of New Castle County, where the county committee levied a one shilling six pence tax on residents in order to properly equip and supply the militia companies that were forming. Rodney informed his brother Thomas that "the people pay it with more cheerfulness than they have been known to pay any tax."[56] This may not have been altogether accurate, however, for ten days after Rodney's observation, the New Castle County Committee acknowledged some difficulty with raising revenue from the new tax.[57]

With the provincial assembly adjourned until June and no colony-wide extralegal body in existence in Delaware, the three county committees led Delaware's response to events. The New Castle County Committee, which five months earlier in December had boldly recommended that all men between the ages of sixteen and fifty assemble themselves into companies and "use the utmost endeavors to make themselves masters of the military exercise" had significant success raising troops in the spring because of the groundwork the committee laid the previous December.[58] Kent and Sussex Counties, animated by the news from Massachusetts, were not far behind New Castle County in their recruitment of militia in the spring of 1775.[59] While the colonists of Delaware prepared to fight, they also looked to the Continental Congress to take the lead on policy. As in the other colonies, unity remained essential to the inhabitants of Delaware.

MARYLAND

In Maryland, the reaction to the news of Lexington and Concord, which arrived in Annapolis on April 26, was similar to the other mid-Atlantic colonies. Governor Robert Eden lamented to his brother William that all was "In a thorough State of Confusion, in Maryland, due to the news from Massachusetts.[60] Eden speculated that a majority of Maryland's populace remained loyal to the British government, but that did not prevent him from expecting "an Uproar of some Sort or another" at any moment.[61]

Based on the reception that William Caswell and several other southern delegates to the Continental Congress received when they passed through Baltimore in early May, Governor Eden's confidence of strong loyalist support may have been ill founded. Caswell noted that upon their arrival at Baltimore,

> We were received by four Independent Companies who Conducted us with their Colours Flying, drums Beating & Fifes playing to our Lodgings [in Baltimore]. The next day . . . Colo. Washington . . . reviewed the Troops. They have four Companies of 68 Men each Compleat, who go thro their Exercises extremely Clever, they are raising in that Town three other Companies which they say will soon be full.[62]

Over a hundred representatives from Maryland's sixteen counties were two days into another convention in Annapolis when the news about Lexington and Concord arrived.[63] Having adopted one of the boldest militia measures at the previous convention in December, the delegates reacted to the news from Massachusetts by reiterating their recommendation to "continue the regulation of the militia . . . [with] particular attention . . . paid to forming and exercising the militia throughout the province." [64]

The Convention also reappointed the colony's delegates to Congress and emphasized their wish for "a happy reconciliation . . . upon a firm basis of constitutional freedom."[65] Acknowledging that this might not be possible, the convention reminded the delegates headed to Philadelphia not to resort to the last extremity [independence] unless such measure is "indispensably necessary for the safety and preservation of our liberties and privileges."[66] It was up to the Continental Congress to decide if or when that point was reached; the Convention pledged to execute whatever measures Congress adopted.[67]

Governor Eden was encouraged with the moderation exercised by the Third Maryland Convention and informed his superior, Lord Dartmouth, the day after the Convention adjourned that "I think I can affirm that the delegates of Maryland (or a very great majority of them) go from hence fully determined to do all in their power to bring about a reconciliation."[68]

Most eyes now turned toward Philadelphia, where the Second Continental Congress convened on May 10.

THE CONTINENTAL CONGRESS ACTS

The delegates to the Second Continental Congress gathered in Philadelphia in early May, many greeted along their journey by enthusiastic crowds of well-wishers. The first few days of the session were spent getting organized; the first significant resolution was adopted five days in, on May 15, when Congress advised New York (in response to reports that a large British military force was sailing to New York) that the colony "act on the defensive."[69] At issue was how to deal with the one hundred British Redcoats garrisoned in New York City, a rather awkward situation given the outbreak of hostilities in Massachusetts. Congress recommended that the troops be permitted to stay in the barracks in the city unmolested so long as they remained peaceable. If they became hostile in any way, however, Congress recommended that New Yorkers "repel force by force."[70]

On May 17, Congress voted to expand its embargo on exports to several colonies that had yet to support the Continental Association, specifically Canada, most of Georgia, and East and West Florida. British fishing vessels operating off the colonies were also to be denied provisions and necessaries, but this did not extend to British warships.[71] Thus, an awkward situation existed where British warships continued to purchase provisions from colonial merchants, while those same merchants were prohibited from exporting provisions to England.

Congress learned of the capture of Fort Ticonderoga on May 18 and scrambled to justify what was obviously an escalation of the conflict. Claiming self-defense with the charge that "a design is formed by the British Ministry of making a cruel invasion from the province of Quebec, upon these colonies, for the purpose of destroying our lives and liberties," Congress asserted that the inhabitants simply seized "a quantity of cannon and military stores, that would certainly have been used in the intended invasion of these colonies."[72]

Still hoping, and for some expecting, reconciliation with Great Britain, Congress ordered that the cannon and ordnance be removed from Fort Ticonderoga and stored at the southern end of Lake George where it would be secured, inventoried, and returned "when the restoration of the former harmony between Great Britain and these colonies so ardently wished for by the latter shall render it prudent and consistent with the overruling law of self preservation."[73]

On May 25, a week after Congress justified the seizure of Fort Ticonderoga, it sent specific instructions to New York to secure King's Bridge connecting Manhattan Island with the mainland and create posts along the Hudson River to block British navigation up the river.[74] Congress did leave the decision on the number of troops to be raised in New York to the Provincial Congress, but by specifying that they should not exceed three thousand and that the troops raised should serve until the end of the year "unless this Congress shall direct that they be sooner disbanded," the Continental Congress essentially took the first step toward assuming direct responsibility and authority for troops in the field.[75]

The next day, Congress called for all of the colonies to put themselves into "a state of defense," but added that reconciliation remained its goal. As a result, Congress agreed to send yet another petition (the Olive Branch Petition) directly to the King.[76] Three days later, Congress appealed to the inhabitants of Canada for their support. On the last day of May Congress learned from Benedict Arnold that the British were preparing to retake Crown Point and Fort Ticonderoga and reversed its decision to remove the cannon and stores from Fort Ticonderoga. Congress instead requested that reinforcements from Connecticut and New York be sent to defend both forts.[77]

Wishing to prevent any misunderstandings with its instructions, Congress specified the following day that "No expedition or incursion ought to be undertaken or made, by any colony, or body of colonists, against or into Canada . . . ."[78] This directive lasted less than a month.

Two

Summer

I N THE WEEKS THAT FOLLOWED THE COMMENCEMENT OF HOSTILITIES
between the British army and Massachusetts militia, a tense stand-
off occurred in Massachusetts. Thousands of British troops remained
in Boston, protected by both the geography of the city (it was hard to
attack) and the British navy (whose firepower made an attack unlikely
to succeed). Outside of Boston, in the towns and hills surrounding the
city, thousands of New England militia gathered, determined to challenge the British if they dared attempt to march out of the city again.

Managing the thousands of militia from several colonies who
were encamped around Boston was a daunting task, and in early
June, Massachusetts turned to the Continental Congress for help.
Noting that the colonial army outside of Boston comprised troops
from several colonies and was formed to protect the rights of all
American colonists, Massachusetts's leaders wrote to Congress to
"beg leave to suggest to your consideration the propriety of your
[Congress] taking the regulation and general direction of it."[1]

Two weeks of debate in Congress concluded with the formation
of continental rifle companies in Pennsylvania, Maryland, and Virginia on June 14, and the appointment of George Washington of Vir-

ginia on June 15, to command "the continental forces raised, or to be raised, for the defence of American liberty."[2] The thousands of troops posted outside of Boston fell into the category of "raised" troops and represented the bulk of the newly formed Continental Army. Up to three thousand troops in New York also apparently fell under continental establishment and by all accounts, it looked as though they would surely be needed.

NEW YORK

An incident occurred in New York City a week before General Washington was appointed commander-in-chief of the Continental Army that nearly sparked armed conflict in New York. The arrival of the HMS *Asia* in New York Harbor in late May offered an opportunity for Major Isaac Hamilton to relocate his one hundred redcoats of the Royal Irish Regiment from their barracks in the city, where they were endlessly harangued and encouraged to desert, to the more secure British warship.

With the blessing of the New York Provincial Congress, which pledged no interference, Major Hamilton and his men marched from their barracks on June 7 to board the *Asia*. The Provincial Congress's pledge of no interference did not stop Colonel Marinus Willett from confronting the British on their march when he noticed several carts loaded with muskets and gunpowder accompanying the column.[3] "Stepping in front of the lead cart, which he recalled was in the front of the column but others reported was in the rear, Willett declared that the Provincial Congress had not granted permission for the British troops to take their spare arms with them."[4]

Several gentlemen, including New York's Mayor Whitehead Hicks, urged Willett to let the column pass, but he was supported by an influential member of the Provincial Congress, John Morin Scott, as well as a large and vocal crowd ready to intervene on Willett's behalf.[5] When some in the crowd seized the carts and diverted them into a side street, effectively confiscating the muskets and gunpowder, Major Hamilton and his troops restrained themselves and did nothing to regain them. Nor did Hamilton or his troops respond when Colonel Willett climbed atop a wagon and urged the soldiers to desert, prompting one to do so.[6]

Assured by the mayor and several other gentlemen that their seized baggage would be returned, Major Hamilton and his men continued their march to the dock and embarked onboard the *Asia*. The fuming British officer noted to Lieutenant Governor Colden the next day that "Had we been equally prone to Acts of violence, and which indeed we had sufficient provocation to justify us in, the consequences might have been fatal to many."[7]

In Philadelphia, the Continental Congress continued its work on forming a Continental Army and appointed Philip Schuyler to serve as one of four major generals. Well aware of Schuyler's strong sentiments and views through his service in Congress as a delegate for New York and also aware of his military experience and reputation (he served as a captain of New York militia during the French and Indian War), Congress accepted Schuyler's nomination by the New York Provincial Congress for the post.[8]

Congress chose another New Yorker to serve as one of eight brigadier generals in the Continental Army. Richard Montgomery was born in Ireland and had far more military experience than most American generals, including General Schuyler. He had served as an ensign in the British 17th Regiment during the French and Indian War and rose to the rank of captain while serving in the Caribbean. He also saw action on the New York frontier during Pontiac's Rebellion.[9]

Returning to England to restore his health, Montgomery remained in the army until 1772, selling his commission and settling in New York. He married into the prominent Livingston family, was selected as a delegate to New York's Provincial Congress, and was nominated by that body to serve as New York's first brigadier general in the Continental Army.[10]

Both men were ordered to proceed to Fort Ticonderoga and assume command of the troops there. Schuyler travelled from Philadelphia to New York with General Washington and several other recently appointed Continental officers, including Major General Charles Lee, who were riding north to assume command of the army in Massachusetts. Schuyler parted company with them in New York City on June 25, but only after they were welcomed into the city by a large, enthusiastic crowd.[11]

Offshore upon a British ship sat Governor William Tryon who, after a long stay in England, had also arrived in New York on June 25. He landed in the city several hours after Washington's procession and was also welcomed by the city's inhabitants with a procession of his own.[12]

Both Washington and Tryon likely learned of the bloody battle of Bunker Hill that occurred in mid-June when they arrived in New York City. For the next few weeks news of the battle appeared in the weekly newspapers, and the bloody accounts may have helped influence Congress's decision to reverse itself on June 27 and authorize an attack upon Canada. Alarming reports of British preparations to attack New York from Canada most certainly influenced Congress's reversal.

> Resolved, That as Governor [Guy] Carleton is making preparations to invade these colonies and is instigating the Indian Nations to take up the Hatchet against them, Major Genl. Schuyler do exert his utmost power to destroy or take all vessels, boats or floating batteries [being prepared by Governor Carleton].
>
> Resolved, That if General Schuyler finds it practicable, and that it will not be disagreeable to the Canadians, he do immediately take possession of St. Johns, Montreal, and any other parts of the country, and pursue any other measures in Canada, which may have a tendency to promote the peace and security of these Colonies.[13]

With these two resolves, the Continental Congress authorized an invasion of Canada and troops from New York, commanded by generals from New York, were to lead the way.

In early July, just a week after his return to New York, Governor Tryon wrote to Lord Dartmouth in England to describe the state of the colony.

> The general revolt that has taken place in the colonies has put His Majesty's civil governors in the most degraded situation, left [to] exercise . . . feeble executive powers.[14]

Noting that nearly all of the colonies deferred to the Continental Congress concerning the dispute with Britain, Governor Tryon declared that, "Oceans of blood may be spilt but in my opinion America will never [accept] Parliamentary taxation."[15]

He added that 5,000 men were being raised in New York, paid for by the Continental Congress, which had voted to issue two million dollars in paper currency to pay for the war effort. There were also nearly 2,000 Connecticut troops posted on Manhattan Island, less than two miles from the city.[16]

The governor actually exaggerated the number of New York troops being raised on continental establishment. It was not 5,000 but 3,000, and on June 30, the New York Provincial Congress organized them into four regiments of 750 officers and men each, commanded by Colonels Alexander McDougall, Goose van Schaick, James Clinton, and James Holmes.[17] Colonel van Schaick had originally been appointed lieutenant colonel of the 2nd New York Regiment, but was elevated when the Provincial Congress's original choice for colonel of the unit declined to serve. The New York Congress also agreed with the Continental Congress's recommendation to raise five hundred Green Mountain Boys as an additional unit, leaving to those troops the selection of their officers.[18]

Governor Tryon wrote to Lord Dartmouth again in early August to warn that "Independency is shooting from the root of the present contest."[19] He acknowledged later in his letter that support for independence among New Yorkers was far from universal or even a majority, but it existed to some degree and would grow as time went on unless Parliament dropped its effort to tax the American colonies.

After the enormous losses suffered at Bunker Hill and Lexington and Concord, British leaders were not about to cave in to the Americans. Determined to settle the matter on the battlefield, Britain continued with preparations to subdue the rebellious colonies with military might and New York continued with its preparations to resist.

On August 11, the Provincial Congress ordered that Colonels McDougall, Clinton, and Holmes march their regiments to Albany to unite with General Schuyler and Colonel Van Schaick's 2nd New

York Regiment, which was already there recruiting from the region.[20] Four days later, General Schuyler informed the Provincial Congress of a surprising result among the election for commander of the Green Mountain Boys. Seth Warner was selected instead of Ethan Allen, not by the troops but by a meeting of committees of the several townships that comprised the New Hampshire grants.[21]

On August 22, the Provincial Congress passed a new militia bill that called for every man in the colony between the ages of 16 and 50 to furnish himself as soon as possible with a good musket, bayonet, or tomahawk, and cartridge box.[22] Fines would be levied for noncompliance. The men were to be formed into militia companies that would meet once a month for drill. One-fourth of the militia were to be selected as minutemen, to be subject to both the authority of the Provincial and Continental Congresses.[23] They were expected to drill once a week.

Those units in New York that had formed prior to the militia bill were exempted from the new arrangement and were allowed to continue as formed. One of those units, Captain John Lamb's artillery company, took action the very next night that resulted in the first bloodshed between New York troops and the British navy.

On the evening of August 23, Captain Lamb led a detachment of his colonial artillery, supported by a detachment of infantry, to the Battery at the southern tip of Manhattan Island, to remove a number of cannon posted there. Warned in advance that the colonists might attempt such a feat, Captain George Vandeput of the HMS *Asia* posted a boat from his ship near the Battery to keep watch.[24] When the British boat detected Captain Lamb's men working on the cannon at the Battery, one of its crew fired a musket to warn the *Asia*. Captain Vandeput insisted later that this shot was not fired at the city, but rather in the air to serve as a warning to his ship, but Captain Lamb's troops interpreted the shot differently and opened fire with their muskets. Shooting into the darkness at what was now a moving target rowing back to the *Asia*, they somehow hit and killed one of the sailors in the boat.[25]

The militia fire prompted Captain Vandeput to respond with three cannon shots at the Battery. With drums beating to arms in the city,

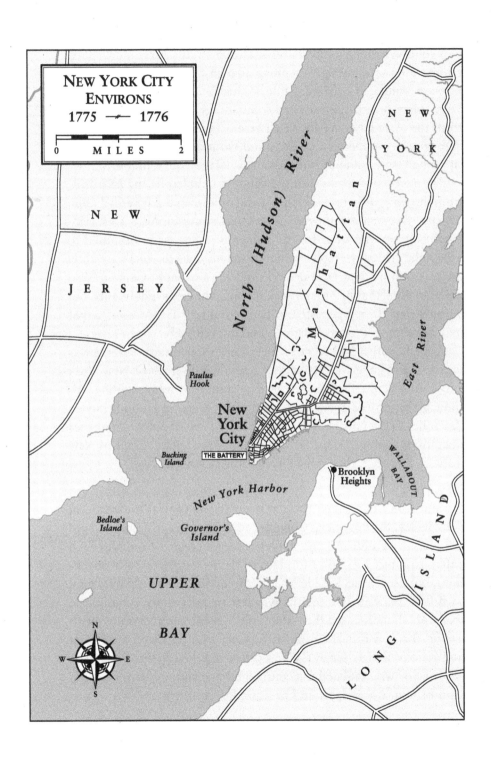

more militia rushing to the Battery to fire upon the *Asia*, and Captain Lamb's men scrambling to remove as many cannon as they could, Captain Vandeput ordered a full broadside directed at the Battery. Over thirty British cannon fired solid and grape shot at the Battery from the *Asia's* twenty-four-, eighteen-, and nine-pound cannon, damaging a number of buildings and wounding three men but not stopping Captain Lamb from removing twenty-one cannon.[26]

The successful removal of the cannon, coupled by the broadside from the *Asia*, dispersed the militia and quiet eventually settled upon the city. The next day the mayor and magistrates of New York criticized Captain Vandeput for his actions, but he was in no mood to accept the criticism. Replying that it was his duty to repel the militia attack upon his boat and defend the King's cannon, Captain Vandeput insisted that he did not seek to harm the city's inhabitants, but warned that if they persisted in their conduct "The Mischiefs that may arise must lie at their Doors, and not mine."[27]

Armed conflict had come to New York three months after it was initiated in Massachusetts and as a result, hundreds of New York City's inhabitants fled the city in expectation of more fighting. Although this proved premature for the city, General Philip Schuyler, 250 miles to the north at Fort Ticonderoga, was about to commence operations against the British in Canada, drawing hundreds of New Yorkers directly into combat against British troops.

NEW JERSEY

For much of the summer there was no strong central leadership in New Jersey; the Provincial Congress adjourned in early June and did not reconvene until August. Other colonies created Committees of Safety to direct resistance in place of their congresses and conventions, but New Jersey's leaders had yet to do so. As a result, resistance to British policies and actions was left to the county committees, many of whom focused their attention over the summer upon loyalists or Tories within their midst. Anyone who criticized the efforts and actions of New Jersey's Whigs (those opposed to the British Parliament) or who violated the continental association (ban) on trade with Britain, was suspect and pressured to conform.

Daniel Coxe, a loyalist member of the Governor's council, lamented over the hostile climate in the colony in a letter to Cortlandt Skinner, the loyalist Attorney General of New Jersey.

> Such is the present infatuated temper of the times and the minds of men daily increasing in madness and frenzy that they are ready to enter upon daring and desperate attempts . . . . What then have men of property . . . who happen and are known to differ in sentiment from the generality? They become a mark at once for popular fury . . . . They are not even allowed to preserve a neutrality, and passiveness becomes a crime. Those who are not for us are against us, is the cry; and public necessity calls for and will justify their destruction, both life and property. In short those deemed Tories have everything to fear from the political persecuting spirit now prevailing.[28]

Governor Franklin agreed with Daniel Coxe's concerns and forwarded a copy of Coxe's letter to Lord Dartmouth in early August. Noting that Coxe's letter highlighted the "critical situation the officers of [royal] government are in, having no kind of protection," Governor Franklin added his view that "There are many friends of government still remaining in the several provinces but they are too scattered to venture into forming themselves into a body especially as they have no place of strength or security to resort to."[29] Franklin went on, noting that,

> There is indeed a dread in the minds of many here that some of the leaders of the people are aiming to establish a republic, rather than submit . . . .[30]

The New Jersey Provincial Congress convened again in August and focused much of its attention on strengthening the colony's military preparedness. But first, it took a step toward a more republican form of government, just as Governor Franklin had feared, by declaring that,

> At a time when this Province is likely to be involved in all of the horrors of a civil war, and when it has become absolutely necessary to increase the burthen of taxes . . . upon the good people of this Colony for the just defence of their invaluable rights and privileges . . . the inhabitants . . . should have frequent opportunities of renewing their choice and approbation of the Representation in Provincial Congress.[31]

To provide for such an opportunity, the Provincial Congress decreed that new elections would be held in September to elect delegates to the next Provincial Congress. All inhabitants eligible to vote, not just county committees, would thus have a say in the selection of the next Congress.[32] Four days later, the representatives turned their attention to the better regulation of the provincial militia.

All able-bodied men between the ages of 16 and 50 were ordered to serve in the militia or be fined four shillings a month for non-compliance.[33] The counties, based on their population size, were given a quota of men to raise. Sparsely populated Cape May County was only expected to raise a battalion of militia (which equated to a partial regiment) while Hunterdon County, the most populated county in New Jersey, was instructed to raise four regiments of militia.[34]

Responding to the recommendation of the Continental Congress, the Provincial Congress instructed New Jersey's counties to raise four thousand minutemen from the ranks of the militia.[35] Since these minutemen fell under the authority of both the Provincial and Continental Congresses, were paid and supplied as the Continental Army when called into service, and could be ordered out of the colony, they were essentially Continental soldiers in reserve.[36]

With the colony's militia better organized and regulated, New Jersey's Provincial Congress adjourned, but not before creating an eleven-member Committee of Safety to govern during its month-long adjournment.[37]

PENNSYLVANIA

Pennsylvania's leaders also focused on strengthening the colony's military posture during the summer. Hundreds of men had enthusiastically stepped forward to fight when news of Lexington and Concord arrived in late April and county committees scrambled to form Associator units as a result. On June 14, the Continental Congress looked to Pennsylvania, as well as Virginia and Maryland, to raise a unique body of troops, riflemen.

Smoothbore muskets were the dominant firearm of colonial militia in America and the British army in 1775. Loaded from the muzzle with cartridges of gunpowder and lead ball, a well-trained soldier could load and fire up to four shots a minute (although three shots was more typical). It was admittedly rare to be engaged in such an intense firefight, but with smoothbore muskets, speed in loading was an advantage. What troops gained in rate of fire, however, they sacrificed, compared to rifled weapons, with accuracy. Although a musket ball could travel hundreds of yards depending on how it was aimed, the likelihood of actually hitting your target diminished considerably past one hundred yards. This was one reason armies in the eighteenth century tended to fire volleys on command.

On the colonial frontier of Pennsylvania and the colonies to the south, however, German gunsmiths introduced rifled weapons, primarily for hunting, that were far more accurate. Men bragged of consistently hitting small targets at 250 yards.

The drawback was in loading a rifle. Since it was necessary for the ball to engage the grooves of the rifle barrel in order to create the spin necessary for accuracy, lead rifle balls fit tightly in the muzzle. Wrapped in a greased patch, the tight-fitting ball took more time to ram down the grooved rifle barrel than a cartridge being rammed down a smoothbore musket. This, along with having to measure one's powder from a powder horn with each shot, significantly slowed the loading process to half the rate of a musket. Another drawback of a rifle was that they were custom built and not designed to mount a bayonet, still the weapon of choice of the British army and typically the last thing defeated troops saw before they ran for their lives.

Despite these drawbacks, many in the colonies believed that frontier riflemen were a secret weapon against the British. Virginian Richard Henry Lee declared to his brother Arthur, who had been away in England for several years, that just one county in Virginia,

Can furnish 1000 Rifle Men that for their number make the most formidable light Infantry in the World. The six frontier Counties [of Virginia] can produce 6000 of these Men who from their amazing hardihood, their method of living so long in the woods without carrying provisions with them, the exceeding quickness with which they can march to distant parts, and above all, the dexterity to which they have arrived in the use of the Rifle Gun. There is not one of these Men who wish a distance less than 200 yards or a larger object than an Orange. Every shot is fatal.[38]

Massachusetts delegate John Adams, excited by the reputation of these riflemen, forwarded reports of their good character to New England.

We are told by Gentlemen here that these Riflemen are Men of Property and Family, some of them of independent Fortunes, who go from the purest Motives of Patriotism and Benevolence into this service. I hope they will have Justice done them and Respect shewn them by our People of every Rank and order. I hope also that our People will learn from them the Use of that excellent Weapon a Rifled barrell'd Gun.[39]

When the Continental Congress instructed Pennsylvania to raise six companies of expert riflemen and Virginia and Maryland to raise two companies each on June 14, 1775, it essentially inaugurated the Continental Army. Those who were selected for the rifle companies signed a form attesting that they had voluntarily enlisted "in the American continental army for one year."[40]

Congress left the formation of the actual rifle companies to the three colonies. Pennsylvanians flocked to arms in such numbers that in very short time the colony raised eight rifle companies, two beyond its quota. Congress accepted the additional rifle companies and formed a Pennsylvania Rifle Battalion out of the eight companies.[41] A ninth rifle company from Lancaster County was added to the battalion on July 11.[42]

The Pennsylvania assembly chose one of its own members to command the rifle battalion. Colonel William Thompson had immigrated to Pennsylvania from Ireland with his family when he was a teenager and settled in Cumberland County on the Pennsylvania frontier.[43] A veteran militia officer of the French and Indian War, Thompson held the respect of the inhabitants on the frontier, serving on the county committee of correspondence and safety and ultimately in the Pennsylvania assembly.[44]

Two days before Pennsylvania's rifle battalion was authorized, General Washington reviewed approximately two thousand troops consisting of three battalions of infantry, an artillery company, a troop (detachment) of cavalry, and several companies of light infantry, rangers, and riflemen. They practiced the manual of arms, firing, and marching before Washington and a large crowd of spectators.[45] It is not clear whether any of the rifle companies in attendance were the continental rifle companies, but if they were, their stay in Philadelphia was brief, for all of those companies were ordered to march to Massachusetts to join the army there as soon as possible.

At the end of June, the Pennsylvania Assembly met and passed several measures to strengthen Pennsylvania's defenses. It recommended to all of the counties to form minute companies of troops to respond to threats at a moment's notice. A bounty was also offered for the production of saltpeter to make gunpowder and £35,000 in paper currency (bills of credit) was authorized, paid for by increased taxes.[46] As Quakers made up a substantial portion of Pennsylvania's population, as well as membership of the assembly, the representatives urged, "a tender and brotherly regard," for those whose beliefs forbade them to take up arms.[47] Upon their adjournment, they left a newly formed Committee of Safety, led by Benjamin Franklin, with John Dickinson, Anthony Wayne, and Robert Morris among others, with authority over the colony's military forces.[48]

The Pennsylvania Committee of Safety initially focused its attention on defending the Delaware River. Preventing the British navy from reaching Philadelphia was the goal, so committee members inspected the river below the city to locate the best place to obstruct and prevent their passage.[49] The construction of forts on Mud Island and across the river in New Jersey (with their permission) at Red Bank was begun, as was the construction of water obstacles (chevaux-de-frise) which were a number of spiked barriers sunk in the river channel in order to damage the hulls of passing ships.[50] Armed gondolas which could be rowed or sailed by crews of between thirty to fifty men and armed with several large cannon were also built per the committee's instructions.[51]

The committee also addressed the shortage of muskets and gunpowder for its Associators, reaching out to the French and Spanish West Indies to secure two thousand stand of arms (muskets, bayonets, and cartridge boxes).[52] In mid-August, the committee drafted a set of rules and regulations to properly discipline the troops and near the end of the month it declared that,

> All National distinctions in dress or name [are] to be avoided, it being proper that we should all be united in the general Association for defending our liberties and properties under the sole denomination of Americans.[53]

To address the ongoing shortage of muskets for the troops, the committee recommended the use of fifteen-foot-long pikes, noting that,

> It has been regretted by some great Soldiers . . . that the use of Pikes was ever laid aside, and many Experience'd Officers of the present time agree . . . that it would be very advantageous in our Modern Wars to resume the Weapon.[54]

The troops likely did not share the same enthusiasm for pikes, so the suggestion did not go far.

The first of Pennsylvania's Continental rifle companies reached camp in Cambridge, Massachusetts, in late July and was warmly welcomed. One unidentified American officer noted the high regard shown the riflemen.

> You will think me vain should I tell you how much the Riflemen are esteemed. Their dress, their arms, their size, but above all their eagerness to attack the enemy, entitle them to the first rank. The hunting shirt is like a full suit at St. James's [the English royal

court]. A Rifleman in his dress may pass sentinels and go where he pleases, while officers of other Regiments are stopped.[55]

Surgeon's Mate James Thacher of Massachusetts was also impressed by the riflemen.

[They are] remarkably stout and hardy men; many of them exceeding six feet in height. They are dressed in white frocks, or rifle-shirts, and round hats. These men are remarkable for the accuracy of their aim; striking a mark with great certainty at two hundred yards distance. At a review, a company of them, while on a quick advance, fired their balls into objects of seven inches diameter, at a distance of two hundred and fifty yards. They are now stationed on our lines, and their shot have frequently proved fatal to British officers and soldiers who expose themselves to view, even at more than double the distance of common musket shot.[56]

The rifle companies continued to arrive in camp in early August, sometimes singularly and other days in pairs.[57] Most conducted the long march from Pennsylvania, Virginia, and Maryland at an incredible pace, averaging twenty-five to thirty miles a day. Colonel Thompson and his second in command, Lieutenant Colonel Edward Hand, reached Cambridge soon after the last company in their battalion arrived.[58]

Even before Thompson and Hand reached Cambridge, however, the Pennsylvania riflemen had an impact upon the American army. General Washington reported to Congress on August 4 that,

I last Saturday Evening [July 29], ordered some of the Riffle Men down [toward the British lines] to make a Discovery, or bring off a Prisoner. They were accidently discovered sooner than they expected . . . & obliged to fire upon them. We have Reason to believe they killed several. They brought in two prisoners. . . . Since that Time we have on each Side drawn in our Centries, & there have been scattering Fires along the Line. This Evening we have heard of three Captains who have been taken off by the Riffle Men & one killed by a Cannon Shot from Roxbury besides several Privates.[59]

Although General Washington was impressed by the aggressive-ness and skill of the riflemen, the significant shortage of gunpowder in camp forced him to rein in the men. James Warren explained the situation to John Adams, noting that the limit on firing placed on the American troops by General Washington was not necessarily a sign of his displeasure with their marksmanship, but rather, the result of scores of New England troops joining in whenever the riflemen engaged in a skirmish.

> The General has been obliged from Principles of frugality to re-strain his rifle men. While they were permitted Liberty to fire on the Enemy, a great number of the Army would go and fire away great quantitys of Ammunition to no Purpose.[60]

Whatever the cause for General Washington's orders, it had the effect of restraining the activity of the riflemen. In the few weeks since their arrival the riflemen had seemingly lived up to their exaggerated reputation. An incident in September, however, significantly tarnished their standing in the army, at least temporarily.

DELAWARE

The Delaware colonial assembly convened for just one day on June 5, 1775. Informed by their delegates to Congress that the represen-tatives in Philadelphia were "unanimously of Opinion that it is ab-solutely necessary, for the Preservation of the Lives, Liberties and Properties of the good People of the Twelve United Colonies, and of the Parish of St. John's in Georgia, to have an armed Force, at their general Expense." Delaware's assembly considered its response.[61] The assembly agreed to contribute to the cost of a continental army through a resolution that made "The Inhabitants of this Govern-ment be . . . charged with their Quota or Share of said Expense, to be ascertained by the Congress."[62] In other words, Delaware's three counties would indeed pay their share of the costs of a continental army.

On July 22, the HMS *Nautilus* (16 guns, 100 crew) arrived off Newcastle with orders to "strictly examine all Vessels you meet that none may be upon the Seas illegally."[63] Captain John Collins and his

British crew were to enforce the trade restrictions imposed on the colonies by Parliament and most particularly, seize all weapons or ammunition they discovered. They were also ordered to give assistance to loyalist colonists and most particularly royal officials who were in need of assistance.[64]

Captain Collins, noting the "great dissatisfaction at my being there," among the inhabitants onshore, and recognizing the difficulty of navigating farther up the Delaware River without reliable river pilots, anchored the *Nautilus* off of Newcastle. He reported to Admiral Graves in Boston that "having Command of the Town" by means of aiming his cannon at it, the *Nautilus* had no difficulty obtaining fresh provisions from the town.[65]

About three weeks after the arrival of the *Nautilus*, a British transport ship, the *Hope*, which had recently been seized by American privateers, successfully passed the *Nautilus* unnoticed at night on its way to Philadelphia, much to the chagrin of Captain Collins. Onboard the *Hope* was a supply of British military clothing and more importantly, two captured British officers, a major and lieutenant. Captain Collins of the *Nautilus* sheepishly explained to Vice Admiral Graves that "Had I had the least intimation from the Major or his Party of their Situation, [I] should have . . . followed her up [to Philadelphia]."[66] The American schooner *Tryall*, and a sloop were not so lucky and were seized by the *Nautilus*.

While tensions remained high in Delaware Bay, recruitment and drill of the militia occurred in all three Delaware counties. The colonial assembly convened in late August and addressed a number of routine matters. One decision that was not routine, however, was the assembly's vote on August 30 to issue £30,000 of paper currency to support the continental cause.[67] As all of the Delaware Assembly's measures needed the governor's consent, several days of negotiation with Governor Penn ensued. It was surprisingly successful and on September 2, Governor Penn affixed the Great Seal of Delaware to the paper currency bill, making it law.[68]

Delaware now had the ability to financially support the American cause and it would soon do so militarily as well.

MARYLAND

Like New Jersey and Delaware, for much of the summer of 1775 there was no central Whig leadership in Maryland to make or direct policy. The Maryland Convention adjourned in early April and did not reconvene in Annapolis until late July. Once again, county committees took the lead in overseeing opposition to Great Britain, but only in terms of their own county.

When Congress allotted two continental rifle companies to Maryland in mid-June, the Maryland delegation in Philadelphia knew immediately where they would come from—Frederick County. Comprised of the western third of Maryland, leaders had little trouble raising two companies of expert riflemen.

Forty-three-year-old Thomas Price, a veteran of the French and Indian War and member of the Maryland Conventions of 1774, commanded one company.[69] Michael Cresap, ten years Price's junior and the youngest son of Colonel Thomas Cresap, a prominent leader in Frederick County, commanded the other Maryland rifle company.[70]

Although all of the rifle companies from Pennsylvania, Maryland, and Virginia marched hundreds of miles to reach Cambridge, a fascinating account of Captain Cresap's march north from an unknown observer provides a vivid description of how they looked and how they were received along the march.

I have had the happiness of seeing [Captain Michael Cresap] marching at the head of a formidable company of upwards of 130 men from the mountains and back woods, painted like Indians, armed with scalping knives, tomahawks and rifles, dressed in hunting shirts and moccasins, and though some of them had travelled near 300 miles from the banks of the Ohio, they seemed to walk light and easy, and not with less spirit than at the first hour of their march. Health and vigor, after what they had undergone, declared them to be intimate with hardship and familiar with danger; Joy and satisfaction were visible in the crowd that met them.[71]

Cresap's men dazzled the assembled crowd with their marksmanship.

A clapboard with a mark, the size of a dollar, was put up; they began to fire off-hand, and the standers by were surprised, few shots being made that were not close or into the paper. When they had shot for some time in this way, some lay on their backs, some on their breasts or sides; others ran 20 or 30 steps, and firing appeared to be equally certain of the mark. With this performance the company were more than satisfied, when a young man took up the board in his hand, not by the end but by the side, and holding it up, his brother walked to the distance and coolly shot into the white.[72]

The brothers changed roles and repeated the feat, but that was not the most astonishing thing witnessed.

Will you believe me when I tell you that one of the men took the board, and placing it between his legs, stood with his back to the tree while another drove his ball thro' the centre? What would a regular army . . . do with a thousand of these men who want nothing to preserve their health and courage but water from the spring, with a little parched corn, and what they can easily procure in hunting; and who, wrapped in their blankets, in the damp of the night, would choose the shade of a tree for their cover and the earth for their bed.[73]

The Maryland rifle companies covered the 550 miles to Cambridge in just over three weeks, arriving in camp on August 9, to an enthusiastic welcome.[74]

In late July, the Fifth Maryland Convention convened in Annapolis. Over a hundred delegates from Maryland's sixteen counties gathered to discuss a plan to better defend the colony. They quickly approved funds to pay for forty-eight tons of lead and two tons of cannon powder, as well as an unspecified amount of musket powder and gun flints.[75]

The Convention also took up the issue of loyalists (Tories) within the colony. Its resolution regarding James Christie of Baltimore was representative of how Tories were treated in Maryland in the summer of 1775. A letter written by Christie on February 22, 1775, to Lieutenant Colonel Gabriel Christie (likely a relative) was intercepted by Baltimore's committee of observation and forwarded to the Convention. It revealed Christie's view that "the inhabitants of [Baltimore are] concerned in measures . . . treasonable and rebellious; and that a number of [British] Soldiers would keep them very quiet."[76] Finding that Mr. Christie "Is and ought to be considered as an enemy to America," the Convention ordered that no person trade or barter with him and that he "be Expelled and banished from this Province, forever, and that he depart this Province before the first Day of September."[77]

The Convention turned its attention to the details of defending Maryland in mid-August, approving an "Association of the Freemen of Maryland" that vowed to "repel Force by Force" and to unite with the other colonies to "promote and support the present opposition, carrying on as well by Arms, as by the Continental Association restraining our Commerce."[78]

Forty companies of minutemen were authorized for the sixteen counties. They were to comprise sixty-eight men each in addition to officers and NCOs. Although they were not considered full time, "regular" soldiers, their term of service was to last until next March, six months away. They were to muster twice a week and could be ordered to march to neighboring colonies if necessary.[79]

The convention also ordered that "every able bodied effective Freeman within this Province between Sixteen and fifty years of age" shall enroll in their county militia by mid-September. Exemptions were made for several groups including clergy, physicians, and those whose religious principles forbade them from bearing arms.[80] This force was designed for home defense, within the colony only, and would muster to train once a week.[81]

To pay for the troops and the equipment and supplies needed, the Convention resolved to issue bills of credit totaling $266,666 in paper currency, each dollar being equivalent to four shillings, six pence sterling of English money.[82] The Convention, realizing that the struggle against Britain would be a long and difficult one, estimated that increased taxes would pay off the paper currency by January 1786.[83]

A sixteen member Council of Safety was formed to govern the colony when the Convention was not in session. Eight members were to be selected from the eastern side of Chesapeake Bay and eight members selected from the western side. This council, as well as the county committees of observation, were directed to enforce all of the measures adopted by the Convention and Continental Congress. The Council of Safety and the Convention had authority over the minutemen and militia.[84] Although an actual threat had yet to appear in Maryland, the colony was ready to fight!

Three

Fall

B Y THE END OF SUMMER, GENERAL PHILIP SCHUYLER WAS READY
to move his force of New York and Connecticut Continentals
northward, up Lake Champlain from Fort Ticonderoga to attack
British posts in Canada and prevent them from staging an attack
upon New York. Congress had instructed General Schuyler to do his
utmost to destroy or capture whatever watercraft the British might
use in such an attack and to "take possession of St. John's, Montreal,
and any other parts of [Canada]," which may promote the security
of the colonies.[1] This authorization was contingent on General
Schuyler finding such effort practicable and not disagreeable to the
Canadians.

For much of the summer, such an enterprise was anything but
practicable for General Schuyler. He informed General Washington
in late July of his struggles to build enough boats to transport his
army north as well as obtain enough provisions to adequately feed
his men.[2] A week later he declared that he was ready to follow either
General Washington's or Congress's instructions, yet lamented that
most of his promised troops and supplies had yet to reach Fort Ticonderoga and he had not a single artillery carriage for his cannon.[3]

Despite such a bleak assessment of his condition, General Washington had determined to strike at Canada, not just with Schuyler's troops, but with a second detachment of 1,200 troops from his own army under Colonel Benedict Arnold. This second force was to march through the Maine wilderness and either catch Governor Guy Carleton and the defenders of Quebec by surprise, or draw forces opposing Schuyler toward Quebec, allowing Schuyler to advance deep into Canada against reduced opposition.[4]

With elements of the four New York Continental regiments scattered from Long Island to Crown Point, only a portion of General Schuyler's troops proceeded north at the end of August. They sailed not under Schuyler, but under General Richard Montgomery. Schuyler had been detained by an important conference with Indian leaders of the Six Nations in Albany where he happily learned of their desire to remain neutral in this "family quarrel" between Britain and her colonies.[5] General Montgomery, alarmed by reports that newly constructed British ships were about to enter Lake Champlain, left Crown Point by boat on August 31 with 1,200 troops from the 1st New York and 5th Connecticut regiments and four twelve-pound cannon.[6] General Schuyler caught up with Montgomery near the Canadian border on September 4 and the Americans continued northward another ten miles down the Richelieu River to the island of Isle-aux-Noix. When they arrived, they fired three cannon, the prearranged signal of their arrival to the Canadians they hoped would turn out to support them.[7] Although Isle-aux-Noix was far from an ideal base of operation for the Americans, plagued as it was with marshy land and swarming insects, it provided Schuyler's force with a strong position to prevent British ships from reaching Lake Champlain. It was also just twelve miles away from Schuyler's first objective, the town of St-Jean, the same Canadian town that Colonel Arnold successfully raided back in May. This time the Americans intended to capture and hold the town as well as the British troops, boats, and equipment that were there.

St-Jean was protected by a strong fort garrisoned by six hundred British, Canadian, and Indian defenders, approximately two-thirds of whom were British redcoats.[8] With few British redcoats in Quebec or Montreal, St-Jean was the strongest British post in Canada at the time. Securing it would go far in securing Lake Champlain and ultimately, New York, at least from threats to the north.

General Schuyler had been assured by several Canadian leaders of strong support among the populace for an American effort against the British. The day after his arrival on Isle-aux-Noix he sent out copies of a declaration amongst the Canadians explaining the American presence in Canada (hoping many Canadians would join his force). On September 6, Schuyler ordered the bulk of his force to proceed downstream to St-Jean. He recounted to Congress that,

> When we arrived in Sight of and at the Distance of about two Miles, the Enemy began a Fire from their Fortress, but without doing any Damage, we approached half a Mile nearer & then landed without Opposition in a close deep Swamp, after being formed, we marched in the best Order we could in Grounds marshy and covered with Woods, in order to approach & Reconnoitre the Fortress.[9]

As they advanced, a party of approximately one hundred Indians struck the Connecticut troops on Schuyler's left flank, inflicting over a dozen casualties. The Americans pressed on, however, inflicting nearly as many losses on the Indians, who fell back and broke off the engagement.[10] With nightfall descending, the Americans halted and hastily fortified their position.

Later in the evening, General Schuyler received detailed information about the enemy garrison at St-Jean from Moses Hazen, a native of Massachusetts who had settled in St-Jean in 1763. He was a retired British officer on half pay who was sympathetic to the American cause. Hazen confirmed that the bulk of the British regulars in Canada were in the strongly built fort at St-Jean, supported by approximately one hundred Indians. Despite the fact that one of the two boats being constructed by the British at St-Jean was just days away from completion and mounted sixteen cannon, Hazen recommended against an attack upon the fort in part because he did not believe any Canadians would join in such an attempt. They wished to remain neutral, claimed Hazen, although his recommendation for Schuyler to send parties amongst the inhabitants suggests that Hazen believed many could be persuaded to join the American effort.[11]

An officer's council the next morning agreed to follow Hazen's advice and General Schuyler ordered a return to Isle-aux-Noix, leaving small parties behind to try to persuade the inhabitants to join the American cause. While the Americans waited for Canadian support to materialize, they fortified their position on Isle-aux-Noix, erected a boom across the Richelieu River to obstruct navigation, and welcomed reinforcements from New York and Connecticut. General Schuyler reported on his return to Isle-aux-Noix that his force had grown to approximately 1,700 men with five cannon and two mortars.[12]

Just two days after his return, Schuyler, who had been ill since late August and would soon be forced to relinquish command to General Montgomery and return to Fort Ticonderoga, received an appeal for support from Canadian James Livingston in Chambly, located downriver from St-Jean. Livingston desired to cut communication between the British at St-Jean and the inhabitants at Chambly and the lower Richelieu River valley as well as Montreal and he requested American troops to join his force of several hundred Canadians to the north of St-Jean.[13]

General Montgomery sailed north with eight hundred troops to support Livingston and landed three miles south of St-Jean under cover of darkness. Lieutenant Colonel Rudolphus Ritzema of the 1st New York Regiment was then sent with approximately five hundred New York and Connecticut troops to march around St-Jean and cut all communication from the British garrison to the north and west, but in doing so some of his troops became startled by their own flank guard (who they mistook for the enemy in the darkness) and retreated in disarray. Order was restored in the detachment and a second attempt to pass the fort and town was made before dawn, but British cannon fire prompted another disorderly retreat. General Montgomery, in frustration, ended the operation and returned to Isle-aux-Noix.[14]

Although the Americans were frustrated and embarrassed by this development, they remained determined to take St-Jean. Several days of poor weather delayed their next attempt, during which General Schuyler's declining health forced him to return to Fort Ticonderoga, but the day before he left, Major John Brown was sent back to St-Jean with one hundred men and thirty Canadian volunteers to bolster the spirits of the friendly Canadians in the region.[15] On the evening of September 17, Brown's force ambushed a small British supply convoy northwest of St-Jean, but they were themselves surprised and dispersed early the next morning by a British sortie from St-Jean.[16] To the south of St-Jean, General Richard Montgomery with hundreds of troops from New York, Connecticut, New Hampshire, Vermont, and Massachusetts, landed once again, resolved to lay siege upon St-Jean. They were joined by Captain John Lamb's Continental artillery company of New Yorkers who were "indispensably necessary," reported General Schuyler, "as we had none that knew any Thing of [artillery]."[17]

General Montgomery sent five hundred troops to cut and hold the roads to St-Jean from Montreal and Chambly. They encountered the British force that had dispersed Major Brown and after "an ill directed Fire for some Minutes [from the British, who] retired with Precipitation," the crossroad was firmly in the possession of the Americans.[18] Montgomery sent Major Brown and his force, which had re-formed after the ambush, down the road to the village of Laprairie on the south bank of the St. Lawrence River across from the Island of Montreal (upon which the town of Montreal was). When they arrived at the outskirts of Laprairie, they encountered a small force of loyalist Canadians and Indians escorting ten carts of supplies to St-Jean. The loyalist militia and Indians abandoned the carts and fled to the river, crossing back to Montreal, where they alarmed the whole city with news of the rebels' appearance on the opposite shore.[19]

Ethan Allen, who continued to serve as a volunteer guide to the northern army after he lost command of the Green Mountain Boys to Seth Warner, was sent by General Montgomery down the Richelieu River to raise a corps of Canadians. In usual Ethan Allen fashion, he exceeded his orders and led nearly 250 men (many without arms) to the mouth of the Richelieu River, then followed the St. Lawrence

River to the town of Longeuil, directly across from Montreal, where he linked up with Major Brown, who had moved there from Laprairie. Without consulting with General Montgomery, Brown and Allen agreed to attack the lightly defended town. They believed that once they crossed onto Montreal Island, Allen to the north of Montreal and Brown to the south of the city, hundreds of Canadians would join them to help secure the town.

Nothing, however, went as planned. Allen's small force of approximately a hundred men crossed onto the island on September 25, but neither Brown nor the Canadians joined him. It appears that they expected the attack to occur the following day and were unaware of Allen's movement until it was too late.[20] Thus, Ethan Allen and his men were on their own.

Governor Carleton and the residents of Montreal learned of Allen's presence on the morning of September 25 and the governor dispatched a small detachment of thirty-four British soldiers (for he had but few redcoats in Montreal) supported by two hundred Canadian militia, to confront Allen. A skirmish ensued outside the town gates in which Allen's men were routed. He and thirty-five of his men were captured. When General Montgomery learned of the debacle, he worried about the effect it would have on Canadian support for the Americans.[21]

Despite the disappointment of Allen's actions at Montreal, St-Jean remained General Montgomery's prime objective, and most of his attention remained focused on besieging the British garrison there. Artillery batteries to the south and north of St-Jean were erected and began firing upon the fort in late September. In early October, Canadian troops cooperating with the Americans erected a battery of artillery to the east of the fort, across the Richelieu River. The fort's commander, Major Charles Preston, sent a detachment of troops on a row galley to drive off the Canadians with cannon, swivel, and musket fire, but the Canadians held firm and the British withdrew.[22]

Despite this successful stand, the American and Canadian troops, and particularly many officers under Montgomery, grew weary of the siege and in mid-October Major Brown informed General Montgomery that "a general Dissatisfaction prevailed, [and] that unless something was undertaken in a few Days there would be a Meeting."[23] At dispute was Montgomery's decision to erect another artillery battery to the west of the fort; his officers all believed such a battery should be erected to the east, across the river, and they used their disagreement to question Montgomery's competence. The frustrated general complained to General Schuyler at Fort Ticonderoga that "I did not consider I was at the Head of Troops who carry the Spirit of Freedom into the Field & think for themselves."[24] He explained that,

> Upon considering the fatal Consequences which might flow from a Want of Subordination & Discipline should this ill Humour continue my unstable Authority over the Troops of different Colonies, the Insufficiency of the military Law, & my own Want of Power to enforce it, weak as it is, I thought it expedient to call the Field officers together.[25]

General Montgomery explained his rationale for erecting a new artillery battery to the west of the British fort, but his officers unanimously opposed it in favor of a new battery to the east, across the river. Montgomery reluctantly acquiesced, and then complained further to General Schuyler.

> I cannot help observing to how little purpose I am here. Were I not afraid the example would be too generally followed & that the publick service might suffer, I would not stay an hour at the head of Troops whose operation I cannon direct.[26]

As things stood at the time, neither battery would have made much difference in the siege because the American army was running low on ammunition and the entire siege was in danger of failing. This ammunition shortage was resolved, however, on October 18, when a combined force of three hundred Canadian militia under Jeremiah Duggan and fifty American Continentals under Major Brown, captured a British fort in the town of Chambly, about twelve miles downriver from St-Jean, without a casualty on either side.[27] Two cannon employed by Duggan's Canadians proved to be the deciding factor, breaching the thin walls of the British fort and convincing its commander, Major Joseph Stopford, to surrender.[28]

While the eighty-three British redcoat prisoners at Chambly were a welcome catch, it was the six tons of gunpowder within the fort that was most welcome by General Montgomery.[29] He exuberantly declared to General Schuyler that "We have Gotten 6 Tons of Powder, which with the Blessing of God will Finish this Business here."[30]

In Montreal, General Carleton grew ever anxious about his situation and realized he needed to act to save the garrison at St-Jean. He organized a force of six hundred Canadian militia, eighty Indians, and 130 British redcoats and attempted to cross the St. Lawrence River at Longueuil on October 30. Waiting for Carleton and his men was Lieutenant Colonel Seth Warner with approximately three hundred Green Mountain Boys and 2nd New Yorkers, along with a single cannon.[31] Although outnumbered more than two to one, the heavy Continental musket and cannon fire of Warner's force prevented Carleton and his troops from landing and after several attempts, he gave up and returned to Montreal.

When General Montgomery learned of Carleton's defeat, he sent a flag of truce to Major Prescott at Fort St-Jean demanding the garrison's surrender. Negotiations commenced and on November 3, Prescott, realizing that no relief was coming, surrendered the fort. In doing so, the bulk of Governor Carleton's British regulars, his best soldiers, fell into American hands.

General Montgomery immediately turned his attention to Montreal and moved the bulk of his army to the southern bank of the St. Lawrence River, extending all the way north to the mouth of the Richelieu River at Sorel, where Colonel James Easton's Massachusetts Continentals established a strong artillery battery overlooking the St. Lawrence River.

Governor Carleton realized that he had little chance to hold Montreal and made preparations to sail to Quebec. He departed by ship on November 11, with less than 150 British redcoats and eight transports loaded with supplies. They were escorted by three armed vessels and slowly made their way downriver against the wind. When they reached Sorel, Colonel Easton's battery of six cannon, along with several armed boats, obstructed their passage.

Determining that it was too dangerous for the British flotilla to attempt to pass Sorel, Governor Carleton was placed in a rowboat and rowed under cover of darkness past Sorel, to make his way to Quebec without the transports. It was left to General Richard Prescott to surrender the ships, crew, and British redcoats, along with a thousand barrels of provisions, to the Americans on November 19, but not before all of the gunpowder and ordnance aboard the vessels was thrown overboard.[32] Governor Carleton encountered a friendly ship past Sorel on November 17, and reached Quebec on the same day that Prescott surrendered the flotilla.

In Montreal, General Montgomery, who had triumphantly entered the town on November 13 with his troops against no opposition, scrambled to retain enough men in the army to continue operations in Canada. The enlistments for many of the men were about to expire and most were determined to return home. Montgomery's recruitment efforts managed to convince approximately seven hundred men to remain with the army until April.[33] Although this was far from a desirable number, Montgomery determined that it was enough to hold Montreal and several other key Canadian posts and still assist Colonel Benedict Arnold in his efforts against Quebec.

New York

Nearly three months earlier in New York City, blood had been shed between the British navy and inhabitants of the city when the HMS *Asia* attempted to stop the removal of a number of mounted cannon on the battery at the tip of Manhattan Island. Governor Tryon, who was away on Long Island when the incident occurred, immediately returned to the city, despite reports that a mob looked to seize him and had searched his residence. He called a meeting of city leaders where he warned them to act cautiously and not provoke Captain Vandeput upon the *Asia* any further. Tryon urged city leaders to leave the cannon on the city common where they had been placed after their removal from the Battery, and continue to furnish the King's ship with fresh provisions.[34] He insisted that news from England of a new plan of accommodation might arrive at any moment to reconcile the two sides.

Provisioning the King's ships became a key issue for both sides. Several boats that had reportedly delivered provisions to the *Asia* had been seized and burned by New Yorkers in early September, and when Vice Admiral Graves learned of the unrest in New York, he instructed Captain Vandeput to demand provisions from the city and if refused, to "fire upon the Town," taking particular aim "upon the House of that Traitor [Isaac] Sears, which I am told stands very conspicuous and beat it down, to convince the Inhabitants you will put your Threats into Execution."[35]

Three days later, Admiral Graves instructed Captain Vandeput to take efforts to seize "any of the Delegates to the Congress at Philadelphia, and any of the Rebel General Officers" if they pass through New York.[36] Captain Vandeput had little opportunity to act on either order; there were no delegates or officers passing through New York to seize, and provisions continued to flow to the *Asia* from the city and countryside. They were not directly transported to the ship, however, but deposited on Governor's Island at the mouth of the East River and then retrieved by the *Asia*.[37]

While tension in New York City remained high, fifty miles up the Hudson River laborers began work on a fort in the Highlands authorized by the Continental Congress. The location selected to obstruct navigation on the river was West Point, or more specifically, Martelaer's Island, a rocky island along the east bank of the Hudson River across from West Point. The narrow river made a ninety degree turn to the west at this point, making it one of the most difficult navigation points on the Hudson, and the rugged island with its steep cliffs was positioned perfectly for artillery to blast approaching ships with cannon fire while repelling assaults from both river and land.

Bernard Romans, a Dutch engineer, selected the site in September and then supervised the construction of a fort, which began in October upon the renamed Constitution Island.[38] Within a few months however, the effort was halted and a new location was selected five miles downriver.

In mid-October, reports that the Continental Congress had instructed the New York Provincial Congress to seize Governor Tryon and other royal officials prompted the governor to seek assurances from city leaders of their safety. Tryon included a veiled threat to city leaders, declaring that should he be seized,

The Commander of his Majesty's Ships of War, in the harbour, will demand that the Inhabitants deliver me on board the Fleet, and, on Refusal, enforce the Demand with their whole Power.[39]

In other words, the city would be shelled by the British navy if Governor Tryon was seized by the rebels.

Dissatisfied by the apparent unwillingness, or inability, of city leaders to ensure the safety of royal officials, Tryon removed himself to the packet ship *Halifax* on October 18, declaring that he was "Ready to do such Business of the Country, as the Situation of the Times will permit."[40] His statement was meaningless, for he had long since lost any influence over New York and his flight from the city was the symbolic end of royal rule in New York.

NEW JERSEY

With the New Jersey Provincial Congress adjourned and few meetings of the Council of Safety, September 1775 was a relatively quiet month in New Jersey, at least compared to the other American colonies. Governor Franklin expressed his impatience to Lord Dartmouth in London for guidance from England, "that we may know what Line of Conduct is to be pursued." [41] He also shared rumors that royal officials might soon be seized and held as hostages. Franklin declared that he would remain in New Jersey, but wished a British warship (which he had requested from General Gage in Boston) would take station at Perth Amboy to offer refuge should he or the other royal officials in New Jersey need to flee for their safety.[42]

In early October, New Jersey's Provincial Congress gathered again in Trenton and focused much of its attention on militia issues that had arisen since the last Congress. Objections to some of the field officers selected to lead militia battalions, concern about how to pay for all of the militia expenses, and questions about company grade officers dominated the first few days of the session.

The Continental Congress in Philadelphia added to the Provincial Congress's work when it recommended on October 9 that New Jersey raise two regiments of Continental infantry to serve for a year. Each regiment was to consist of eight companies of sixty-eight men each, plus the necessary officers and non-commissioned officers and staff (surgeon, musicians, a minister).[43]

New Jersey's leaders readily agreed to raise the two regiments, but voiced concern over the selection of the field officers for each unit. Granted authority to select company grade officers, the New Jersey Provincial Congress wanted the authority to select the regimental field officers as well (rather than submit recommendations to the Continental Congress). Two weeks of silence from Congress ensued before New Jersey's leaders moved forward with efforts to raise the regiments, resigned that their request had been ignored.[44]

While New Jersey's leaders worked to improve the colony's military capabilities, two incidents with support craft of the British navy occurred along the coast that nearly triggered armed conflict. The first occurred on October 7, when a captured prize vessel belonging to the HMS *Viper* (ten guns, eighty crew) was seized by inhabitants of Monmouth County. It is unclear whether the vessel's three-man crew was forced to surrender to armed militia on shore or whether it became grounded while avoiding inclement weather in Barnegat Bay and was seized, but upon its capture the Provincial Congress instructed the Monmouth Committee to "publish an advertisement in the newspapers, describing the sloop, so that the owner may know where to apply; and that the men and arms found on board the said sloop, be taken proper care of by that Committee, until this Congress or the Committee of Safety shall give further orders."[45]

The other incident involved a British transport ship, the *Rebecca & Francis*, which was sailing to New York from Boston to recruit for a new provincial regiment being raised in America. Twenty-one recruits were aboard as well as two sergeants and a lieutenant, all under the command of Captain Duncan Campbell.[46] When the ship grounded on the New Jersey shore (near present day Atlantic City), the passengers and crew all went ashore.

Captain Campbell and Lieutenant Smith attempted to make their way by small boat to the HMS *Asia* in New York but after a two night pursuit, they were taken by a party of New Jersey militia.[47] The grounded transport's captain, crew, and remaining passengers were all taken by another party of militia and brought to Philadelphia where they admitted throwing several cannon, sixty muskets, and two and a half barrels of gunpowder overboard.[48] In both instances, New Jersey militia had successfully threatened force to capture British military personnel and property, actions that were no doubt viewed unfavorably by British officials.

The New Jersey Provincial Congress directed its efforts in late October to pay for the increased expenses of an expanded military force in the colony. Three thousand stand of arms (muskets and bayonets), ten tons of gunpowder, twenty tons of lead, two thousand cartridge boxes, eight hundred tents, one thousand hunting shirts, and four thousand blankets were some of the items the Provincial Congress authorized.[49] The representatives also set aside money to pay the militia, purchase entrenching tools and artillery, and construct saltpeter works to allow for the production of gunpowder.[50] On the last day of the session, 30,000 pounds of additional paper currency was authorized and the names of William Alexander (Lord Stirling) and William Maxwell were submitted to the Continental Congress to command New Jersey's two continental regiments.[51]

Forty-nine-year-old William Alexander, who preferred the title Lord Stirling because of his contested claim to a Scottish earldom, was a well-educated and prominent leader in New Jersey who had served as an aide-de-camp to Massachusetts Governor William Shirley during the French and Indian War. Appointed to New Jersey's Provincial Council (a privy council to the royal governor) prior to the outbreak of hostilities, Governor Franklin removed Stirling from the Council when he accepted an officer's commission to command one of New Jersey's militia battalions.[52] Stirling was a fierce patriot who rose in rank over the course of the war to major general in the Continental Army.

Forty-two-year-old Irish-born William Maxwell had much more military experience than Lord Stirling, but not nearly the social standing. Maxwell's involvement in the French and Indian War, in which he rose to the rank of a militia lieutenant, and his continued involvement with the British army on the frontier after the war, provided him with the experience the Provincial Congress sought in a regimental commander.[53]

In mid-November, the New Jersey assembly convened in Burlington to conduct its duties as the colonial legislature. Many of the assembly's members had served in the Provincial Congress three weeks earlier. The session began with an address by Governor Franklin. Acknowledging his disagreement with the "destructive measures . . . adopted in the colonies," yet admitting that further discussion on that topic was fruitless and would only "endanger the harmony of the present session," Governor Franklin avoided further comment on New Jersey's actions and shared with the assembly the King's disappointment that reconciliation had yet to be achieved.[54]

Franklin reminded the legislators that the King viewed their actions as rebellion, "which menaces to overthrow the Constitution," and that he was determined "that the most vigorous efforts should be made, both by sea and land, to reduce his rebellious subjects to obedience."[55] Governor Franklin urged the legislators to exert themselves to dissuade the populace from threatening British authorities because the British navy had instructions to respond with harsh measures in any situation in which royal officials were threatened or harmed.[56]

Believing that a majority of colonists opposed independence, Franklin closed his address by asking the legislatures to reveal their position on independence (a topic that had appeared several times in the newspapers of late). He hoped to pressure many to publicly dismiss the idea of independence. In a sense, Franklin got what he wanted.

It took the legislature two weeks to respond, during which they voted to fund the government for another year and instructed the delegates to the Continental Congress to oppose independence should the issue be considered in Philadelphia.[57] The assembly's response to the governor at the end of November included the expression of surprise that Franklin and his fellow royal officials ever felt threatened as well as their own continued hope for reconciliation.[58] Whether they actually meant either claim was anyone's guess.

PENNSYLVANIA

As fall approached in Massachusetts, the luster of the independent rifle companies began to wear off for General Washington and his army, in large part due to the conduct of a number of Pennsylvania riflemen. Discipline among the New England troops had long perplexed General Washington. He candidly described the New England troops to his cousin and caretaker of Mount Vernon, Lund Washington, as "an exceeding dirty & nasty people."[59] Washington blamed most of the problem on the officers, whom he found indifferent to their duty and in some cases, corrupt and cowardly.[60] Washington speculated that the New England troops would likely "fight very well if properly Officered," but few officers showed any inclination to contribute toward instilling better discipline among the men.[61] As a result, Washington lamented to Richard Henry Lee in a letter a few days later that it fell to him to strictly enforce discipline, making him "very obnoxious to the greater part of these people."[62]

Washington's struggle to discipline the troops only increased with the arrival of the riflemen who, for all of their skill and energy, chafed at military discipline. This led to an incident of near mutiny among a group of Pennsylvania riflemen in September. Jesse Lukens, a Pennsylvania rifle officer, blamed preferential treatment of the riflemen and lax discipline from their officers as the cause of the insubordination.

> Our camp is separate from all others about 100 yards—all our courts martial and duty was separate—we were excused from all working parties, camp guards, and camp duty. This indulgence, together with the remissness of discipline and care in our young officers, had rendered the men rather insolent for good soldiers. They had twice before broke open our guard house and released their companions who were confined there for small crimes, and once when an offender was brought to the post to be whipped, it was with the utmost difficulty they were kept from rescuing him in the presence of all their officers—they openly damned them and behaved with great insolence. However the colonel was pleased to pardon the man and all remained quiet.[63]

Such lenient treatment and lack of discipline among the Pennsylvania riflemen eventually created a serious problem. An attempt by the officers to exercise their authority caused some of them to resist in early September. Lieutenant Lukens recounted the incident:

> On Sunday last, the adjutant having confined a serjeant for neglect of duty and murmuring, the men began again and threatened to take him out. The adjutant, being a man of spirit, seized the principal mutineer and put him in also, and coming to report the matter to the colonel, where we, all sitting down after dinner, were alarmed with a huzzaing and upon going out found they had broke open the guard house and taken the man out. The colonel and lieutenant colonel with several of the officers and friends seized the fellow from amongst them and ordered a guard to take him to Cambridge at the Main Guard, which was done without any violent opposition, but in about 20 minutes 32 of Capt. Ross's company with their loaded rifles swore by God they would go to the Main Guard and release the man or lose their lives, and set off as hard as they could run—it was in vain to attempt stopping them.
>
> We stayed in camp and kept the others quiet—sent word to General Washington, who reinforced the guard to five hundred men with fixed bayonets and loaded pieces. Col. Hitchcock's regiment [of Rhode Islanders] (being the one next to us) was ordered under arms and some part of General Green's brigade (as the generals were determined to subdue by force the mutineers and did not know how far it might spread in our battalion). Generals Washington, Lee, and Green came immediately, and our 32 mutineers who had gone about half a mile toward Cambridge and taken possession of a hill and woods, beginning to be frightened by the proceedings, were not so hardened but upon the General's ordering them to ground their arms they did it immediately. The General then ordered another of our company's (Capt. Nagles) to surround them with their loaded guns, which was immediately done and . . . he ordered two of the ring leaders to be bound. I was glad to find our men all true and ready to do their duty except these 32 rascals—26 were conveyed to the Quarter Guard on Prospect Hill and 6 of the principals to the Main Guard.

You cannot conceive what disgrace we are all in and how much the General is chagrined that only one regiment should come from the South and that set so infamous an example: and in order that idleness shall not be a further bane to us, the general orders on Monday were "That Col. Thompson's regiment shall be upon all parties of fatigue [work parties] and do all other camp duty with any other regiment."[64]

General Washington, perhaps out of gratitude to the Pennsylvanians for coming to Boston, was surprisingly lenient on the mutineers and only fined them twenty shillings each.[65] Lukens noted that further punishment appeared unnecessary, for "the men are returned to their camp, seem exceedingly sorry for their misbehavior and promise amendment."[66]

Fortunately for the reputation of the Pennsylvania riflemen, Captain Ross's mutineers were not the only noteworthy Pennsylvanians in General Washington's army that autumn. Two companies of Pennsylvania riflemen had been selected at the start of September to participate in a daring expedition to Quebec. Captain William Hendricks and Captain Matthew Smith led their rifle companies to Cambridge the day before the mutinous incident and joined Colonel Benedict Arnold's 1,200-man expedition for Quebec. A third rifle company from Virginia under Captain Daniel Morgan joined the Pennsylvanians at Cambridge.

General Washington had pondered an expedition through the Maine wilderness to Quebec for weeks to either assist or exploit General Schuyler's expedition into Canada from New York. Such a move would place Governor Carleton and his limited forces in Canada in a pincer movement. Although it was late in the season to launch such an expedition, Washington ordered Colonel Arnold to proceed, and his force of three rifle companies and ten musket companies formed in Cambridge. From there they marched to Newburyport, then sailed to the Kennebec River and made their way to Fort Western in modern-day Augusta, Maine. Approximately two hundred hastily built bateaux were waiting for them just below the fort, and the plan called for Arnold's force to use these watercraft to continue up the Kennebec and Dead Rivers and into Canada.

To avoid bottlenecks, Arnold formed four detachments and sent them upriver days apart. The three rifle companies comprised the first division and they started upriver on September 25. Captain Daniel Morgan, destined to become a legend in the war, assumed command of the three rifle companies, apparently with the approval of Captains Hendricks and Smith. It became clear almost immediately that the movement upriver was to be challenging.

Pennsylvania rifleman George Morison of Captain Hendricks's rifle company recalled in his journal that,

> The water in many places being so shallow, that we were often obliged to haul the boats after us through rock and shoals, frequently up to our middle and over our heads in the water; and some of us with difficulty escaped being drowned.[67]

While the men in the bateaux battled the swift current and rocky shoals, the rest of the expedition marched alongside the river. They were frequently called upon to assist with the boats, especially when difficult rapids or waterfalls were encountered. The weather also challenged the men, turning cold and raw. Captain Simeon Thayer, commanding a company of Rhode Island troops who followed a day behind the riflemen, noted on September 30 that "Last night, our clothes being wet, were frozen a pane of glass thick, which proved very disagreeable, being obliged to lie in them."[68]

Arnold's scattered force slowly struggled north, the divisions strung out for miles. On October 7, the rifle division reached the Great Carrying Place. This was the location of a twelve-mile portage route that connected the Kennebec and Dead Rivers. Three ponds linked the route and made the overland trek a bit easier. Nevertheless, hauling the heavy boats and supplies over the rough terrain was a daunting task. The riflemen were given the added responsibility of clearing and improving the path for the detachments to come. Rifleman Morison described the difficulties they endured:

> This morning we hauled out our Batteaux from the river and carried thro' brush and mire, over hills and swamps . . . to a pond which we crossed, and encamped for the night. This transporta-

tion occupied us three whole days, during which time we advanced but five miles. This was by far the most fatiguing movement that had yet befell us. The rains had rendered the earth a complete bog; insomuch that we were often half leg deep in the mud, stumbling over all fallen logs. . . . Our encampments these two last nights were almost insupportable; for the ground was so soaked with rain that the driest situation we could find was too wet to lay upon any length of time; so that we got but little rest. Leaves to bed us could not be obtained and we amused ourselves around our fires most all the night. . . . The incessant toil we experienced in ascending the river, as well as the still more fatiguing method of carrying our boats, laden with the provisions, camp equipage etc., from place to place, might have subdued the resolution of men less patient and less persevering than we were. . . . Our gallant officers, who partook of all our hardships left nothing unsaid or undone that might hearten us to the enterprise.[69]

After days of backbreaking work, the riflemen reached the Dead River. The expedition made good progress for a few days on this river, but the weather eventually deteriorated and the Americans were forced to halt and endure the remnants of a hurricane. Sixteen-year-old John Henry of Captain Smith's Pennsylvania rifle company described the storm's impact:

A most heavy torrent of rain fell upon us, which continued all night . . . toward morning we were awakened by the water that flowed in upon us from the river. We fled to high ground. When morning came, the river presented a most frightful aspect: it had risen at least eight feet, and flowed with terrifying rapidity. None but the most strong and active boatmen entered the boats. The army marched on the south side of the river, making large circuits to avoid the overflowing [river]. . . . This was one of the most fatiguing marches we had as yet performed, though the distance was not great in a direct line.[70]

To make matters worse, much of the food was spoiled by the wet weather. Surgeon Isaac Senter noted,

The bread casks not being water-proof, admitted the water in plenty, swelled the bread, burst the casks, as well as soured the whole bread. The same fate attended a number of fine casks of peas. These with the others were condemned. We were now curtailed of a very valuable and large part of our provisions. . . . Our fare was now reduced to salt pork and flour. Beef we had now and then, when we could purchase a fat creature, but that was seldom. A few barrels of salt beef remained on hand, but of so indifferent quality, as scarce to be eaten, being killed in the heat of summer, took much damage after salting, that rendered it not only very unwholesome, but very unpalatable.[71]

Despite the difficult conditions, the expedition continued onward. On October 25, a heavy snowfall hit the men, adding to their misery.[72]

When the riflemen reached the area known as the Height of Land (the highest point of the march) the two Pennsylvania companies abandoned all but one of their bateaux. The Virginians, however, carried their remaining seven boats over the difficult portage. John Henry described how the Virginians struggled to haul the boats overland.

It would have made your heart ache to view the intolerable labors of these fine fellows. Some of them, it was said, had the flesh worn from their shoulders, even to the bone.[73]

The Virginians were not alone in their suffering. The constant physical exertion and lack of provisions took its toll on all the men. George Morison reported,

The time had now arrived when our suffering began to assume a different shape. Famine stared us in the face. Our provisions began to grow scarce, many of our men too sick, and the whole of us much reduced by our fatigues; and this too in the midst of a horrid wilderness, far distant from any inhabitation.[74]

A week later, Morison recorded in his journal that,

Never perhaps was there a more forlorn set of human beings.
. . . Every one of us shivering from head to foot, as hungry as
wolves, and nothing to eat save a little flour we had left, which
we made dough of and baked in the fires . . . .[75]

The expedition's ordeal peaked in early November. Dr. Senter recalled,

We had now arrived . . . to almost the zenith of distress. Several
had been entirely destitute of either meat or bread for many days.
. . . The voracious disposition many of us had now arrived at, rendered almost anything admissible. . . . In company was a poor
dog, [who had] hitherto lived through all the tribulations. . . . This
poor animal was instantly devoured, without leaving any vestige
of the sacrifice. Nor did the shaving soap, pomatum, and even the
lip salve, leather of their shoes, cartridge boxes, &c., share any
better fate.[76]

Private Morison had a similar meal on November 2.

This morning when we arose to resume our march, many of us
were so weak as to be unable to stand without the support of our
guns. I myself . . . staggered about like a drunken man. . . . This
day I roasted my shot-pouch and eat it. It was now four days since
I had eat anything save the skin of a squirrel. . . . A number re-
sorted to the same expedient; and in a short time there was not a
shot-pouch to be seen among all those within my view. . . . This
was the last resort. . . . Hope was now partly extinguished; and
its place was supplied with deep insensibility.[77]

The expedition had degenerated into a disorganized band of starv-
ing men, scattered along a twenty mile stretch of land. Many fell out
of the march, resigned to die in the wilderness. The last three musket
companies of the column actually turned back without orders. Yet
the rest of the expedition carried on.

Their perseverance was rewarded on November 3, when the expedition sighted cattle being driven toward them by an American ad-

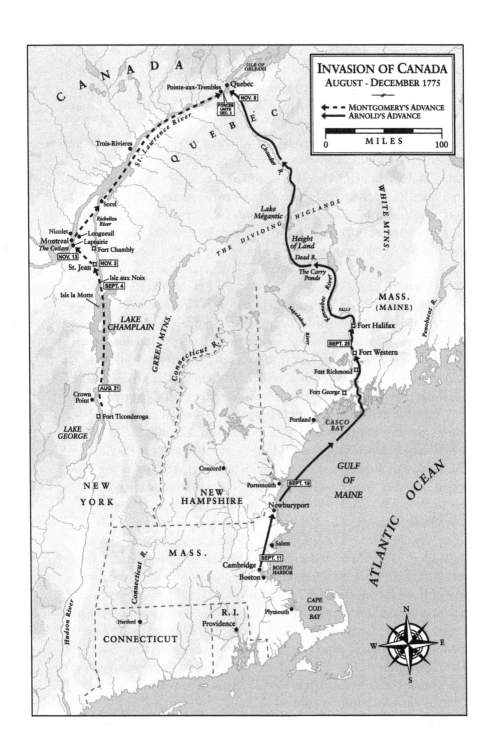

INVASION OF CANADA
AUGUST - DECEMBER 1775

◄--- MONTGOMERY'S ADVANCE
◄— ARNOLD'S ADVANCE

MILES
0   100

vance party. The cattle were immediately butchered, and the famished men gorged themselves on fresh beef and other provisions. Many of the rejuvenated men returned to the wilderness to assist their exhausted comrades. Arnold's march through the wilderness was over, but more challenges lay ahead.

While hundreds of Pennsylvania riflemen struggled through the wilderness of Maine and manned the siege lines of the Continental Army in Boston, Pennsylvania's Committee of Safety in Philadelphia continued its efforts to defend the Delaware River (and Philadelphia) and raise and supply additional troops. The committee had authorized the construction of thirteen river gondolas over the summer, and most were ready for service by September, so the committee appointed commanders for the vessels. Work also continued on river obstacles and forts along the river south of Philadelphia.

The mood in Philadelphia in September 1775 was one of intolerance to anyone with loyalist sympathies. Samuel Morris described an incident in early September where two suspected loyalists were, "paraded in a Cart through all the Streets to their great Mortification and unpitied by every person who saw them. Their Crimes were speaking disrespectfully of the present Measures [of Congress]."[78]

As the Pennsylvania Assembly prepared to meet in late September, the Committee of Safety offered several recommendations for the assembly to consider. One was to build several powder magazines in the colony to store the gunpowder that was frantically being collected. Another was to address a situation that bothered a large number of Pennsylvanians who had sacrificed their personal comfort to serve in the militia. The Committee of Safety noted that while the troops in the field "Are subjected to Expenses to accoutre [equip] themselves as Soldiers, and their affairs suffer considerably . . . very many of their Country Men, who have not associated, are entirely free of these Inconveniences."[79] Those of the Quaker faith were particularly absent among the troops, despite the initial enthusiasm of some to oppose Great Britain. The Associators believed that "Where the Liberty of all is at stake, every Man should assist in its support."[80] The Committee of Safety agreed and proposed to the assembly that a tax on any able body man in Pennsylvania who was not willing to serve as an Associator be applied to them.

The Committee of Safety also included an estimate of the money it had expended through September as well as that which it expected to still spend. It amounted to over £87,000.[81] Muskets and powder accounted for more than half of the expenditures. The thirteen armed boats authorized by the committee to patrol the Delaware River and defend Philadelphia came to over £7,000, money well spent in the minds of the committee, since its priority, as evidenced by the amount of time the committee spent on matters pertaining to river defenses, was to stop the British navy from threatening Philadelphia.[82]

On October 16, the committee instructed the thirteen armed vessels built and outfitted over the summer to "repel force by force," should any of the King's ships, "proceed up the river in a hostile manner or with hostile intentions."[83] Pennsylvanians had been fighting in Massachusetts with the Continental Army for two months and now they were authorized to do so in their own colony.

Four days prior to the committee's instructions, the Continental Congress called upon Pennsylvania to raise a regiment of Continental infantry upon the same terms as New Jersey, namely eight companies of men for one year. The Committee of Safety referred the request to the Pennsylvania Assembly which agreed to the recommendation and began the process of selecting officers for the unit in late October.[84] John Bull was nominated by the assembly to command the regiment and was appointed colonel by the Continental Congress in late November.[85] He resigned his commission just two months later and was replaced by John Philip De Haas.[86]

DELAWARE

As any British warship that attempted to sail up the Delaware River would first have to pass the Lower Three Counties of Delaware, the Pennsylvania Committee of Safety depended on the Lower Counties to remain vigilant and if need be, resist the British should they attempt to land or pass with hostile intentions. The Pennsylvania committee voted to lend the inhabitants of Lewis Town (present day Lewes, Delaware) six six-pound cannon and ammunition, "to defend themselves from any Hostile attacks."[87] It was contingent on the inhabitants agreeing to return the cannon on demand and the Delaware Committee of Safety agreeing to repay the quantity of ammunition in a reasonable time.

At almost the same time as this arrangement was made in mid-September, Vice Admiral Graves in Boston justified the action of the Pennsylvania Committee of Safety by reminding Captain John Collins, the commander of HMS *Nautilus*, to "exert your utmost Endeavours to . . . restrict the Trade of the Colonies and to prevent the importation of Gunpowder, Arms, and Ammunition and every kind of illegal Commerce or Communication." The admiral added,

> And whereas almost the whole Continent is in open Rebellion against his Majesty, and the Rebels have fitted out armed Vessels, and are endeavouring to equip a naval force to oppose and annoy the King's Ships; You are hereby required and directed to take, sink, burn and destroy every American armed Vessel you meet.[88]

Ships loaded with provisions or supplies of any sort useful for the British navy or army in Boston were also to be seized and sent to Boston. Fortunately for the inhabitants of Delaware and Pennsylvania, the *Nautilus* was diverted to duties off of New England before it could begin its mission, and with the British navy stretched thin in North America, no British warship was posted in Delaware Bay for the remainder of 1775.

The lack of British activity near Delaware, coupled with the limited activity of Governor Penn and the fact that Delaware men had not been sent out of the colony yet, meant that the situation remained relatively calm in the Lower Three Counties on the Delaware River. Militia continued to form and drill; six hundred reportedly exercised under Colonel Thomas Cooch in early November, watched by two thousand spectators.[89] Efforts throughout the three counties to obtain additional gunpowder and weapons also continued, but with no British or even Tory force to confront, the situation in Delaware remained calm.

MARYLAND

Maryland's two rifle companies in Massachusetts managed to avoid the controversy and derision created by some of the Pennsylvania riflemen in General Washington's army. Posted near Roxbury with Captain Hugh Stephenson's Virginia rifle company, the three companies served admirably. Tragedy struck the Maryland troops in mid-October when Captain Cresap died of illness in New York City on his way back to Maryland to recover his health. Lieutenant Moses Rawlings took command of the rifle company in Cresap's absence.

With no British military presence in Maryland and a royal governor, Robert Eden, who still had some influence with the population, Maryland, like Delaware, was relatively, but not completely, quiet in the fall of 1775. The seizure of a pilot boat from Annapolis near the Virginia capes in mid-September by the HMS *King-Fisher* may have triggered an attempt at retaliation in the city against suspected Tories. Governor Eden described the incident to Lord Dartmouth.

> Some few, but very few of the most violent here, made an Attempt . . . to collect the people of the City together, in Order to drive, or cart, out of the Town all of the Tories, as they term those who will not muster, nor sign the Association . . . . On my Speaking to many of them, and desiring their Attendance, they made a Point of being present at the meeting under Liberty Tree, and with Spirit, Resolution, and Threats of Force, totally overset a madheaded Scheme, set on foot by only eight or nine very worthless idle Fellows, and I hope have put an End to any future internal Attempts of a similar Nature in this City.[90]

Although Governor Eden had managed to retain more influence in his colony than nearly any other royal governor, he could not stop the Maryland Council of Safety from procuring muskets, accoutrements, and gunpowder, something the council worked hard to do throughout the fall.

In mid-November, an incident occurred in western Maryland that further worsened colonial relations with Great Britain. Dr. John Connolly had been a land agent for Virginia's royal governor, Lord Dunmore, and had participated in Dunmore's expedition against the Shawnee Indians in 1774. Commanding a company of militia at Fort Pitt when word of hostilities at Lexington and Concord arrived in the spring, Connolly remained loyal to the British and immediately saw an opportunity to recruit western Indians to fight for the Crown.

He travelled to Virginia in the summer of 1775 to consult with Lord Dunmore, who had fled Virginia's capital in June and was aboard a British warship off of Norfolk. Dunmore approved Connolly's plan and sent him to Boston to consult with General Gage. The British commander also saw the benefit of recruiting western Indians and offered Connolly a lieutenant colonel's commission along with weapons and gunpowder to arm his western force. Connolly then returned to Virginia to apprize Governor Dunmore of the status of his plan.[91]

He was to make his way to Detroit to take command of a detachment of British troops posted there. Supported by a large number of Indians that he planned to recruit, Connolly would then march on Pittsburgh. After capturing that important post, he planned to take Cumberland, Maryland, and then, sometime in April, rendezvous with Governor Dunmore in Alexandria.[92]

Alas, Connolly revealed his intentions to the wrong person in Boston and word of the plot reached General Washington. He informed the Continental Congress which in turn informed the different Committees of Safety to be on the lookout for Connolly. After his second meeting with Lord Dunmore in Norfolk, Connolly made his way up the Chesapeake Bay and Potomac River, then went by land to Hagerstown, Maryland, where he was recognized and arrested by the local militia. Brought to Philadelphia in chains, Connolly remained imprisoned for nearly five years before finally being paroled.[93]

The psychological impact of the news of Connolly's plot upon the colonists was enormous. Many were enraged that British authorities would unleash Indians upon their fellow Englishmen and the incident was cited as justification for continued colonial resistance, and for some, independence.[94]

Four

Winter

December 1775–February 1776

WHILE EACH COLONY DEALT WITH ITS OWN INTERNAL ISSUES, most of the American colonies also maintained a keen interest on events in Canada. News of General Montgomery's success at St-Jean and Montreal, and of Arnold's arrival at Quebec in November, elevated the hopes of many that the Americans were on the verge of expelling the British completely from Canada. Colonel Arnold's force, however, was not sufficient to effectively besiege the walled city of Quebec, much less storm it, so he withdrew upriver to Point aux Tremble to unite with Montgomery.[1]

General Montgomery, in Montreal, scrambled to take advantage of his success at St. Jean and Montreal before winter put a halt to operations in Canada. With offers of a general bounty and the distribution of captured clothing from the British, he had managed to convince seven hundred men to extend their enlistments until April.[2] About three hundred of these men were from New England, the rest, approximately four hundred, were New Yorkers.[3] They were supported by a newly raised Continental regiment of Canadians under Colonel James Livingston of approximately two hundred men.[4]

Montgomery loaded a portion of his New York troops, approximately three hundred men, aboard the British transport ships captured near Sorel and sailed downriver to Pointe aux Trembles. Major John Brown's small force of Massachusetts and New Hampshire men and several cannon at Sorel joined Montgomery. Colonel Livingston's two hundred Canadian Continentals marched by land to Pointe aux Trembles.[5] They united with Montgomery and Arnold in early December.

Soon after their arrival at Pointe aux Trembles, Montgomery, supported by a number of Canadian civilians who provided sleighs to transport men and supplies, moved his united command to the outskirts of Quebec to sever all land access to the city. Several calls to surrender were rejected by Governor Carleton and efforts to bombard the city into submission proved fruitless given the small number of cannon Montgomery had. With weather conditions deteriorating, Montgomery decided that taking the city by storm was his only viable option.[6] It was decided to use the cover of night, and the next winter storm, to do so. Early in the morning of December 31, with a winter storm howling, Montgomery commenced his attack.

His plan called for a pincer strike against the lower town of Quebec from two directions while a third detachment feigned an attack on the western approaches of Quebec (the Plains of Abraham) to distract the enemy's attention away from the lower town. Montgomery led approximately two hundred New York troops along the shore of the St. Lawrence River to approach the lower town from the south while Colonel Arnold led his troops, 350 strong, through the suburbs of Saint Roche and along the St. Charles River to approach the lower town of Quebec from the north.[7] Once the lower town was captured, the united American force would storm the upper town. Since they were significantly outnumbered, the American plan depended on both surprise and decisive execution.

The attack began at 5:00 a.m. when Colonel Livingston and Major Brown led their detachments toward St. John's Gate (at the center of the western wall) and Cape Diamond (on the southwest corner of the wall) and commenced firing on the British sentinels.[8] While Quebec's defenders raced to their alarm posts, Montgomery led his detachment from the Plains of Abraham down to Wolf's Cove and then along the St. Lawrence River toward the lower town. He led them through a palisaded barrier and toward a guardhouse. A blast of grapeshot erupted from the guardhouse and smashed into the advancing Americans, killing Montgomery and several of his officers and men. The shock of the blast, coupled with the loss of Montgomery, unnerved the surviving officers and they hastily aborted the attack and withdrew, abandoning Colonel Arnold and his detachment to their fate.[9]

Arnold's column approached the lower town of Quebec through the northern suburbs and along the St. Charles River. Arnold accompanied a thirty man advance guard at the head of the column. A single six pound brass cannon on a sled followed, its crew struggling to move it through the snow. The remainder of Arnold's force, with Captain Morgan of Virginia and his rifle company in the lead, followed. Charles Porterfield was with Morgan and described the march to the lower town in his diary:

> We paraded at 4 o' clock, A.M. . . . The signal given, with shouts we set out. In passing by the Palace gate, they fired, and the bells rung an alarm. We marched with as much precipitancy as possible, sustaining a heavy fire for some distance, without the opportunity to return it, being close under the wall.[10]

Pennsylvania rifleman John Joseph Henry, who was alongside or right behind the Virginians, provided a bit more description of the approach through the storm:

> Covering the locks of our guns with the lappets of our coats, and holding down our heads, (for it was impossible to bear up our faces against the imperious storm of wind and snow,) we ran along the foot of the hill in single file . . . we received a tremendous fire of musketry from the ramparts above us. Here we lost some brave men, when powerless to return the salutes we received, as the enemy was covered by his impregnable defences. They were even sightless to us—we could see nothing but the blaze from the muzzles of their muskets.[11]

Arnold's detachment continued on through the storm until it reached an enemy barricade (wooden wall), with two cannon blocking the approach. The original plan called for the six pound American field piece to be brought forth to blast the barricade. Dragging the heavy cannon through the deep snow, however, proved too difficult and it was abandoned along the route. Complicating matters further, much of Arnold's force, which had become spread out in the difficult march, went astray in the blinding storm and narrow streets of Saint Roche and the lower town. Despite this, Arnold led the troops that kept up with him forward, toward the barricade. Before he reached it, he was wounded in the leg, yet the advance continued without him. Virginian Charles Porterfield described what happened:

> Coming to the barrier of the entrance of the lower town, guarded by a captain and 50 men, with two pieces of cannon, one of which they discharged and killed two men, we forced them from the cannon, firing in at the port-holes, all the time exposed to the fire of the musketry from the bank above us in the upper town. Here, Colonel Arnold was wounded in the leg and had to retire. The scaling ladders being brought up, if there was any honor in being first over the barrier, I had it. I was immediately followed by Captain Morgan. Upon our approach the guards fled, and we followed close to the guard-house, when, making a halt till some more men should come up, we sallied through into the street. We took thirty men and a captain.[12]

Captain Daniel Morgan gave a similar account of the assault.

> I had to attack a two-gun battery, supported by Captain M'Leod and 50 regular troops. The first gun that was fired missed us, the second flashed, when I ordered the ladder, which was on two men's shoulders, to be placed; (every two men carried a ladder.) This order was immediately obeyed, and, for fear the business might not be executed with spirit, I mounted myself, and was the first man who leaped into the town, among M'Leod's guard, who were panic struck, and, after a faint resistance, ran into a house that joined the battery and platform. I [landed] on the end

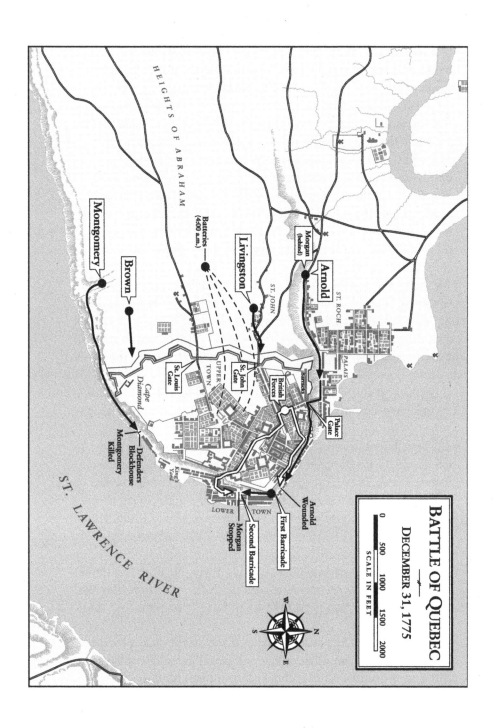

BATTLE OF QUEBEC
DECEMBER 31, 1775

SCALE IN FEET

0 500 1000 1500 2000

of a heavy piece of artillery, which hurt me exceedingly and perhaps saved my life, as I fell from the gun upon the platform, where
the bayonets were not directed. Charles Porterfield, who was then
a Cadet in my company, was the first man who followed me; the
rest lost not a moment, but sprang in as fast as they could find
room; all this was performed in a few seconds. I ordered the men
to fire into the house, and follow up their fire with their pikes (for
besides our rifles we were furnished with long espontoons) this
was done, and the guard was driven into the street. I went through
a sally-port at the end of the platform; met them in the street; and
ordered them to lay down their arms, if they expected quarter;
they took me at my word and every man threw down his gun.[13]

Although they had captured the first enemy barricade, Arnold's
troops were scattered about the lower town in disarray and their
wounded commander taken to the rear. A delay in the assault ensued
as the officers with Morgan decided to wait for their men to re-form
and for Montgomery and his detachment to arrive from the other
side of the Lower Town.

Unwilling to stand idle, Morgan advanced ahead of the stalled
Americans to reconnoiter the second barricade. He observed that,

The sally-port through the barrier was standing open; the guard
left it; and the people came running, in seeming platoon, and gave
themselves up, in order to get out of the way of the confusion that
was likely to ensue. I went up to the edge of the upper town, with
an interpreter, to observe what was going on, as the firing had
ceased. I found no person in arms at all.[14]

Morgan returned and called a council of war. He urged an immediate advance on the second barricade with the men that they had
(approximately two hundred).[15] Morgan bitterly remembered that,

I was overruled by hard reasoning; it was stated that, if I went
on, I would break an order, in the first place; in the next place, I
had more prisoners than I had men; that if I left them, they might
break out, retake the battery, and cut off our retreat; that General

Montgomery was certainly coming down the River St. Lawrence, and would join us in a few minutes, so that we were sure of conquest if we acted with caution. To these arguments I sacrificed my own opinion and lost the town.[16]

Charles Porterfield remembered that nearly an hour passed before the attack was finally resumed.[17]

During this delay, the British rushed men to the second barrier. Lieutenant Colonel Henry Caldwell, the commander of the British militia in Quebec, described what he found there when he arrived with reinforcements from the upper town:

> The enemy had got in [the Lower Town] at the Sault-au-Matelot, [first barricade] but neglecting to push on, as they should have done, were stopped at the second barrier which our people got shut just as I arrived.[18]

Caldwell's timely arrival at the second barricade bolstered the spirits of its defenders. Caldwell posted men inside buildings overlooking the barricade (and Sault-au-Matelot Street, the only avenue of approach for the Americans) and placed a detachment at the foot of the barricade with fixed bayonets, ready to fall upon any rebel who dared scale the twelve-foot high wall.[19]

As daylight approached, Arnold's detachment finally advanced down Sault-au-Matelot Street toward the second barricade, some three hundred yards away.[20] As they rounded a curve, Captain Morgan, at the head of the column, was hailed by a detachment of the enemy that had sallied forth from the second barricade. Captain Abner Stocking recorded what happened in his journal:

> We . . . were proceeding to the second barrier, when on turning an angle in the street, we were hailed by a Captain Anderson who had just issued from the gate with a body of troops to attack us. Captain Morgan who led our little band in this forlorn hope, answered the British Captain by a ball through his head, his soldiers drew him within the barricade and closed the gate; a tremendous fire from the windows of the buildings and port holes of the wall was directed against [us].[21]

Charles Porterfield, still with Captain Morgan, described the heavy fire the Americans faced at the second barricade:

> On approaching the second barrier, [the enemy] hailed us. We immediately fired; they returned it with a shower of shot. Being planted in houses on the opposite side of the barrier, a continual fire ensued for some time, while we rushed up to the barrier, set up our ladder, and, at the same instant, Captain Morgan mounted one, I the other, to force our way, spear in hand, but we were obliged to draw back. Here we were at a disadvantage. Our guns being wet, could not return the fire we were subject to; [we] were obliged to retreat into the street.[22]

Pennsylvania rifleman George Morison also described the assault on the second barricade.

> The ladders are laid to the wall—our gallant officers are mounting followed by several men when a furious discharge of musketry is let loose upon us from behind houses; in an instant we are assailed from different quarters with a deadly fire. We now find it impossible to force the battery or guard the port-holes any longer. We rush on to every part, rouse the enemy from their coverts, and force a body of them to an open fight, some of our riflemen take to houses and do considerable execution. We are now attacked by thrice our number; the battle becomes hot, and is much scattered; but we distinguish each other by hemlock springs previously placed in our hats. All our officers act most gallantly. Betwixt every peal the awful voice of Morgan is heard, whose gigantic stature and terrible appearance carries dismay among the foe wherever he comes.[23]

Despite Morgan's bold leadership and effort, the American situation was critical. "Confined in a narrow street hardly more than twenty feet wide, and on the lower ground, scarcely a ball, well aimed or otherwise, but must take effect upon us," recalled John Joseph Henry.[24] American losses quickly mounted. Lieutenant William Humphreys, Morgan's friend and first lieutenant, fell as did

Captain William Hendricks of the Pennsylvania riflemen, both mortally wounded. Bodies of dead and wounded men littered the narrow street before the barricade. Those who were unhurt sought shelter in nearby buildings and fought on, encouraged by Captain Morgan who "stormed and raged" at both his men and the enemy.[25] Charles Porterfield found cover inside one such building with fellow Virginian Peter Bruin and seven or eight other men and recalled that,

> We fired . . . from the windows, determined to stand it out or die. . . . Upon seeing Colonel Green and others give up their arms, we held a council what to do, Bruin declaring to the men that, if they thought proper to risk it, he was willing to fight our way out—that he should stand or fall with them.[26]

Inside one building that comprised part of the barricade, the struggle became hand to hand as combatants from both sides entered simultaneously, the Americans through the front door and the British via a ladder through an upstairs window. The British emerged victorious in this clash, driving the Americans back into the street.[27]

While the fight raged on at the second barrier, hundreds of enemy troops recaptured the first barricade behind the Americans and advanced on them from the rear. Trapped in the lower town between two strong enemy forces, the Americans fought on, hoping that Montgomery's detachment would arrive to relieve them. By 10:00 a.m., however, it was evident that Montgomery was not coming and that the attack had failed. With no hope of holding on until nightfall and a promise of good treatment from their captors, Arnold's men surrendered.

Over three hundred Americans were captured in the attack on Quebec including the bulk of the Virginia and Pennsylvania riflemen attached to Arnold. Another sixty were killed or wounded.[28] The British lost only a handful of men. Yet, Governor Carleton opted not to press his advantage and remained behind the city's walls. Colonel Arnold, who was seriously wounded in the leg, assumed command of the remnants of the American army outside of Quebec. Although he could not breach the walls of Quebec, he could still disrupt Carleton's communication and the commerce of the city and posted his remaining troops to do so. Arnold also appealed to the new ranking commander of American troops in Canada, Brigadier-General David Wooster of Connecticut, for reinforcements.

Sixty-five year old General Wooster, who had remained in Montreal upon his arrival in the late fall, had few troops to spare, but he did forward nearly two hundred New York troops to Arnold at the end of January. Like Arnold, Wooster requested reinforcements from General Schuyler in Albany who in turn requested assistance from the Continental Congress as well as from leaders in New England. A trickle of troops from Massachusetts arrived over the next month and Congress passed bold resolutions to hold Canada, but with winter firmly in place, there was little to be done until spring.

NEW YORK
The focus of New York's leaders prior to the disastrous news of Quebec was on suppressing Tory sentiment in the colony. Although Isaac Sears, one of New York's most ardent opponents to Britain, had actually relocated to Connecticut in September, he led several attacks on suspected Tories in New York. In November, Sears led one hundred men on horseback into Westchester County, seized several prominent Loyalists and burned a sloop used for supplying the HMS *Asia*.[29] Sears and his men then rode into New York City and pillaged James Rivington's loyalist newspaper, stealing his type.[30]

General Schuyler in Albany was instructed by the Continental Congress in late December to disarm the numerous loyalists in Tryon County (which spanned much of New York's frontier and included the Mohawk Valley) and apprehend their leaders.[31] In late January he reported to General Washington that,

> I returned last Night from Tryon County into which I marched a Body of Militia, to disarm the Malignants, which I have [done]. Six of the [leaders] of about two hundred and fifty or three hundred Scotch Highlanders are to go [as] Prisoners to Pennsylvania, as are six Others of the English & Dutch Inhabitants of that County. We have taken four six & four Pounders [cannon] together with a Number of Swivels & Blunderbusses.[32]

Two weeks before General Schuyler's letter, Washington, concerned by reports (many attributed to Isaac Sears) of large scale Tory support on Long Island as well as reports that the British might soon move against New York, sent General Charles Lee to New York with the following instructions:

> Having such information . . . that the Inhabitants (or a great part of them) on Long Island in the Colony of New York, are not only Inemical [hostile] to the Rights and Liberties of America, but by their conduct and Publick Profession's, have discovered a disposition to aid and assist in the reduction of that Colony to Ministerial Tyranny—And as it is a matter of the utmost Importance to prevent the Enemy from taking possession of the City of New York & the North [Hudson] River. . . . You will therefore, with such Volunteers as are willing to join you . . . repair to the City of New York, and calling upon the Commanding Officers of the Forces of New Jersey for such assistance as he can afford . . . you are to put that City in the best posture of Defence which the Season & Circumstances will admit of—Disarming all such persons upon long Island and elsewhere (& if necessary otherwise securing them) whose conduct, and declarations have render'd them justly suspected of Designs unfriendly to the Views of Congress.[33]

General Lee, a former British officer with extensive military service in Europe, was perhaps the most celebrated American officer next to General Washington in the Continental Army. By 1776, Lee was also Washington's second in command. Although Lee was a native of Britain and had only arrived in the colonies in 1773 as a retired British officer on half pay, he had earned the trust and admiration of many in Congress as well as the army over the past eight months.

Prior to Lee's arrival in New York, the Continental Congress reauthorized New York's four Continental battalions for another year (1776). The term of enlistment for the original troops expired in December, so most of the officers who remained in Continental service scrambled in January to recruit new troops to replace those that had returned to their homes.[34]

New York's Committee of Safety was uncomfortable with the apparent blanket authority that General Lee possessed regarding the defense of New York and expressed its displeasure to both Lee and the Continental Congress. Up until Lee's arrival, decisions concerning New York's defensive placements rested with the committee, but General Lee would have none of that. The Continental Congress offered a solution; Lee did not have to answer to the New York Committee of Safety or Congress regarding his decisions, instead, a committee of the Continental Congress was sent to New York to confer with Lee.[35]

Lee, suffering from a severe case of gout that restricted his ability to walk or stand, entered the city on February 4, on a litter. That same day a British warship carrying General Henry Clinton (on his way to command British operations in the Carolinas) was sighted off Sandy Hook, on its way into New York Harbor. Fear that the city was about to be attacked spread quickly, but Clinton's stop in New York Harbor, primarily to meet with Governor Tryon, proved brief and uneventful, and he soon sailed back to sea, leaving the HMS *Asia* and HMS *Phoenix* (44 guns, 250 men), which had joined the *Asia* in December, still menacing the city.

Lee took a number of measures to restrict communication with Governor Tryon from shore and to better prepare the city's defenses. Strong artillery batteries and redoubts were constructed on Brooklyn Heights (a crucial position that overlooked Manhattan) as well as on the east side of Manhattan to restrict navigation of the East River. Other positions were fortified near Hell's Gate to obstruct passage to the East River from Long Island Sound. To better protect the west side of Manhattan, all of the streets that led to the Hudson River were barricaded and King's Bridge, on the northern end of the island was protected by several redoubts.[36] Hundreds of militia from both New York and Connecticut worked on the defenses. Upriver some fifty miles, new forts in the Highlands were begun in place of the disappointing fort on Constitution Island, across from West Point. Construction on Fort Montgomery, named in honor of General Montgomery, was commenced just five miles downriver from West Point on the west bank of the river. It would be the cornerstone of New York's defense of the upper Hudson River.

Although the defensive measures undertaken in early 1776 were largely the result of Lee's orders, he did not remain in New York to see them completed. Aware that the British were planning operations in the South, the Continental Congress instructed Lee to proceed to Virginia in March. Newly promoted Brigadier-General William Alexander, Lord Stirling, was left in charge of fulfilling Lee's defensive plans for New York.

While much of New York was focused on the defense of the city and events in Canada, Colonel Henry Knox of Massachusetts worked assiduously to transport a number of much needed cannon from Fort Ticonderoga to Washington's army outside of Boston. In early January, Knox informed Washington that the lack of snow and unexpected thaw in temperatures had made the roads impassable and slowed his advance considerably. Knox optimistically declared from Albany however, that "the first severe night will make the Ice on the river sufficiently strong" to cross and that he expected to be in Springfield, Massachusetts, within ten days of the next hard freeze.[37] Good to his word, Colonel Knox arrived in Cambridge on January 18, the cannon deposited twenty miles away in Framingham.[38] They would prove pivotal to the American cause in the coming weeks.

New Jersey
New Jersey had benefitted from its relative obscurity compared to Massachusetts, New York, Pennsylvania, and Canada, and with no direct British threat looming over it, the Continental Congress decided that the colony was free to send many of its troops to New York to assist its neighbor. Both of New Jersey's Continental regiments were ordered to New York in December 1775. Several companies were sent to the New York Highlands on the Hudson River to man the forts there. The bulk of the troops, however, were ordered to New York City.[39] A month later the Continental Congress adjusted its instructions and ordered Colonel Maxwell's 2nd New Jersey Regiment to march to Albany to reinforce General Schuyler.[40] Two days after that, on January 10, Congress authorized the formation of a third New Jersey Continental regiment under Colonel Elias Dayton.[41]

Concern over loyalist opposition sparked several county committees in New Jersey to call out their militia to suppress loyalist sentiment and activity over the winter. In Sussex County hundreds of militia rounded up forty suspected Tories and forced most to sign the continental association.[42] The handful who refused to do so were sent to Philadelphia to face the Continental Congress.

New Jersey's efforts against Tories extended into neighboring New York in early January when the colony sent six hundred militia under Colonel Nathaniel Heard, per the Continental Congress's request, to Queen Anne County on Long Island to help quell Tory sentiment there.[43]

Just one day before Congress made its request to New Jersey, it passed a resolution on suspected Tories that aimed, "to frustrate the mischievous machinations, and restrain the wicked practices of these men."[44] Congress advised that such men were to be disarmed, "and the more dangerous among them . . . kept in safe custody."[45]

Colonel Alexander (Lord Stirling) of the First New Jersey Regiment interpreted the resolve to apply to royal officials as well as ordinary colonists, so when incriminating letters Governor Franklin had written to Lord Dartmouth fell into Stirling's hands, he ordered Franklin's arrest. For a moment it looked as if Governor Franklin was to be held in the town of Elizabeth, but instructions from the Committee of Safety allowed him to remain at his residence in Perth Amboy under house arrest, instead.[46]

The New Jersey Provincial Congress met in February and approved additional funds for the defense of the colony. It also appointed delegates to the next Continental Congress and most interestingly, called for an election of delegates for the Third Provincial Congress scheduled for May.[47] This was important because unlike previous conventions, whose delegations were selected by county committees, delegates for the Third Convention would be elected within their counties directly by the inhabitants of each county. As the issue of independence, which loomed larger than ever thanks to the publication of Thomas Paine's pamphlet, *Common Sense*, would undoubtedly be the issue for the Third Convention to address, the election of its delegates would serve as a referendum on independence for the people of New Jersey.

PENNSYLVANIA

In Pennsylvania, much had been accomplished on the Delaware River to protect Philadelphia from attack. The river galleys, each with an 18 pound cannon on its bow and a crew of fifty, along with the submerged river obstacles (which had already sunk several civilian vessels who carelessly tried to pass them) and the artillery batteries built onshore to defend the submerged obstacles, presented a powerful deterrent for any British attempt to sail upriver to attack Philadelphia.[48]

The Continental Congress had authorized the origins of a continental navy in mid-October when it determined that, "a swift sailing vessel, to carry ten carriage guns . . . with eighty men, be fitted . . . for a cruise of three months . . . for intercepting such transports as may be laden with warlike stores and other supplies for our enemies."[49] A second vessel was added the same day and in late October, Congress authorized two additional ships.[50] A fifth ship, the *Providence* from Rhode Island, was added in December and by January a squadron of five Continental ships was ready to sail from Philadelphia. The *Alfred* (30 guns, 220 crew) and the *Columbus*, (28 guns, 220 crew) were the largest vessels in the squadron, followed by the *Andrew Doria* (16 guns, 130 crew), the *Cabot* (14 guns, 120 crew), and the *Providence* (12 guns, 90 crew).[51] Each vessel also had a contingent of marines onboard (ranging from twenty-eight to sixty marines depending on the ship).[52]

Congress also called on Pennsylvania to raise four new Continental regiments in December.[53] Arthur St. Clair, John Shee, Anthony Wayne, and Robert Magaw were nominated by the Pennsylvania Council of Safety and approved by Congress to command the new regiments.[54] An additional regiment was authorized by Congress in early January, bringing Pennsylvania's total of Continental regiments in 1776 to seven, counting the 1775 Pennsylvania rifle battalion that was renamed the First Continental Regiment at the start of 1776.[55] Each of Pennsylvania's Continental regiments (except the First Continental Regiment who were all riflemen) consisted of seven companies of musket troops and one company of riflemen.[56] Colonel William Irvine was selected by Pennsylvania to command the newest regiment, the 6th Pennsylvania.[57]

On January 8, the Continental Congress, still unaware of General Montgomery's death and defeat at Quebec but aware of the severe reduction of troops under General Schuyler, voted to send the 1st and 2nd Pennsylvania Regiments to Albany as reinforcements to counter an expected British push in the spring to recapture Canada.[58]

Growing concern for the security of New York City prompted the Continental Congress to order Colonel Anthony Wayne's 4th Pennsylvania Regiment to the city on February 20.[59] A week earlier Congress had urged Pennsylvania's Committee of Safety to send detachments of militia there.[60]

In Massachusetts, Colonel William Thompson's 1st Pennsylvania Regiment (his old rifle battalion) continued to serve in the lines outside Boston. They had performed admirably since the mutinous affair in September and as their enlistments lasted into the summer of 1776, Thompson's battalion was one of the few experienced units remaining in Washington's army in January 1776. The other New England regiments that had served outside of Boston in 1775 underwent substantial change in their ranks when the enlistments of their men expired in December.

Congress decided to rename the regiments with General Washington at the start of 1776. They all became known as Continental Regiments, without any reference to their place of origin. The units were labeled 1st, or 2nd, or 3rd Continental Regiment based on the date the original unit began its service in the Continental Army in 1775. As a result, Colonel William Thompson's Pennsylvania riflemen were given the honor of serving in the re-designated 1st Continental Regiment.

In Quebec, most of the survivors of Captain Hendricks and Captain Smith's Pennsylvania rifle companies languished as prisoners, adequately cared for, but still imprisoned by the British. Just a handful of riflemen evaded capture, and they waited with the rest of Colonel Benedict Arnold's small force outside of Quebec for the winter to subside and reinforcements to arrive.

DELAWARE

In early December, the Continental Congress, likely with the blessing and encouragement of Delaware's delegates, instructed the three lower counties of the Delaware to raise a regiment of Continental soldiers.[61] Eight companies were to be recruited from the three counties to serve for one year. Irish born Colonel John Haslet was selected by the Delaware Council of Safety and approved by the Continental Congress to command the regiment.[62] He had previous militia command experience in the colony, but none in armed conflict. Nevertheless, Haslet, who was educated for the Presbyterian ministry but practiced medicine in Dover prior to his appointment, was well regarded among Delaware's leaders and population and proved to be an excellent choice to lead the regiment.

As in the other colonies, loyalist sentiment appeared to grow in Delaware over the winter as talk of colonial independence increased. It would erupt in the spring with further talk of independence and the arrival of the HMS *Roebuck* (44 guns, 250 men) in Delaware Bay.

MARYLAND

The increased attention directed toward the question of independence for the colonies seems to have startled Maryland's leaders in the winter of 1775-76. When the Maryland Convention met in December, it voted to restrict its delegates to the Continental Congress from supporting any movement toward independence.[63] Despite being one of the first colonies outside of New England to call for stronger measures to enhance colonial militias, reconciliation was still the preferred goal of most Marylanders.

Maryland was not averse to preparing to fight, however, and joined Pennsylvania in building warships to do so. A 28 gun frigate, christened the *Virginia*, was fitted out in Baltimore in December and Maryland sailors manned the cruisers *Hornet* and *Wasp*, which were also fitted out in Baltimore in the fall. They joined the newly created Continental Navy under Commodore Hopkins in January.[64]

At the start of 1776, the Maryland Convention voted to strengthen the colony's defenses by raising 1,444 regular (full time) soldiers. About a third of these troops (eight companies of sixty-eight men) were formed into a regiment under the command of Colonel William Smallwood, a prominent member of the Maryland Convention.[65] Nine other independent companies of one hundred men each accounted for the rest of the 1,444 regulars. Two of the independent companies were to be artillery companies.[66]

Five of Colonel Smallwood's companies were posted in Annapolis along with one of the two artillery companies. His remaining three companies of regulars were posted in Baltimore with the other artillery company. The counties of Worcester, Somerset, Dorchester, Tabot, and St. Mary's received one full independent company of regulars while Queen Anne and Kent split a company and Calvert and Charles County split the last remaining company of regulars.[67]

Although these troops were to serve continuously (as opposed to militia who were called to action when needed or to drill occasionally) they were not Continental soldiers because the Continental Congress had yet to authorize the formation of a Continental regiment in Maryland. The two rifle companies Maryland sent to Boston in the summer continued to serve as Maryland's only Continental soldiers.

While Maryland strove to raise nearly 1,500 regular troops at the start of 1776, two companies of Maryland minutemen were sent to Northumberland County on the eastern shore of Virginia, at the request of the Continental Congress to counteract mounting Tory sentiment and activity there.[68] They were eagerly received by the Northampton County Committee in mid-February, who apologized for the indifferent accommodations that were offered to the troops. The Virginians assured them that "nothing in our power shall be wanting to promote your convenience and happiness" during their stay.[69]

By mid-January the Continental sloop *Hornet* (eight 4 pound cannon) and schooner *Wasp*, (eight 2 pound cannon) were ready to sail from Baltimore. They were ordered by the Continental Congress to "take under . . . convoy such vessels as are ready for the Sea, as shall be committed to your Care . . . & see them safe through the Capes of Virginia."[70] The two warships were then to proceed north to Delaware Bay to rendezvous with Commodore Ezek Hopkins and his squadron of Continental ships sailing from Philadelphia.[71] They joined Commodore Hopkins on February 13.[72]

Part II

1776

Five

Spring

THE ARRIVAL OF CANNON FROM FORT TICONDEROGA IN JANUARY, followed by a supply of gunpowder and ordnance for the cannon from New York City, provided General Washington with an opportunity to finally seize the initiative in the stalemated siege of Boston. Washington broached the idea of a direct assault upon Boston to a council of war in mid-February, but it was strongly opposed by his officers as too hazardous and unlikely to succeed. Instead, the war council called for the fortification and bombardment of Boston from Dorchester Heights, unoccupied high ground that overlooked the southern section of Boston and the harbor.[1]

To erect fortifications upon the frozen ground and in the face of the enemy required more than the usual preparation. Lieutenant Colonel Rufus Putnam provided the solution from a book on field engineers. Prior to occupying Dorchester Heights, the army constructed a number of chandeliers (wooden cribs) to hold fascines (wooden sticks tightly tied together into bundles). Screwed Hay (hay that was twisted into a thick rope and then laid in stacks) was also used to shield the army's movement along a causeway to Dorchester Heights.[2]

Washington did not seek to build an impenetrable fortress upon Dorchester Heights, but rather, simply provoke the British to leave their secure position in Boston and fight the Americans outside of Boston. He was confident that if they did so, the American army would emerge victorious.

Washington ordered 2,000 troops forward to occupy Dorchester Heights on the evening of March 4. They were not discovered by the British until the next morning. General Howe's first inclination was to drive the Americans from the heights and he made preparations to do so. His experience at Bunker Hill, combined with a belief that Boston was of little further use to the British, caused Howe to change his mind and he resolved instead to evacuate Boston.

Washington, who had waited several days for the British to attack, received word of Howe's intention to abandon Boston through a letter from several of the city's selectmen on March 8. The town would be spared, reported the selectmen, if the British evacuation went unmolested by Washington's forces.[3]

Washington withheld fire and watched the British conduct their evacuation, which took over a week to accomplish. The American commander and his troops were not idle during this time. Washington's attention swung to New York, where he expected Howe to go, and Washington made preparations to march the bulk of his army there as soon as possible.

Howe did indeed have plans to go to New York, but first he sailed with his army to Halifax, Nova Scotia, to reorganize and await further assistance from Britain.

New York

Waiting for Washington and his army in New York was Brigadier General William Alexander (Lord Stirling) of New Jersey. He had assumed command of New York's defenses on the departure of General Charles Lee, who was sent to Virginia in early March to shore up the defenses there. General Stirling reported to the New York Committee of Safety in mid-March that approximately one hundred cannon, ranging from thirty-eight 32 pound cannon to three 3 pound cannon, were available for the defense of the city.[4] Another 124 cannon needed repair (they had been spiked and thus damaged by the British troops upon their departure the previous summer).[5] One of the offi-cers in command of a company of provincial artillerists was young Captain Alexander Hamilton, who was appointed by the New York Provincial Congress on March 14.[6]

Word of Howe's departure from Boston initially alarmed New Yorkers; many assumed that he was headed to New York with his army. Colonel Gold Silliman of the Connecticut militia reported in early April that the city "Is almost deserted by the Inhabitants so that there is a great Plenty of empty Houses into which the Officers & Soldiers are put."[7]

Five days earlier, on March 29, a committee sent by the Continen-tal Congress to inspect the progress of the city's defenses reached New York. Charles Carroll of Maryland, a member of the committee, did not take notice of the missing residents, but instead, reported that,

> The ardor of the citizens is astonishing, gentlemen of the first and men of all ranks, work on these fortifications. . . . I was told by a gentleman, that some gentlemen not used to work with a spade, worked so long, to set an example, that the blood gushed out of their fingers.[8]

Carroll added that, "While this spirit continues the Americans will ever remain unconquerable."[9]

Colonel Silliman, writing to his wife on the same day, also ex-pressed confidence in the city's defenses.

> I . . . have taken a View of the greater Part of our Fortifications in this City, and am of Opinion that it would be extreamly difficult for an Army to force its Way into this Town from the Water for there are strong Breast Works raised across every Street that leads down to the Water . . . behind each of which a considerable Num-ber of Men may be placed and be kept covered from the Fire of the Enemy.[10]

With 6,000 troops from New York, New Jersey, and Connecticut already in and around the city and many more on the way, the con-fidence of Charles Carroll and Colonel Silliman seemed justified.[11]

The first of Washington's troops from Massachusetts reached New York the day after Colonel Silliman and Charles Carroll made their observations.[12] Major General Israel Putnam of Connecticut, a veteran of the French and Indian War and a hero of Bunker Hill, arrived a few days later on April 3, and assumed command.

Four days after Putnam's arrival, a skirmish erupted on Staten Island between a party of Continental riflemen and a watering party of British sailors and marines from the two British warships anchored in New York Harbor. The British lost three men killed, an unknown number wounded, and ten captured, all without the loss of a single American rifleman.[13] General Putnam reported the engagement to the Continental Congress and added, "As Hostilities are now Commenced In this Province I have tho't fit to order no more Provision to be sent the Men at War [British warships]."[14] The New York Provincial Congress was no longer in session, so it was the Committee of Safety that bristled at General Putnam's decree. Whether Putnam's decision would remain or not would be up to the American commander-in-chief when he arrived just a week later.

Washington arrived on April 13 and assumed responsibility for the defense of New York City.[15] Although a number of units had yet to arrive from Massachusetts, Washington complied with instructions from the Continental Congress on April 15 and sent four regiments north under General William Thompson, who had been promoted by Congress in the spring, to reinforce General Schuyler's troops in Canada. Six other regiments followed under General John Sullivan of New Hampshire at the end of April.[16]

Washington understood the importance of reinforcing the army in Canada, but he warned Congress upon the departure of the six additional regiments that if General Howe's force from Boston, or another of similar size from Great Britain, should attack New York, the troops that remained under Washington's command were insufficient to defend the city. He therefore called upon Congress to authorize another 10,000 troops for New York City.[17]

Washington, ever sensitive to the authority of civil bodies, wrote frequently to the New York Committee of Safety to solicit their support and cooperation. His first letter to the committee, just four days after his arrival, established where he stood on the question of who had the ultimate authority for the defense of New York City. Declaring that he would always prefer to "go hand in hand with the Civil Authority," he acknowledged that sometimes that was not possible. In such circumstances, wrote Washington, where local interests must be inconvenienced to promote the interest of the American Cause, "the least of two Evils must be preferred."[18]

Washington had in mind the confounding situation of New York's continued willingness to supply British warships with necessary provisions (food and water), nearly a full year after the bloodshed of Lexington and Concord. General Lee had addressed this issue in mid-February, proposing to halt the practice of selling provisions to the warships, but New York's Provincial Congress rebuffed him, claiming that "it is totally impossible to prevent the *Asia* and *Phoenix* from supplying themselves with provisions."[19] The Provincial Congress argued that to block provisions to the warships would only cause the British navy to retaliate and seize provisions destined to the city that were transported by boat from New Jersey and Connecticut. The city's inhabitants, who depended to a large degree upon these foodstuffs from the neighboring colonies, would thus be the ones to suffer food shortages or worse, perhaps bombardment from the British in retaliation for the stoppage of provisions from shore. Furthermore, noted the Provincial Congress,

> If we provoke the captains of the ships of war . . . the inhabitants [of this city] will not only be destitute, but our commissary will be incapacitated from procuring the necessary supplies for the army now in town. You will please to consider that the ships of war have it in their power to seize all the provisions that they may find afloat, by which means they will have an opportunity of supplying the enemy at Boston.[20]

General Lee ignored the views of the Provincial Congress and ordered his troops to stop any attempt by New Yorkers to furnish provisions to or communicate with the British ships. Lee informed Washington that this measure had, "thrown the Mayor, Council and Tories into agonies."[21]

Lee's departure in early March left General Stirling in charge of the defense of New York. The Provincial Congress convinced Lord Stirling to allow a resumption of the provisioning of British warships in the harbor. It was no longer to be haphazard, however, but occur solely through the port master and his assistants, who were sworn not to divulge any useful information to the British navy during the transfer of provisions.[22]

When he arrived in New York in mid-April, Washington, backed by thousands of newly arrived troops, was determined to end this practice, with or without the approval and support of New York's civilian leaders.

Washington acknowledged that the policy of providing provisions to the British warships may have been justified earlier when the city was in a weak and defenseless state, but that was no longer the situation. The American army was now able to defend the city against the handful of British warships in the harbor, so Washington saw no reason to continue the practice of supplying the ships with provision, a practice that not only allowed the warships to remain a threat in New York Harbor, but also provided them with useful information on developments in the city and with the American army. Washington asserted that it was therefore his "incumbent duty" to end the practice and he hoped New York's civil authorities would support his decision.[23]

The Committee of Safety responded to Washington's "recommendations" (as they called them) the following day with their full support. All communication and trade with the British warships was to cease immediately.[24]

Washington continued to work with the New York Committee of Safety, as well as the Provincial Congress when it met, to establish a system of lookouts and signals to warn of the expected arrival of a British fleet with General Howe and his army. Washington also worked with New York's leaders to better organize the local militia.[25] Near the end of April a little spat occurred between Washington and the Committee of Safety regarding the four Continental regiments that the Continental Congress had reauthorized for New York in January.

In reporting on the progress of recruitment of these four regiments, the Committee of Safety wrote to Washington that "Congress has tho't proper to put them under our immediate direction. . . ."[26] It is likely that the committee was referring to the recruitment and formation of the regiments, but Washington wrote back to the committee two days later asking for clarification.

> If the four Battalions . . . are placed under the immediate care of the [Committee] of safety for this Colony, by Congress, I should be glad to know how far it is conceived that my powers over them extend, or whether I have any at all.[27]

Washington insisted that it was not practical to subject the four Continental regiments to both his direction and that of the Committee of Safety and wished to know, "whether these Regiments cannot be ordered out of the Colony—for Instance to New Jersey—if necessity should require it."[28]

The Committee of Safety sheepishly assured Washington that "We never considered [the regiments in question] under our Direction except so far as concerned the forming and equipping them."[29] They fully recognized that the regiments were formed "for the command of the continental General."[30] In other words, Washington had the authority to command the four New York regiments as he pleased.

As with all people, there was a public face and a private face to Washington, and not surprisingly, the latter provided greater insight into the American commander. Washington's letter to his brother John Augustine at the end of April provides a good example.

> We have already gone great lengths in fortifying this City & the Hudsons River—a fortnight more will put us in a very respectable posture of Defence. The Works we have already constructed, and which they found we were about to erect, have put the King's Ships to flight; for instead of laying within Pistol shot of our Wharves, & their Centrys conversing with ours (whilst they received every necessary that the Country afforded) they have now gone down to the Hook, near 30 Miles from this place—the last Harbour they can get to –and I have prevaild upon the [Committee]

of safety to forbid every kind of Intercourse between the Inhabitants of this Colony and the Enemy; this I was resolved upon effecting; but thought it best to bring it about through that Channel, as I can now pursue my own measures in support of their resolves.[31]

In this letter, Washington expressed a degree of confidence about the strength of the city's defenses, despite his concern about the loss of ten regiments to Canada. Washington's political savvy is also evident in his interaction with the Committee of Safety.

Work on the fortifications continued unabated in May. Fortified positions were constructed on the heights of Brooklyn on Long Island (which overlooked the East River and New York City) and on Governor's Island (which lay in the mouth of the East River between the city and the heights of Brooklyn).

In the middle of May the Congress in Philadelphia summoned Washington to confer with him in person. He departed New York on May 21, leaving General Putnam in command of the army. By the time Washington returned to New York in early June, a gigantic step toward American independence had been taken in Congress.

New Jersey

With Governor Franklin under house arrest in Perth Amboy, the New Jersey Provincial Congress assembled in New Brunswick in February. When reports reached the Congress in mid-February that the British warship HMS *Asia* had seized several boats with foodstuffs from New Jersey on their way to New York City, the delegates voted to prohibit any further trade with the city.[32] The ban was rescinded after a week on the justification that the initial reports about the *Asia* were untrue.[33] In reality, the Congress also likely realized the futility of enforcing such an unpopular measure.

Although there was no significant British presence or threat to New Jersey, other than the several British warships in New York Harbor, the Provincial Congress was concerned about the vulnerability of Perth Amboy as well as its shoreline along the Delaware River to a sudden British attack. With two of their three Continental regiments posted outside of the colony, in New York and Canada, the Provincial Congress asked the Continental Congress to authorize (and pay for) the formation of two additional regiments and two companies of artillery.[34]

The delegates in Philadelphia declined to do so, leaving New Jersey to authorize just the artillery companies (with a total of 12 cannon) at their own expense.[35] The Provincial Congress also reorganized the militia, dissolving the minute companies that were formed in 1775 (which had lost much of their manpower to Continental recruitment) and incorporating the few minutemen that remained into the general militia.[36] In late March, the Provincial Congress, responding to concern that the British might strike at New York City at any moment, ordered a draft from all of the colony's militia in order to send three militia battalions to help defend New York.[37]

To reduce the threat posed by those with loyalist sentiments, militia officers in New Jersey were ordered to disarm any inhabitant of the colony who refused to sign the Continental Association established by the First Continental Congress in 1774.[38]

One such resident of New Jersey who refused to sign the Association was Governor Franklin. In a long letter to Lord George Germain, the new British Colonial Secretary, Franklin detailed his mistreatment and continued refusal to cooperate with the Provincial Congress. Governor Franklin lamented the impact of Thomas Paine's recent pamphlet, *Common Sense*, and reported that a majority of delegates to the Provincial Congress "appeared inclined to adopt independency should it be recommended by the Continental Congress in Philadelphia."[39] With the Provincial Congress adjourned until May, it would be nearly two months before Governor Franklin's speculation could be confirmed.

Prior to Franklin's letter to London, the Continental Congress ordered New Jersey's only Continental regiment still in the colony, Colonel Dayton's 3rd New Jersey, to New York City to help defend against the expected arrival of the British army from Boston.[40] The 1st New Jersey Regiment was already in New York City while the 2nd New Jersey was in Albany making preparations to join the American forces in Canada. The defense of New Jersey was left to its militia, who fended off occasional British naval forage parties that snuck ashore to gather water, provision, and cattle.[41]

PENNSYLVANIA

The defense of the Delaware River and Philadelphia remained the priority of Pennsylvania's leaders over the winter of 1776. With the need for reinforcements in both Canada and New York City drawing all seven of Pennsylvania's Continental regiments out of the colony by March, the defense of the river and city of Philadelphia was left to provincial troops and sailors. In a close vote, decided by the Speaker of the legislative assembly, Pennsylvania voted to raise two battalions of riflemen and one battalion of musketmen, totally 1,500 soldiers, to serve as provincial regulars. They were to remain on active service in Pennsylvania until the end of the year, or the end of the war, whichever came first.[42]

Much progress on the river defenses protecting Philadelphia was made over the winter and work continued in the spring to better obstruct the river channel and build cannon batteries to stop the British navy from reaching the city. In mid-February, the Continental naval squadron that was formed in Philadelphia went on the offensive against the British. Commodore Esek Hopkins of Rhode Island commanded the squadron that included the frigates *Alfred* (30 guns, 280 crew and marines) and *Columbus* (28 guns, 280 crew and marines), the brigs *Andrew Doria* (16 guns, 160 crew and marines) and *Cabot* (14 guns, 150 crew and marines), the sloops *Providence* (12 guns, 118 crew and marines) and *Hornet* (8 guns, 60 crew), the schooner *Wasp* (8 guns and 60 crew), and the sloop-tender *Fly* (4 guns, 29 crew).[43] Hopkins's squadron set sail for the Bahamas in mid-February and arrived on March 1.

Commodore Hopkins recounted to Congress what occurred after the fleet captured two sloops and learned that a large supply of gunpowder and war material was to be had at New Providence, on Nassau Island.

> I formed an expedition against New Providence which I put into execution on March 3 by landing two hundred Marines . . . and 50 Sailors . . . . They took Possession of a small Fort of Seventeen Pieces of Cannon without any Opposition [except] five Guns which were fired at them without doing any damage.[44]

Commodore Hopkins was informed that over two hundred men still manned the main fort, and rather than risk significant bloodshed by storming it, Hopkins summoned the garrison to surrender the next day. He included a promise that the garrison and their personal property would all remain safe if they did not oppose the seizure of the fort and the King's stores within it. The fort's defenders (all civilians) accepted the terms and abandoned the fort. The Royal Governor, Montfort Browne, was seized and relinquished the keys of the fort. A search found a disappointing amount of military stores; 150 barrels of gunpowder had eluded the Americans when Governor Browne ordered it loaded aboard a small sloop that sailed unnoticed from the island under cover of darkness the night before.[45]

The Americans had to content themselves with the capture of Governor Browne and several other British officials, as well as a handful of cannon and military supplies. The boldness and audacity the American fleet displayed in attacking and briefly holding a British post in the Bahamas was probably the most significant result of the raid on New Providence. The rebel navy proved it could threaten British interests in the Caribbean and would have to be dealt with.

The American squadron sailed back toward the continent in mid-March and captured a British tender and bomb brig off Rhode Island in early April. On April 6, the fleet encountered the HMS *Glasgow* (20 guns, 160 crew), and a fierce battle erupted for several hours. Lieutenant John Paul Jones, who was destined to be America's greatest naval hero in the Revolutionary War, served on the *Alfred* and noted that the engagement lasted an hour and a half before the *Glasgow* broke off and sailed for Rhode Island and the support of additional British warships. Commodore Hopkins chose not to pursue and sailed for New London, Connecticut. Lieutenant Jones recorded in the *Alfred*'s log that

> The *Cabot* was Disabled at the 2d broadside, the Capt. being dangerously Wounded; the Master and several Men killed. The Enemys whole Fire was then Directed at us and an unlucky Shot having carried away our Wheel Block & Ropes, the Ship broached too and gave the Enemy an Opportunity of Raking us with several

Broadsides before we were again in Condition to steer the Stick
& Return the Fire. In the Action we Received Several Shot under
Water which made the Ship Verry Leaky. We had besides the
Mainmast Shot Thro' and the Upperworks and Rigging very con-
siderable damaged. Yet, it is Surprising that we only lost the 2d
lieutenant of Marines & 4 Men.[46]

Captain Howe of the *Glasgow* described the engagement as "a
very hot action" that killed one British marine and wounded another.
All of the lower masts on the *Glasgow* were disabled and most of
the rigging shot away.[47] The *Newport Mercury* newspaper printed
an account of the battle just two days after it occurred and included
the observation that based on the holes in her sails, "and by the hanging of her yards . . . she had been treated in a very rough manner."[48]

Not to be outdone by the Continental Navy, Pennsylvania's own
state navy of 13 river galleys, each mounting a large cannon on its
bow (ranging from 18 pounders to 32 pounders), as well as a floating
battery of ten 18 pound cannon, engaged the 44 gun HMS *Roebuck*
and 28 gun *Liverpool* when the British ships sailed up the Delaware
River in early May.

The *Roebuck* had arrived in Delaware Bay in late March, thor-
oughly alarming the inhabitants of Delaware with its presence. It remained on station in the bay through April, capturing a number of
small prizes (civilian boats). On May 7, the *Roebuck,* joined by the
HMS *Liverpool* and several tenders, sailed up the Delaware River to
obtain fresh water and spotted the Continental schooner *Wasp.* The
British ships gave chase and although they failed to catch the *Wasp,*
they forced a civilian schooner aground near Wilmington and proceeded to unload its cargo of bread and flour.[49]

Upriver at Mud Island (which was also referred to as Fort Island
because of the earthworks erected on it) Pennsylvania's thirteen river
galleys prepared for action. They were joined by a floating battery
of ten cannon, all of which made their way downriver, past the river
obstructions, to challenge the British warships. Captain Andrew Hamond of the *Roebuck* provided an account of the engagement that
ensued.

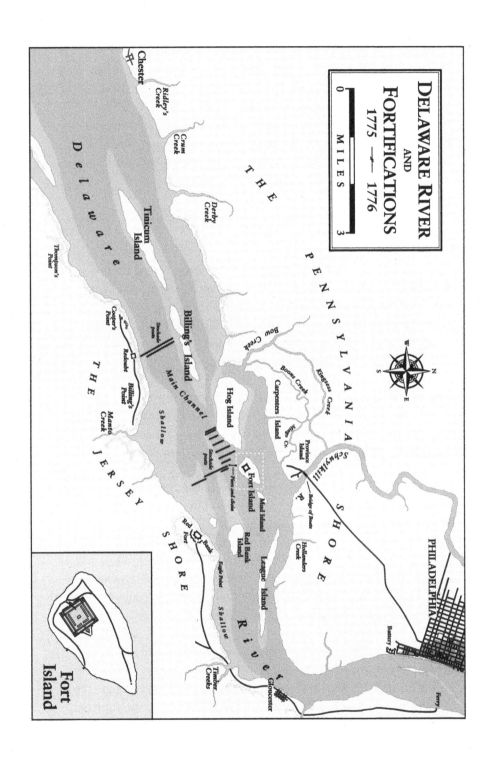

About 1 in the afternoon, I perceived the Arm'd craft of the River coming down, before the wind, with an appearance of attacking us. . . . We met them under sail . . . and lay under the disadvantage of being obliged to engage them at the distance they chose to fix on, which was scarcely within point blank Shot; and being such low objects on the water, it was with some difficulty that we could strike them, so that we fired upon them near two hours before they thought proper to retire, and row off.[50]

Colonel Samuel Miles commanded Pennsylvania riflemen onshore and witnessed the engagement.

Our Boats and the two men of war have been ingaged for two hours at long shot. I believe there is no damage done on either side, tho' I suppose three or four hundred shot have past between them. . . . Our Boats fire much better than the other Vessels, but in my opinion ingage at too great a distance. . . . A great deal of ammunition has been wasted.[51]

The Pennsylvanians let an excellent opportunity to damage or even destroy the *Roebuck* pass when that vessel became grounded on the New Jersey shoreline. A sailor aboard one of the river galleys recognized the opportunity.

In the course of the engagement the *Roebuck* ran ashore, and is now fast on the Jersey shore. . . . Our fleet has suffered no injury but by a single shot which struck the *Camden*, but has done her little damage. We expect in a hour's time she will be on the careen [tilted on its side exposing the hull below the waterline], when a second attack will be made upon her, and hope it will be crowned with success. The other ship [HMS *Liverpool*] has come too, under the *Roebuck*'s stern within musket shot.[52]

No attack from the river galleys ensued and the *Roebuck* was refloated before dawn of the next day. When the early fog burned off at mid-morning, the *Roebuck* and *Liverpool* set sail to re-engage the river galleys, which had remained anchored about two miles upriver all evening. Captain Hamond recalled that the Pennsylvanians "industriously plied their Oars and Sails to avoid us."[53]

When the wind ceased in the early afternoon and the ebb tide commenced, the British ended their chase and instead, tried to draw the river galleys back downriver where there was more room to maneuver. Their ploy worked, the Pennsylvania navy now gave chase, but at a safe distance. Several hours of cannon fire ensued but with little effect. The river galleys ended their pursuit in the evening near New Castle, Delaware. The British ships dropped their anchors as soon as they noticed, hoping to draw the Pennsylvanians farther into Delaware Bay, but the river galleys remained at a safe distance and returned upriver the next day.[54]

Although little of real consequence occurred as a result of this two day naval engagement, newspaper accounts of the battle left readers with the impression that the river galleys had thrashed the British warships and proven their ability to defend the Delaware River against the mighty British navy.[55]

DELAWARE

The arrival of the HMS *Roebuck* in Delaware Bay in late March sparked alarm in the three Lower Counties of Delaware. Henry Fisher, a resident of Lewes in Sussex County and a local river pilot with detailed knowledge of Delaware Bay and the river, was hired by the Pennsylvania Committee of Safety in September 1775 to serve as a lookout for British warships entering Delaware Bay.[56] Fisher sighted the *Roebuck* approaching the Delaware Capes in the early evening of March 25, and sent an express to Philadelphia, some 120 miles away. It passed through Dover by 4:30 a.m. the following morning, Wilmington by 1 p.m., and reached Philadelphia later that afternoon, around twenty hours after it was sent.[57]

Back in Lewes, local militia answered the call to arms. Fisher updated the Pennsylvania Committee of Safety a week after first sighting the *Roebuck* and reported that,

> Several Companies of Militia from all Parts of [Sussex] County who live within [twenty-five] miles of Lewes came in as soon as they could be expected, seemed all quite unanimous and hearty in

the Cause determined to defend their Country. There has been near 1000 Men in at times the last Week so that we were obliged to discharge Many of them not having Occasion for half the Number. We prevailed on those [who] lived at a distance to leave some of their Best . . . Arms (for Numbers of them want Firelocks) which are not to be purchased.[58]

A company of "well equipped" Delaware Continentals under Captain Charles Pope joined the militia at Lewes on March 30. A second company soon followed.[59]

The assembled troops were of course powerless to stop the *Roebuck* and its tender from seizing several vessels in the bay and along the coast, including Henry Fisher's pilot boat, but they could at least resist any landing by the British and it looked to Fisher that they intended to do so.

When the British helmsman in Fisher's captured pilot boat fell asleep and let the craft become beached, the militia seized the small crew of four, a 3rd lieutenant, two sailors, and a civilian pilot. Ten muskets and five pistols that had been thrown overboard were also recovered.[60]

On Easter Sunday, April 7, a heated engagement erupted between the *Roebuck*'s tender and Captain Pope's company of Continentals, supported by militia. A schooner had arrived from the Caribbean loaded with coarse linen and signaled to the guard posted at the light house at Cape Henlopen that it needed assistance to unload about seven miles south of the lighthouse. Time was of the essence as the *Roebuck* and its tender were nearby. The ship's captain had hoped to unload and be on his way before the British discovered him, but the tender spotted the ship and bore down on it. Informed of the situation, Captain Pope led his company of Delaware Continentals, joined by militia, in a dash to reach the schooner, which was aground to expedite the unloading, before the tender could capture it. Pope recalled that,

> Our troops were outgone by the tender, though they marched at the rate of seven miles per hour. Just before our arrival the tender gave [the lighthouse] guard (who was at the schooner) a

broadside with swivels and musquetry, which they returned. On our junction a constant fire was kept up for some time, till we perceived the distance too great. We then left off firing, and unloaded the schooner, though several hundred shots were fired at us, to prevent it. Our people picked up many of their balls rolling in the sand. . . . About this time the [*Roebuck*] turned the cape. The tender anchored within musket shot of the schooner, and kept up a continual fire with her swivels. We had by this time got two swivels in the schooner loaded with grape shot, and a constant fire for two hours was kept up on both sides. We undoubtedly wounded their men, for we perceived some to fall, and others ran to their assistance; they made several efforts to [haul] their anchor, which we prevented with our fire, but at last they succeeded; fortunately however one of our swivel shot cut their halyards and down came their mainsail, which obliged them to anchor once more. . . . They had a boat to tow them off; we then turned our fire on the boat, when two men were seen to fall; the barge returning from the [*Roebuck*] joined to tow them out. Our men escaped unhurt. The militia officers, at Lewes, acted with a spirit which does honor to their county.[61]

Two weeks after this engagement, the *Pennsylvania Evening Post* printed a letter from an inhabitant in Lewes, dated April 17, that described the confident mood there.

Lewestown is at this time made up of officers and soldiers, and the people altogether seem determined to defend our little place. As for Tories, there are none such among us. That infamous name is quite done away since danger comes so nigh us. . . . We have between fifty and a hundred men on guard [each] night. [The British] have application to fish on our beach, we would not let them, but desired them to go to Newfoundland for that purpose. If they should attempt to fish on the beach, we are determined to shew them Yankee play, as we did on Easter Sunday.[62]

The rest of April was relatively quiet in Delaware. The *Roebuck* remained on station in Delaware Bay, occasionally sailing out to sea for brief periods, only to return to the bay with several prizes (captured vessels). By the first of May there were three Continental companies stationed at Lewes as well as militia, all standing guard against the *Roebuck*. Henry Fisher requested that the Pennsylvania Committee of Safety inform the Continental Congress that there were only enough muskets to arm one of the three companies of Continentals posted in Sussex County and that only a trifling of gunpowder and lead was available to them.[63] Fisher urged the committee to "use your Interest with the Congress to have the Companys Equipt, as they are a parcel of fine fellows."[64]

Concern that the British would soon discover the weak condition of Delaware's defenders and take advantage of it prompted Colonel John Haslet to implore Congress to rescind its order to exchange the British officer captured at Lewes in early April, Lieutenant George Ball, for a captured American merchant captain. Noting the freedom and humanity shown to Lieutenant Ball during his captivity at Dover, which allowed the British officer to observe "very little Zeal [among those he encountered for the] Defence of American Liberty," and knowing that Lieutenant Ball was fully aware of "our Naked & defenseless Situation," Colonel Haslet feared what the British officers aboard the *Roebuck* and *Liverpool* would do with such information.[65] "[Lt. Ball] knows it is in his power with 150 men well armed to desolate great parts of this Seemingly Devoted Country," stressed Haslet, who then reminded Congress that,

> Popes Company is armed by us for the Defence of Lewes; Capt Caldwell marched a Detachment of 150 men completed for the Field by my Orders, as soon as Intelligence was had of the Men of War going up the River, which leaves us without a sufficient Number of Guns to mount a Sergeants Guard—all this is known to Mr. Ball.[66]

When Henry Fisher learned of the planned exchange of Lieutenant Ball, he too urged that it not proceed, citing the same concerns as Colonel Haslet.[67] Their appeals worked, and Ball was sent to Germantown, where he gave his parole, but remained out of contact with his ship.

The concern of both Colonel Haslet and Henry Fisher highlights a disturbing situation in the Lower Counties of Delaware in the spring of 1776. A large portion of the population had seemingly yet to embrace the patriot side of the dispute and many were downright loyalist. This became alarmingly obvious in the coming weeks as talk of independence intensified.

MARYLAND

Two months before the naval engagement in the Delaware River, the inhabitants of Maryland had their own encounter with the British navy. On March 4, reports circulated in Maryland that a British warship, escorted by several tenders, was sailing up Chesapeake Bay. It was the HMS *Otter* (14 guns, 125 men) commanded by Captain Mathew Squire. After months of duty in Virginia, where Captain Squire and his men opened hostilities in Virginia by attacking Hampton in October 1775, the *Otter* was ordered to sail to Baltimore and "use every means in your power to take or destroy" two armed vessels belonging to the rebels.[68] Captain Squire was also ordered to "procure a quantity of livestock" either peacefully with ready money, or, if refused, then by force. "You are to annoy the Rebels," continued his orders, "by every means in your power, and to Seize and detain all American Vessels you may meet with, as well as those of any other Country that may be Trading with the Americans . . . ."[69]

On his return down the bay, Squire was to stop in Annapolis and deliver a packet of letters to the royal governor, Robert Eden, who although powerless, maintained his position in Maryland. Captain Squire was given two weeks to complete his mission.

The first reports of his approach up the bay reached the Maryland Council of Safety in Annapolis on the evening of March 5, and they spread the alarm.[70] One observer in Annapolis recalled that fear that the British intended to destroy the city "threw the inhabitants into the greatest confusion, what with the darkness of the night, thunder, lightning, and rain, cries of women and children, people hurrying their effects into the country, drums beating to arms. &c. I can assure you it was by no means an agreeable scene."[71]

As in every colony, a shortage of arms and gunpowder forced Maryland's leaders to scramble. To better arm at least some of the Maryland regular troops posted at Annapolis, the Council of Safety ordered a militia captain there to deliver the eighty stand of public arms in the possession of his company to Major Thomas Price, who in turn was instructed to provide a receipt to the captain and a list of the arms provided to the council.[72]

The *Otter* passed Annapolis on March 7 and continued up the bay, suggesting to all that Baltimore was its target. Governor Eden had sent a message to Captain Squire when the *Otter* was off of Annapolis. Squire halted several hours to reply and also delivered the packet of letters he had planned to deliver to the Governor on his way back down the bay. Knowing that his correspondence would likely be read by the Committee of Safety, Captain Squire explained that his appearance was solely to obtain fresh provision for the navy, for which he was eager to pay. "I am sorry to find by our Letter," wrote Captain Squire, "that the People of Annapolis Should be under any Apprehensions from their Town being burnt or beat down. I must beg Leave to assure you Nothing of that Kind will happen from Me."[73] Squire added that he expected to be back in Annapolis in a few days, hopefully to purchase provisions.

Baltimore's leaders intensified preparations for the *Otter*'s arrival. The town committee sent an express to Philadelphia to solicit gunpowder and arms and ordered a breastwork with cannon built at Fells Point, just outside of Baltimore on the Patapsco River to protect the harbor and town.[74] Samuel Purviance Jr., a successful Baltimore shipper, reported that the militia in town paraded in the afternoon and seemed ready to fight. "The Ardor & Spirit of our Inhabitants has convinced Me They will behave bravely."[75]

The actual target of the *Otter* was not Baltimore, but the schooner *Defense*, an 18 gun vessel being fitted out for service in Baltimore. Although the ship still needed work and was armed with 6 and 9 pound cannon in bad condition, a crew was hastily assembled and made preparations to sail under Captain James Nicholson. A company of Maryland regulars joined the crew and the *Defense* sailed out of Baltimore Harbor on March 8.[76] Lieutenant Joseph Smith, a marine aboard the *Defense*, described to his brother what transpired after they set sail.

We went down the river in a fog with 220 men & had proceeded about ten miles when we discovered the enemy [several
tenders] & the ship they had taken [a large vessel loaded with
wheat and flour that had grounded] within two miles. As soon as
we saw them all hands gave three loud cheers . . . but the enemy
immediately made sail, and left all their prizes in our possession.
Another vessel of the enemy [the *Otter*] lay four miles below, and
we waited for them to come and give battle . . . . Though our ship
was inferior to that of the enemy, we were much disappointed in
not attacking them, for some time before night the British made
sail & we have not seen them since.[77]

Amazingly, Captain Squire declined to engage the *Defence* and sailed
back down the bay to Annapolis. He sent a boat ashore under a flag of
truce with a request to purchase provisions, which was denied by the
Council of Safety. Expecting a hostile response, the committee was surprised to find a second flag come ashore accompanied by several prisoners that the *Otter* had detained on its voyage. The released captives
reported that they had been very civilly treated and as a gesture of
thanks, the Council of Safety sent two quarters of beef to Captain
Squire.[78] The *Otter* and its tenders then set sail farther down the bay.

Many Marylanders could not believe that Squire's departure was
the end of it; they expected a return of the British navy with a
stronger force, but that did not occur. Praise for Captain Nicholson
and his crew, as well as for the militia and regulars who turned out
to face the British navy, was universal, and confidence grew among
the patriot ranks in Maryland that, despite the widespread shortage
of weapons, powder, gear and clothing, they were ready to defend
themselves against another such British attack.

In early April, Captain James Barron of the Virginia State Navy
intercepted a packet ship with correspondence between the British
Secretary of State, Lord George Germain, and Maryland's royal governor, Robert Eden. Governor Eden had managed to avoid the displeasure of Maryland patriot leaders by appearing sympathetic to
their views, but the intercepted letters suggested that Eden had been
conspiring with the British Ministry all along.

A delegation from the Maryland Council of Safety visited Governor Eden to request he reveal a copy of his August 27, 1775, letter to Lord Dartmouth that was referred to in the captured letters. Eden claimed no copy existed, to which the skeptical delegation asked Governor Eden to give his parole (promise) not to leave Maryland until the next convention met. Eden assured the delegation that there was nothing in the letter to inflame the British Ministry and asked for a day to consider their parole request.[79]

Noting the inappropriateness of the Governor of Maryland giving his parole to the Council of Safety as if he were a prisoner, Governor Eden refused to comply with the Council's request. He challenged the council to produce definitive evidence that he had acted in a hostile manner against the colony in his correspondence and then assured them that he planned to "remain in my Station, as long as permitted."[80]

The Council sheepishly replied to Governor Eden admitting that "We know of no Information you have given [the British Ministry], countenancing or encouraging the Introduction of Troops into this Province, nor do we know of any measures whatever to have been concerted or pursued by our Excellency injurious to this Province or America."[81] The Council then thanked him for pledging to remain at his station and ended their reply with "[Our] Ardent wishes for a speedy Reconciliation upon honorable and constitutional Terms."[82]

The matter of Governor Eden's conduct did not end there, however. General Charles Lee, who had read the captured letters while posted in Virginia, wrote to Samuel Purviance Jr., the chairman of Baltimore's Committee of Observation, on April 6, and instructed him to direct the commanding officer of the troops in Annapolis to seize the Governor and his papers. "The Sin and Blame be on my Head," wrote Lee, "I will answer for all to the Congress."[83] Purviance strayed from General Lee's instructions by sending Captain Samuel Smith, who commanded a company of regulars in Baltimore, to Annapolis by boat to seize the governor.[84]

When Captain Smith reached Annapolis on April 16, the same day that the Council of Safety's delegation first met with Governor Eden, they found no opportunity to arrest the governor. When the Council of Safety was informed that Captain Smith had been sent by

Baltimore's Committee of Observation to seize Eden, its members were indignant at what they viewed as the Baltimore committee's usurpation of power. Their indignation grew stronger when they learned that the Continental Congress also sought Governor Eden's arrest.[85]

The Council of Safety refused to comply, informing Maryland's delegates to the Continental Congress that "We consider the Congress as having the supreme Authority over the Continent and look up to them with Reverence and Esteem, but that they cannot interfere with uncontrollable Power in the internal Polity of this or any other Province."[86] The Council added that they were confident in Governor Eden's assurances to remain in Maryland.

The Council then turned to Baltimore's Committee of Observation and particularly Samuel Purviance Jr., who admitted that he had acted without his committee's knowledge, on the matter.[87]

Dumbfounded by Purviance's actions and stung by criticism of its leniency toward Governor Eden, the Council of Safety called for another Maryland Convention to meet in early May to consider the entire matter. The Convention that met publicly rebuked Purviance for his actions, but took no further action against him. [88]

Six

Canada

W HILE THE MIDDLE COLONIES SCRAMBLED TO BETTER DEFEND themselves and fend off several British naval incursions in the first half of 1776, thousands of troops from New York, New Jersey, and Pennsylvania were engaged in a much bigger fight to the north in Canada.

General Richard Montgomery's defeat and subsequent death at Quebec at the tail end of 1775 was a significant blow to American efforts to secure Canada from British control. Although a handful of American troops remained in Montreal under General David Wooster and approximately 1,000 more, about half of which were Continental troops from New York, held firm outside of Quebec with Colonel Arnold, American hopes to secure Canada were tenuous.[1]

General Schuyler in Albany sought 3,000 reinforcements from General Washington, who himself had few troops to spare at the start of 1776.[2] Prior to learning of the defeat at Quebec, the Continental Congress voted on January 8, to keep nine regiments in Canada for the upcoming season.[3] If fully manned, they would surpass 6,000 troops, but it would take time to raise them and even longer to equip and march them to Canada.

To expedite the process, Congress ordered two existing Continental regiments, the 1st Pennsylvania under Colonel John De Haas and the 2nd New Jersey under Colonel William Maxwell, to march immediately to Albany to reinforce Schuyler.[4] Colonel James Livingston of Canada was authorized to form all of the Canadian troops then with the American army into a regiment and Congress hoped that two other regiments could be formed from among the American troops still in Canada.[5] The 2nd Pennsylvania Regiment under Colonel Arthur St. Clair, one of Pennsylvania's four new Continental regiments authorized by Congress in December, was also ordered to Canada once it was complete, while New Hampshire, Connecticut, and New York were instructed to each raise a new regiment and march it to Canada as soon as possible.[6] All of this was done before Congress learned of the disastrous defeat at Quebec.

The reaction of Congress to the news of Quebec was restrained. Largely content with the number of reinforcements it had authorized eleven days earlier, Congress requested General Washington in Massachusetts to send just one regiment, if possible, to Canada.[7] The several colonies who were to send reinforcements to Canada were also urged to speed along the process.

In mid-February, Congress ordered General Charles Lee in New York to take command of all of the American troops in Canada.[8] Within two weeks of this decision, however, new intelligence suggesting that the British planned to strike in the southern colonies caused Congress to send Lee to Virginia instead. General John Thomas of Massachusetts was promoted to Major-General and sent from Washington's army in Massachusetts to command in Quebec in Lee's place.[9] A reliable commander who Washington had endorsed for promotion the day after Congress promoted him (and before he was aware of Congress's actions), Washington informed Congress that Thomas, "stands fair in point of reputation and is esteemed a brave and good Officer."[10]

REINFORCEMENTS ARRIVE IN ALBANY

The arrival of some of the first troops from the 1st Pennsylvania and 2nd New Jersey Regiments in mid-February was welcomed by General Schuyler in Albany, although he noted to Washington that more than half of their arms needed repair and nearly all needed shoes, socks, and mittens.[11] Outside Quebec, Brigadier-General Benedict Arnold (who had been promoted by Congress in January) continued his loose siege of the city. He informed Washington at the end of February that "Desertions from [the city] are frequent by which we learn they are much distres'd for [firewood] & must soon Burn their Houses & Ships."[12] Arnold's troops had repulsed two British sorties from the fort which, along with several hundred recent reinforcements, kept the spirits of his men up. Arnold did note, however, that his troops suffered in the severe winter climate because they were still "poorly clad."[13] On a brighter note, Arnold reported that his leg wound, received in the attack on Quebec two months earlier, had entirely healed.

Reinforcements from New Jersey, Pennsylvania, Connecticut, and Massachusetts joined Schuyler in Albany in March, but he complained to Washington that they "arrive here more or less without Arms."[14] Efforts to procure arms for all of the reinforcements proved disappointing, prompting Schuyler to confess to Washington that "we shall not by any Means have that respectable Army, which was intended by Congress."[15]

Two weeks after Schuyler expressed his disappointment, the Continental Congress acted to address his concern. The departure of the British from Boston in mid-March prompted Congress to order General Washington to send four regiments from his army into Canada "as soon as [Washington] shall be of opinion that the safety of New York and the eastern service will permit."[16] On April 15, just two days after Washington arrived in New York City, he ordered three regiments from Massachusetts and one from New Hampshire to prepare to embark upon transports on the Hudson River.[17] Washington formed the units into a brigade under General William Thompson and they departed for Albany by boat on April 21.

Two days after their departure, the Continental Congress instructed Washington to send six more regiments to Canada.[18] He ordered the 1st and 3rd New Jersey Regiments under Colonel William Winds and Colonel Elias Dayton, the 4th and 6th Pennsylvania Regiments under Colonel Anthony Wayne and Colonel William Irvine, and two regiments from New Hampshire to follow in the wake of the troops that departed a week earlier to Canada.[19] Altogether the regiments surpassed 3,000 officers and men, with over 2,200 of them coming from New Jersey and Pennsylvania.[20]

To the north, General David Wooster, the ranking American general in Canada over the winter, finally joined General Arnold outside of Quebec in early April. Arnold's force had grown to approximately 2,500 men. A quarter of the troops with Arnold at Quebec were from New York's four Continental regiments raised in 1775. Parts of Colonel Maxwell's 2nd New Jersey Regiment and Colonel De Haas's 1st Pennsylvania Regiment were also at Quebec by April.[21]

With nearly a quarter of the American troops at Quebec sick with smallpox or under inoculation, their position outside of the fortified city was precarious. Even more troubling was that the enlistments of more than half of the troops, including those from New York, were due to expire in just two weeks. General Wooster offered a bounty to those who agreed to reenlist for a year, but after a harsh winter during which they had been poorly supplied, most declined the offer.[22]

Arnold and Wooster did not get on very well and less than three weeks after Wooster's arrival, Arnold was in Montreal commanding troops there.[23] He was joined by Major-General Thomas on April 26, who took command of all of the American troops in Canada. General Thomas presented a bleak report to Washington.

> I find that the troops who engaged only to the 15th of April are mostly on their return home, and cannot be prevailed on to continue longer in the Country; and by the information given me have no reason to expect, that when those who are on their way here shall arrive, the whole will much exceed 4000. . . . The Artillery, powder &ct. are not yet arrived, and little or no preparation made, as I expected there would have been, for the defence of the Country.[24]

Thomas added that the army in Canada only had enough provisions to last until May 10, and that Continental currency held little weight with the Canadians, who were reluctant to extend any more credit to the Americans for provisions.

Thomas hoped that a committee of commissioners sent by the Continental Congress, made up of Benjamin Franklin, Samuel Chase, and Charles Carroll, might improve the situation. The committee's mission was to "make known to the people of [Canada], the wishes and intentions of the Congress with respect to them."[25] In other words, they were to convince the Canadians to remain on the American side of the conflict with Great Britain.

The commissioners arrived in Montreal on April 29, and reported that the Canadians were largely disillusioned and distrustful of the Americans because of the "lowness of the Continental credit here from the want of hard money."[26] The committee urged that 20,000 pounds of hard money (gold and silver coins) be sent to the army in Canada immediately, "otherwise it will be impossible to continue the war in this Country, or to expect the continuance of our interest with the people here, who begin to consider the Congress bankrupt and their cause desperate."[27] The committee estimated that 8,000 men were needed to properly defend Canada and that currently there were only 3,000 available.

Help was on the way, however. General Sullivan reported from Albany on May 10 that over 5,000 officers and men from sixteen Continental regiments, including all three of New Jersey's Continental regiments, four of the six from Pennsylvania, and one from New York, were either on the march or soon to be on the march to Canada from Albany, Fort George, and Fort Ticonderoga.[28]

RETREAT FROM QUEBEC

Unfortunately for the Americans at Quebec, time had run out for them. When General Thomas arrived at the American encampment outside of Quebec on May 1, he was disappointed at what he found. "I examined into the state of the army," wrote Thomas to Washington, "and found by the returns there were 1900 men. Of this number only 1000 were fit for duty, Officers included; the remainder were Invalids, chiefly confined with the small pox."[29] Several hundred of the troops who were fit for duty were determined to leave on May 15 when their enlistments expired and were loath to do any more duty. Another two hundred men had recently been inoculated for smallpox and were likely to become ill soon.[30] In addition to this, there were only 150 pounds of gunpowder available and six days of provisions left for the army.

A council of war on May 5 unanimously called for the evacuation of the invalids upriver to the settlement of Trois-Rivieres (Three Rivers), eighty miles away. The rest of the army would follow behind.[31] General Thomas believed he still had a couple of days to orderly implement this movement, but British warships appeared off of Quebec the next day and the orderly withdrawal upriver became a disorderly retreat.

The arrival of British reinforcements caused many of the Canadians who had supported and tolerated the Americans all winter and spring to abandon them. "They would neither furnish us with teams [of oxen], nor afford us the least assistance, but kept themselves concealed," reported Thomas to Washington.[32]

Several hundred of the American sick fell into British hands as did most of their cannon and gunpowder at Quebec. Thomas and the remainder of his dispirited force retreated forty miles along the St. Lawrence River, halting at Deschambault, until the lack of provisions forced Thomas to continue on to Trois-Rivieres, midway between Quebec and Montreal. After a few days Thomas continued on to Sorel, leaving Colonel Maxwell of New Jersey in command of a rearguard at Trois-Rivieres.[33]

When the Congressional commissioners in Montreal learned of the retreat from Quebec they were stunned. They could not understand how the American situation had turned so desperate so quickly, but the answer was simple. The lack of military supplies and most particularly provision (food) and the inability to purchase such items from the Canadians because of the lack of hard currency and an enormous debt from earlier purchases on credit, caught up to the Americans in early May. Strengthwise, there were enough American troops assigned to Canada, albeit scattered from Albany to Trois-Rivieres, to give the Americans a chance of success against the British. But logistically, supplying these thousands of troops with weapons, food, clothing, ammunition, and camp gear proved a daunting task that became impossible once the local Canadians stopped accepting American credit for the purchase of food. A letter from an unidentified American officer involved in the withdrawal, shed light on why the Americans kept retreating.

> I wrote you last from Deschambault, where we remained four or five days on a very short allowance [of provision], and left it with half an allowance of flour, and no pork, to serve the men to Trois Rivieres, two good days march. It has since been concluded on to keep no detachment for the present below the Sorel [River], as the Army have been living from hand to mouth for some time past, the supplies of provisions from the other side of the Lakes [in New York] being but small, and very little to be procured [in Canada] without force, or paying hard money for it.[34]

General John Thomas, writing to the Congressional commissioners from Sorel on May 20, also cited the lack of provision, as well as rampant illness, as reasons for the continued retreat of the army.

> The Army here have now for two days been entirely destitute of meat; that no contractor is provided, nor have I any money to purchase provisions, were they to be procured in this country. . . . The want of provisions has made it absolutely necessary for me to order Colonel Maxwell, with the troops under his command at Three Rivers, immediately to join me here. In order to judge truly my situation, you will be pleased to figure to yourselves a retreating Army, disheartened by unavoidable misfortunes, destitute of almost every necessity to render their lives comfortable, or even tolerable, sick, and (as they think) wholly neglected, and no probable prospect of a speedy relief. . . . In short, such are our present circumstances that, unless some effectual spirited steps are immediately undertaken for our relief, it will not be possible to keep the Army together, but we must unavoidably be obliged to abandon a country of infinite importance to the safety of the Colonies, and to leave our friends here a prey to those whose mercies are cruelties.[35]

At first Governor Guy Carleton, reinforced by several thousand British troops under General John Burgoyne and a strong naval squadron, did not press the Americans upon their withdrawal. He blamed strong, steady winds blowing downriver for his inability to pursue the Americans upriver, but the reality was, there was no need to press them, they gave ground without any pressure whatsoever.[36]

Commissioner Samuel Chase, in Montreal, was livid about the American collapse in Canada and wrote a scathing letter to Richard Henry Lee laying much of the blame for the distress upon Congress.

> I am at a Loss to express my Astonishment at the Conduct of Congress. Almost two Months ago they voted 4 Battalions, and since 6 more Battalions for this Country, without the least provisions for their Support. We now have 4,000 Troops in Canada & not a Mouthful of food. Pork is not to be procured. Wheat may be bought for Specie, but we have none. Necessity had compelled Us to take provisions. Will this contribute to regain the Affections of this people?. . . I hope I shall be excused in Saying the Congress are not a fit Body to act as a Council of War. They are too large, too slow and their Resolutions can never be kept secret.[37]

BATTLE OF THE CEDARS

Trouble continued for the Americans when a detachment of 350 troops posted forty miles to the west of Montreal in a location known as the Cedars, was attacked by a combined force of approximately forty British regulars and two hundred Indians.[38] Major Isaac Butterfield commanded the American troops, who were protected by a rough wooden fort. The unit's original commander, Colonel Timothy Bedel, had returned to Montreal to personally warn of the approaching enemy. On his return with 150 reinforcements he fell sick with smallpox.[39]

The British force was commanded by Captain George Forster, who surrounded Major Butterfield with his redcoats and Indians on May 19. The Americans, well protected behind their fortification which stood up against the musket fire of the British and Indians, also had two cannon at their disposal, but they were ill served and largely ineffective.[40]

Nonetheless, the Americans were in a strong position, and yet, when Captain Forster summoned the garrison to surrender the next day or face the wrath of the Indians once the fort was taken by force,

Major Butterfield agreed. The American relief column of 150 men was ambushed the following day by Captain Forster and his party. The outnumbered Americans put up a strong fight for about an hour, but they too were forced to surrender.[41] In two days, Forster had managed to capture nearly five hundred Americans with a force only half that size.

Bearing down upon Forster from Montreal, however, was General Benedict Arnold with 350 troops. Colonel De Haas's 1st Pennsylvania Regiment of 110 riflemen and 300 muskets also rushed west from Sorel to reinforce Arnold.[42]

Captain Forster, burdened with five hundred prisoners, used them as bargaining chips with General Arnold. Forster proposed to parole the prisoners, meaning they would be released under a pledge not to take up arms again until they were officially exchanged for British prisoners held by the Americans. The two sides would then disengage, leaving Forster and his force to return westward. Arnold reluctantly agreed to these terms out of concern that the prisoners would be slaughtered if he attacked Forster.[43] A few prisoners were retained as hostages by Forster to insure implementation of the agreement.

THE AMERICAN ARMY REGROUPS AT SOREL

Back at Sorel, smallpox struck down General Thomas, who relinquished his command and went to Chambly, forty-five miles south of Sorel along the Richelieu River, in an effort to recover. He suffered terribly and died on June 1. Command of the American troops at Sorel passed to General Thompson, who sent Colonel St. Clair with approximately seven hundred troops, including his own 2nd Pennsylvania Regiment and Colonel Maxwell's 2nd New Jersey Regiment, to attack, if possible, a detachment of eight hundred British troops and Canadians reportedly posted at Trois-Rivieres.[44] Thompson, who was himself a Pennsylvanian like St. Clair, assured Washington in a letter that "Col. St Clair is an Officer of great experience and I make no doubt he will acquit himself well of his command."[45]

General Sullivan reached Chambly on June 3, with most of his brigade, including the 1st New Jersey Regiment under Colonel Winds, part of the 4th Pennsylvania Regiment under Colonel Wayne, and the 6th Pennsylvania Regiment under Colonel Irvine.[46] Colonel

Top to Bottom: Quebec in 1775; the Town of Sorel, Lower Canada; the Town of Three Rivers. (*New York Public Library*)

Dayton's 3rd New Jersey Regiment was left behind in New York to help suppress Tory agitators in Tryon County. Command of the American army fell to Sullivan, who was shocked at what he found. He informed Congress two days later from St. Jean that "Every thing is in the utmost Confusion & almost Every one Frightened at they know not what."[47]

Despite his pessimistic report to Congress, Sullivan expressed confidence to Washington that the American army could make a successful stand at Sorel. He ordered the heavy baggage and entrenching tools that had been sent south toward Lake Champlain to return to Sorel and informed Washington that "I am far from fearing 800 men against Such a force as I can muster," referring to the eight hundred British troops reportedly at Trois-Rivieres.[48] Sullivan did not realize that his troops were about to face a much larger British force than he expected.

BATTLE OF THREE RIVERS
On the morning of June 6, two dispatches reached Sullivan informing him that the number of British troops in Trois-Rivieres numbered only three hundred men, supported by several British ships. Sullivan sent General Thompson with "our best troops," Colonel Wayne's 4th Pennsylvania Regiment and Colonel Irvine's 6th Pennsylvania Regiment, to join Colonel St. Clair's 2nd Pennsylvania Regiment and Colonel Maxwell's 2nd New Jersey Regiment (which had not yet attacked the British at Trois-Rivieres). [49] The two American detachments united at the small settlement of Nicolet on the south side of the St. Lawrence River across from Trois-Rivieres. General Sullivan left the decision to attack to General Thompson, stressing that "a Defeat of your party at this time might prove the Total Loss of this Country."[50]

General Thompson and his men arrived at Nicolet late in the evening of June 6-7. He determined that there was not enough time to complete a crossing of the St. Lawrence River and then attack Trois-Rivieres before dawn, so he let his tired men rest. They waited until evening to cross several miles upriver from the British ships at Trois-Rivieres. The plan was to attack the British at dawn of June 8.[51] Thompson informed General Sullivan of his decision and added that the latest reports on British troop strength at Trois-Rivieres ranged from five hundred to 1500 strong. The actual number of British troops at Trois-Rivieres approached two thousand, many who had recently arrived aboard transport ships.[52]

At nightfall on June 7, the Americans, over 1,500 strong and divided into five divisions commanded by Colonels Maxwell, St. Clair, Wayne, Irvine, and Hartley (in reserve), commenced crossing the river, landing nine miles upriver from Trois-Rivieres.[53] They struggled in the darkness to advance, directed by guides who either purposefully misled or incompetently led them. Captain Henry Harvey aboard the HMS *Martin* upriver from Trois-Rivieres, was informed by a local Canadian that the Americans were marching on the town. He sent a boat closer to shore to confirm the report and when its crew did so, he fired an alarm to alert the rest of the fleet and British army. Two British regiments were rushed ashore from transport ships to reinforce the troops already posted in Trois-Rivieres.[54] Captain Harvey recalled that,

> About 5 OClock, a large body of the rebels appear'd opposite to the Ship, at the edge of the woods, marching toward the Town; I immediately fir'd on them which oblig'd them to take shelter in the Woods til they had passed our line of Fire.[55]

Colonel Anthony Wayne with the 4th Pennsylvania came under fire of the *Martin*'s guns and recalled that,

> A Surprise was out of the Question—we therefore put our best face on it and Continued our line of march thro' a thick deep swamp, three miles wide, and after four Hours Arrived at a more open piece of Ground—amidst the thickest firing of the shipping—when all of a sudden a large Body of [British] regulars marched down in good Order Immediately in front of me to prevent our forming.[56]

Colonel Wayne ordered his light infantry and a company of riflemen to "advance and amuse" the British while the rest of his men positioned themselves to attack the British flanks. Wayne proudly reported that his light troops,

> Continued the attack with great spirit until I advanced to support them [on both flanks]. . . . I ordered [the wings] to wheel to the Right & left and flank the Enemy at the same time [the light troops] poured in a well Aimed and heavy fire in front. . . . [The British] attempted to Retreat in good Order at first but in a few minutes broke and ran in the utmost Confusion.[57]

Captain Harvey aboard the HMS *Martin* apparently witnessed this engagement, noting that the Americans, "attack'd the advance guard of our Troops and appear'd to do it, with much resolution."[58]

The American success against the British advance guard was impressive but short-lived. Heavy British cannon and musket fire from the ships and entrenchments at Trois-Rivieres halted the American advance. Colonel Wayne noted that,

> We advanced in Column up to their breastworks . . . Gen'l Thompson with Cols St. Clair, Irvine, & Hartly were marching in full view to our support. Col. Maxwell now began to Engage on the left of me, the fire was so hot he could not maintain his post— the other [American] troops had also filed off to the left—my small Battalion . . . amounting in the whole about 200 were left exposed to the whole fire of the shipping in flank and full three thousand men in front with all their Artillery. . . . Our people taking example by others gave way—Indeed it was impossible for them to stand in longer.[59]

An unidentified American officer involved with the battle, possibly Colonel Maxwell, gave a similar account.

> The great body of the enemy, which we knew nothing of, consisting of two or three thousand men, covered with intrenchments, and assisted with the cannon of the shipping and several field pieces, began a furious fire, and continued it upon our troops in the front; it was so heavy that [Wayne's] division gave way. . . .

Colonel St. Clair's division advanced, but the fire was too heavy. Part of Colonel Irvine's division (especially the Riflemen) went up toward the enemy. Lieutenant Colonel Hartley, understanding the Army was in confusion, led up the reserve within a short distance of the enemy. . . . Under all of these disadvantages, our men would fight, but we had no ground for it. We had no covering, no artillery, and no prospect of succeeding, as the number of the enemy was so much superior to ours.[60]

When a strong British detachment attempted to cut off the Americans from their boats, nine miles upriver, a retreat was ordered. "It was impossible to [retreat orderly] as we could not regain the road," remembered the unidentified American officer, "the shipping and artillery of the enemy being in the way; small parties went through the swamp."[61]

Two hundred and fifty men had been left upriver to guard the American boats and they grew anxious at the first reports of the battle. Several hundred exhausted Americans reached the boats before the detachment guarding them fled across the river, leaving the bulk of General Thompson's force behind to make their escape by foot.[62] One of the American officers left behind recalled that,

Our party advanced within a mile of the place where our boats were, but our guard had carried them off. The English had possessed the ground near the landing, so that we could not get there, but we saw part of them. The enemy had so many men that they sent parties to fortify all the ferries we were to pass, and the shipping proceeded upriver to cover them. Colonel Wayne, with his party, lay near the enemy. We passed through a prodigious swamp, and at night took possession of a hill near the enemy. Our men, without provision, without sleep, and after all this fatigue, required some rest. The mantle of Heaven was our only covering; no fire, and bad water our only food. We mounted a small quarter-guard, fixed our alarm post, and made every man lay down on the ground, on which he was to rise for action in case of an attack. I slept a little by resting my head on a cold bough of spruce. Morning appeared; what was to be done? We consulted our officers and men; they said they were refreshed with sleep; it was agreed to stand together, and that they would effect a passage through the enemy, or die in the attempt.[63]

The Americans continued on and fell in with Colonel Wayne's party, bringing their number to seven hundred desperate but determined men. "We had confidence and agreed to attack them if they fell in our way," remembered one American officer.[64] The British, however, had ended their pursuit, and when they reached their camp at Sorel, much to the relief of General Sullivan, they brought the number of Americans who had returned from the battle to about 1,200.[65]

Those killed or wounded in the Battle of Three Rivers amounted to less than twenty for the British and around fifty for the Americans.[66] Several hundred Americans, including General Thompson and Colonel Irvine, were captured by the British and French Loyalists who scoured the woods and swamp after the battle.[67] Most made it back to Sorel, however, where they soon continued their retreat with the rest of the American army.

CANADA ABANDONED
General Benedict Arnold's letter to General Sullivan just two days after the American defeat at Trois-Rivieres accurately summed up the view of many in the American camp.

> I am fully of opinion not one minute ought to be lost in securing our retreat, and saving our heavy cannon, baggage, and provisions. The enemy . . . is doubtless much superior to ours, and we have no advice of any reinforcements. Shall we sacrifice the few men we have by endeavouring to keep possession of a small part of the country which can be of little or no service to us? The junction of the Canadians with the Colonies—an object which brought us into this country—is now at an end. Let us quit them, and secure our own country before it is too late.[68]

The American army at Sorel, Montreal, and several smaller posts in Canada numbered just over 4,000 officers and men fit for duty in the days following the battle at Trois-Rivieres. Continental troops from New Jersey and Pennsylvania accounted for more than half of that number.[69] Most had only recently arrived in Canada and now they were to retreat.

Although General Sullivan was discouraged by the defeat at Three Rivers, he informed Washington four days after the battle that despite the reports of thousands of British troops now in Canada and the state of his sick and famished army, "I am employ'd day & Night in fortifying & Securing my Camp & am Determin'd to hold it as Long as a person will Stick by me."[70] Sullivan shared similar views with General Schuyler in Albany, prompting Schuyler to respond that "although I applaud your magnanimous spirit, yet I cannot . . . approve that you should think only of a glorious death or a victory obtained against superior numbers."[71] Schuyler declared that the loss of the entire American army in Canada would be a much bigger blow than the loss of Canada, and wrote that "you ought not to remain any longer in Sorel."[72]

By the time Sullivan received Schuyler's reply, his withdrawal was well underway. The American army initially retreated to Isle Au Noix, in the Richelieu River, but it was too marshy and unhealthy, so Sullivan moved farther south down Lake Champlain. He ended his retreat at Crown Point, an abandoned British fort just eleven miles north of Fort Ticonderoga. These two posts, particularly Fort Ticonderoga, were now the anchor of America's defense of upper New York.[73] From here on out, the Americans would fight a defensive war in northern New York.

Seven

Summer

Although the situation in Canada was on the minds of many colonists in May and June 1776, their attention was also drawn to New York, South Carolina, Virginia, and Pennsylvania. It was in Philadelphia, on May 15, that a critical step toward American independence occurred.

Declaring that the King and Parliament had, "excluded the inhabitants of these United Colonies from the protection of his crown," and that their petitions and appeals for reconciliation had gone unanswered and instead, "the whole force of that kingdom, aided by foreign mercenaries, is to be exerted for the destruction of the good people of these colonies," the Continental Congress declared that it was "absolutely irreconcilable to reason" that the colonists could not support "any government under the crown of Great Britain."[1] The Congress therefore announced that all royal authority "should be totally suppressed, and all the powers of government exerted, under the authority of the people of the colonies for the preservation of internal peace, virtue, and good order, as well as for the defence of their lives, liberties, and properties, against the hostile invasions and cruel depredations of their enemies."[2]

This declaration was attached as a preamble to a resolution Congress passed five days earlier that recommended that the colonies, "adopt such government as shall, in the opinion of the representatives of the people, best conduce to the happiness and safety of their constituents in particular, and America in general.[3] Taken together, these statements amounted to a de facto declaration of independence for the colonies.

John Adams of Massachusetts believed that the resolutions merely affirmed what the British Parliament had already accomplished by its passage of the Prohibitory Act the previous December. This act authorized the British navy to seize American vessels and property in an effort to economically strangle the American colonists into obedience. When Adams learned of the measure in March, he announced that it should be called the Act of Independency because "It is a compleat Dismemberment of the British Empire, levels all Distinctions and makes us independent in Spite of all our supplications and Entreaties."[4] Adams, who had become the leading advocate for independence in Congress, added that,

> It might be fortunate that the Act of Independency should come from the British Parliament, rather than the American Congress: But it is very odd that Americans should hesitate at accepting Such a Gift from them.[5]

On the same day that the Continental Congress adopted its bold resolution of May 15, the Fifth Virginia Convention, meeting in Williamsburg, voted unanimously to instruct Virginia's delegates to the Continental Congress to propose that Congress, "declare the United Colonies free and independent states absolved from all allegiance to or dependence upon the crown or parliament of Great Britain."[6] Three weeks later, on June 7, Richard Henry Lee of Virginia introduced a resolution in the Continental Congress calling for American independence from Great Britain. After two days of debate, Congress adjourned for three weeks to allow delegates to better gauge the sense of their constituents back home.

These measures received a mixed reaction among American colonists. Those in favor of independence (patriots) embraced both actions as long overdue. Others believed that although the rights of the colonists had indeed been violated, the time for independence had not yet arrived. They argued that it was not practical to take such a drastic move that would likely end in failure. Yet another group of colonists (Tories) refused to even contemplate independence and were angered by the measures. Many colonists in the Middle Colonies fell in the latter two groups in May and early June 1776 and still had some influence in their colonies.

New York

As the probable epicenter of Britain's retaliatory response against the colonies, the inhabitants of New York were very anxious in the spring of 1776. Tory sentiment had been suppressed on Long Island by force, but the expected arrival of an enormous British invasion force promised to encourage such sentiment again.

On May 27, a committee formed in the Third New York Provincial Congress charged with responding to the Continental Congress's May 15 resolution about forming new colonial governments, delivered its report. It asserted that the hostile actions of the British government toward the colonies had made New York's royal government, "ipso facto dissolved," and the people of New York now needed to institute a new form of government.[7] Until this was done, the Provincial Congress would serve as New York's governing body.

Although the Provincial Congress acknowledged the demise of royal authority, their solution did not explicitly endorse independence. James Duane, one of New York's delegates to the Continental Congress in Philadelphia, likely approved of the half measure of the Provincial Congress. He had written to a fellow delegate, John Jay, who was away from Philadelphia to attend the Provincial Congress, that,

> There seems . . . no Reason that our Colony sho"d be too precipitate in changing the present mode of Government. I would wish first to be well assured of the Opinion of the Inhabitants at large. Let them be rather followed than driven on an Occasion of such momentous Concern. But, above all, let us see the Conduct

of the middle Colonies before we come to a Decision. It cannot injure us to wait a few weeks.[8]

Several of New York's delegates in the Continental Congress apparently disagreed with Duane. They wrote to the Provincial Congress seeking its sentiments on independence.

> Your Delegates here expect that the question of independence will very shortly be agitated in Congress. Some of us consider ourselves as bound by our instructions not to vote on that question & all wish to have your sentiments thereon.[9]

When the issue of independence was addressed by the Provincial Congress on June 11, the delegates followed James Duane's advice and declared that "The good people of this Colony have not, in the opinion of this Congress, authorized this Congress, or the Delegates of this Colony in the Continental Congress, to declare this Colony to be and continue independent of the Crown of Great Britain."[10] The Third New York Provincial Congress thus deferred a decision on the issue of independence and focused instead on preparations for an expected British attack on New York City. New York's decision on independence was to be settled by the Fourth New York Provincial Congress, which was scheduled to convene on July 8.

John Adams was not pleased by the conduct of New York's leaders. He informed a friend on June 23 that,

> New York still acts in Character, like a People without Courage or sense, or Spirit, or in short any one Virtue or Ability. There is neither Spunk nor Gumption, in that Province as a Body. Individuals are very clever. But it is the weakest Province in point of Intellect, Valour, public Spirit, or anything else that is great and good upon the Continent. It is incapable of doing Us much good, or much Hurt, but from its local situation. The low Cunning of Individuals and their Prostitution plagues Us, the Virtues of a few Individuals is of some Service to Us. But as a Province it will be a dead Weight upon any side, ours or that of our Enemies.[11]

Adams privately blasted New York yet again in another letter the following day.

> What is the Reason that New York is still asleep or dead in Politicks and War? Must it always be So? Cannot the whole Congregation of Patriots and Heroes, belonging to the Army, now in that Province, inspire it, with one generous Sentiment? Have they no sense? No Feeling? No sentiment? No Passions? While every other Colony is rapidly advancing [toward independence], their Motions Seem to be rather retrograde . . . . Is there any Thing in the Air, or Soil of New York, unfriendly to the Spirit of Liberty? Are the People destitute of Reason, or of Virtue? Or what is the Cause?[12]

John Adams's disenchantment with New York did not stop him, or Congress, from striving to defend the colony from an expected attack from the British. With alarming reports in early June of an enormous British army of over 30,000 men due to arrive in New York at any moment, the Continental Congress took action to bolster the defense of New York. It called for 13,800 militia from Massachusetts, Connecticut, New York, and New Jersey to reinforce General Washington's army of approximately 8,500 men.[13] New York was to provide 3,000 men and New Jersey 3,300. Congress also formed a reserve force of 10,000 militia, calling it a Flying Camp. Pennsylvania was to provide 6,000 men for this force, Maryland 3,400, and Delaware, six hundred. All of the militia would serve until December 1.[14]

The New York Provincial Congress assigned militia quotas for each county and New York City on June 7 to fill its allotment of 3,000 troops. The men were to be volunteers, not draftees, and were to be organized into four militia battalions of 750 officers and men each.[15] Two days later, acknowledging the need to raise these troops quickly, the Provincial Congress empowered the counties to fill their quotas with draftees, chosen by lot, if necessary.[16] A sense of urgency to do so was supplied by John Hancock, the President of the Continental Congress, who wrote to the leaders of Massachusetts, Connecticut, and New York on June 11 that,

The Congress have this Day received Advices, and are fully convinced, that it is the Design of Genl. Howe to make an Attack upon the City of New York as soon as possible. The Attack, they have Reason to believe, will be made within ten Days.[17]

Hancock "most earnestly" requested that the three colonies call forth their militia and march them to New York City as quickly as possible.[18] The Continental Congress also ordered the two remaining Continental regiments in Pennsylvania, Colonel John Shee's 3rd Pennsylvania and Colonel Robert Magaw's 5th Pennsylvania, to New York upon Washington's request on June 10.[19]

In his request to Congress, Washington mentioned the efforts of Governor Tryon, who was still aboard a ship off New York, to maintain the spirits of the "disaffected" (Tories). "I had no doubt when I left this City, for Philadelphia" wrote Washington, "but that some measures would have been taken to secure the suspected, and dangerous Persons of this Government before now, and left Orders for the Military to give every aid to the Civil Power."[20] To his frustration, little effort to suppress suspected Tories in New York was made by New York's leaders. Washington lamented that "The Subject is delicate & nothing is done in it—we may therefore have Internal, as well as external Enemies to contend with."[21]

Such an internal threat to the army, and to Washington himself, was discovered and thwarted in mid-June. Washington provided the details of the plot to the Continental Congress in late June.

Congress I doubt not will have heard of the plot that was forming among many disaffected persons in this City and Government; for aiding the King's Troops upon their arrival. No regular plan seems to have been digested but several persons have been Inlisted and sworn to Join them—The matter I am in hopes by a timely discovery will be suppressed and put a stop to—Many Citizens & others, among whom is the Mayor, are now in confinement—the matter has been traced to Governor Tryon & the Mayor appears to have been a principal agent or go between him and the persons concerned in It—The plot had been communicated to some in the Army, and part of my Guard engaged in It—Thomas Hickey one of them, has been tried and by the unanimous opinion of a Court Martial is sentenced to die, having Inlisted himself and engaged others.[22]

Newspaper accounts of the plot reported that the conspirators planned to kill Washington and that five hundred Tories were involved.[23] Although many people, including the city's mayor, David Mathews, were detained and investigated, Thomas Hickey was the only one convicted for his involvement. Washington hoped that his execution, by hanging, would suffice to deter future plots.

Troubling as the conspiratorial news was to Washington and the army, the arrival of a massive British naval fleet attracted most of New York's attention at the end of June. Washington reported to Congress on June 30 that 110 British ships, presumably carrying thousands of British troops under General William Howe, had arrived off New York Harbor.[24] A troop return of his army dated June 29 revealed that Washington had only 10,394 officers and men fit for duty to challenge the British.[25] The recent arrival of Pennsylvania's two Continental regiments (the 3rd and 5th Pennsylvania) added one thousand men, and approximately 1,800 New York militia had also recently arrived per the Continental Congress's June 3 resolution, but the militia from Massachusetts, Connecticut, and New Jersey, which represented potentially ten thousand troops, had yet to arrive, and even when they did, assuming they did, the Americans defending New York would still be significantly outnumbered when the remainder of Britain's invasion force arrived from England.[26]

NEW JERSEY

Overshadowed by its neighbor to the east, New Jersey did not address the May 15 resolves of the Continental Congress until its own Provincial Congress, elected in late May, convened in Burlington. The first business of this Congress was to address, yet again, Governor Franklin's conduct. Two weeks after the Continental Congress called on all of the colonies to replace their royal forms of government, Governor Franklin, from his residence in Perth Amboy, called for the New Jersey Assembly to meet.

The Provincial Congress met instead and rejected Franklin's call for the assembly to meet. Furthermore, the convention deemed Franklin's action as a sign of contempt for the Continental Congress (which it surely was), and labeled him an "enemy of the liberties of this country," who needed to be secured.[27] The Provincial Congress gave Colonel Nathaniel Heard of Middlesex County specific instructions on how to secure Franklin.

> It is the desire of Congress that this necessary business be conducted with all the delicacy and tenderness which the nature of the business can possibly admit. For this end you will find among the papers the form of a written parole, in which there is left a blank space for you to fill up, at the choice of Mr. Franklin, with the name of Princeton, Bordentown, or his own farm at Rancocus. When he shall have signed the parole, the Congress will rely upon his honour for the faithful performance of his engagements; but should he refuse to sign the parole, you are desired to put him under strong guard, and keep him in close custody, until the further order of this Congress.[28]

Colonel Heard reported back to the Provincial Congress on June 18, that Franklin had refused to sign the parole. Heard ordered a company of militia (sixty strong) to stand guard of Franklin's residence until he received further instructions from the Congress.[29] They ordered Colonel Heard to bring Franklin to Burlington, where they were assembled. The Provincial Congress also wrote to the Continental Congress to suggest that it might be best to send Franklin to another colony where he could do less mischief.[30]

Governor Franklin, indignant at what he viewed as the usurpation of the King's government by the Provincial Congress, refused to answer any questions when he was brought before the Provincial Congress.[31] The Congress once again turned to the Continental Congress for guidance, and their solution was to send Franklin, under guard, to Connecticut where it was hoped he would give his parole (promising good conduct). If he still refused to do so, Congress instructed that he be treated as a prisoner under close guard.[32]

On the same day that New Jersey's Provincial Congress solicited guidance from the Continental Congress about Governor Franklin, the delegates voted overwhelmingly, 54 to 3, to follow the May 15 recommendation of Congress to form a new government.[33] More importantly, the Provincial Congress gave New Jersey's five delegates to the Continental Congress, which was to reconvene on July 1, the authority to,

> Join with the Delegates of the other Colonies in Continental Congress, in the most vigorous measures for supporting the just rights and liberties of America. And if you shall judge it necessary and expedient for this purpose, we empower you to join with them in declaring the United Colonies independent of Great Britain, entering into a confederacy for union and common defence . . . .[34]

It was not a specific instruction to vote for independence, but rather, the authority to vote for independence, which, according to John Adams, all of New Jersey's delegates were inclined to do.[35]

At the end of June an incident occurred off Cape May that cost the British a number of sailors and the colonists a ship and over a hundred barrels of gunpowder. The brig *Nancy,* loaded with four hundred barrels of gunpowder from the Caribbean, was spotted by the HMS *Kingfisher* and HMS *Orpheus* entering Delaware Bay. It was driven ashore off Cape May and the crew, assisted by the crew of two Continental warships that had been blocked up along the coast by the British navy for days, hurriedly unloaded barrels of gunpowder, muskets, and dry goods as fast as they could.[36] Several boats from the *Kingfisher* approached the *Nancy,* but were driven off by fire from the beached brig and the shore. The *Kingfisher* then drew closer, some three to four hundred yards from the brig, and "returned their Fire with redoubled fury."[37] Five boats from the *Kingfisher* and *Orpheus* were then sent to secure the *Nancy.* The Americans onboard fled ashore, but continued to fire upon the British.

Suddenly, a tremendous explosion ripped the *Nancy* apart, blowing British sailors forty yards into the air.[38] The Americans had managed to save 265 barrels of gunpowder, 50 muskets, and some valuable dry goods, but another 135 barrels of powder were left behind and had exploded.[39] Accounts of the engagement in the newspapers claimed the Americans had rigged the powder to explode.[40] The British described it as an accident. Whatever the cause, strewn about the wreckage in the water were the "heads, arms, legs, and entrails of British sailors."[41] The logs of the two British vessels recorded seven sailors killed and one wounded. The Americans lost one man killed and one wounded in the fighting that occurred before the explosion.[42]

The New Jersey Provincial Congress received word of the arrival of the British fleet outside of New York the same day as the engagement at Cape May. It immediately ordered all of the militia that had been raised to reinforce New York City to march there immediately.[43] Within a month, 1,675 New Jersey militia were in the city to help defend it.[44] That was barely over half the militia the Continental Congress had called for in early June.

PENNSYLVANIA

On the day that the Continental Congress passed its May 15 resolution calling on the colonies to adopt new government to replace the former royal governments, the Pennsylvania Assembly was five days away from convening. The Pennsylvania Committee of Safety remained in session, but its focus was almost solely on improving the defenses for Philadelphia and the Delaware River. Pennsylvania had done much already, at great cost, but the committee desired further improvements and wrote to the Continental Congress on May 20 to request that that body pay for additional ships and artillery batteries on and along the river.[45] To justify its request that Congress pay for these new measures, the committee listed all that Pennsylvania had taken upon itself at its own cost.

> That the General Assembly of this Province having . . . caused thirteen Armed Boats or Gondolas to be built, equipped, and manned, and have since built, fitted and manned a large Ship, Floating Battery, several Guard Boats, and a great number of Fire Rafts, erected Fortifications on Deepwater Island, raised a large Artillery Company for their defence, and sunk Chevaux-de fries

in the Channel of the River; that the Assembly have raised two Battalions of Riflemen and one of Musketry, stationed on the banks of the River Delaware.[46]

The Committee of Safety believed that Pennsylvania, by paying for such measures, had greatly exceeded the effort and contribution of the other colonies. It was only appropriate, therefore, given the importance of the city of Philadelphia to all the colonies, that the Continental Congress pay for additional defensive measures that the committee believed were needed. Three weeks passed before Congress replied and agreed to pay for some of the additional measures.[47]

Although the Pennsylvania Committee of Safety did not address the May 15 recommendation of the Continental Congress to form new governments, Philadelphia's Committee of Observation met on May 22, and read the resolution aloud to the cheers of a large crowd in attendance. The committee then proposed that a Provincial Convention be chosen by the people with the express purpose of carrying the resolve of Congress into action. [48]

Given the Pennsylvania Assembly's refusal just six weeks earlier to alter its instructions to Pennsylvania's delegates in the Continental Congress, instructions that opposed any move toward independence, Philadelphia's committee and others who supported independence realized it was crucial to remove the assembly from any further decision on the issue.[49] The assembly had reconvened on May 20 and coolly received the Philadelphia Committee's petition calling for a Provincial Convention two days later. Claiming uncertainty about the meaning of the Continental Congress's May 15 resolution, it formed a committee to study it and determine what the Congress meant by it.[50]

While the assembly waited for the committee's findings, which were presented on June 6 and after a lengthy debate, referred back to the committee for further consideration, it went on with its work, much of which involved the consideration of petitions on both sides of the independence issue. On June 5, the assembly took a big step toward independence by forming a committee to develop new instructions to Pennsylvania's delegates in the Continental Congress.

The motion to form the committee, chaired by John Dickinson, long a leader against Britain's policies but also an opponent of independence, passed "by a large Majority."[51]

The committee presented its first draft of instructions the following day. A full day of debate ensued on June 7, the very day Richard Henry Lee proposed independence for the colonies in the Continental Congress. The assembly approved the new instructions the following day.[52]

> When by our instructions of last November, we strictly enjoined you, in Behalf of this Colony, to dissent from and utterly reject any Propositions, should such be made, that might cause or lead to a Separation from Great-Britain, or a Change of the Form of this Government, our Restrictions did not arise from any Dissidence of your Ability, Prudence or Integrity, but from an earnest Desire to serve the good People of Pennsylvania with Fidelity, in Times so full of alarming Dangers and perplexing Difficulties. The Situation of public Affairs is since so greatly altered, that we now think ourselves justifiable in removing the Restrictions laid upon you.[53]

The assembly then outlined many of the wrongs the British government, King and Parliament, had committed against the colonists, and declared,

> We therefore hereby authorize you to concur with the other Delegates in Congress, in forming such further Compacts between the United Colonies, concluding such Treaties with foreign Kingdoms and States, and in adopting such other Measures as, upon a View of all Circumstances, shall be judged necessary for promoting the Liberty, Safety and Interests of America.[54]

The Pennsylvania Assembly had thus given its delegates to the Continental Congress permission to vote for independence. It was not, however, a directive, but rather, an option.

On June 18, representatives from a number of county committees met in Carpenter Hall, site of the First Continental Congress, to form a Provincial Conference of Committees. The Philadelphia Committee of Observation, frustrated at the assembly's refusal to act upon the Continental Congress's May 15 resolve, organized the meeting as a sort of shadow governing body. Nearly a hundred men from twelve counties and Philadelphia met and immediately approved the May 15 resolution, essentially declaring independence for Pennsylvania.[55]

The next step of these delegates was to call for the creation of a Provincial Convention, tasked with forming a new government for Pennsylvania. Two days were spent determining who was eligible to vote for delegates to the Provincial Convention. The requirements were largely the same as for those who could vote for the Pennsylvania Assembly, namely freemen over 21 years of age. What was new, however, was an oath declaring that,

> I do not hold myself bound to bear allegiance to George, the Third, King of Great Britain, and that I will steadily and firmly . . . oppose the tyrannical proceedings of the King and Parliament of Great Britain against the American Colonies, and to establish and support a Government in this Province on the authority of the people only.[56]

The next thing the Conference of Committees did was fill a vacuum caused by the inability of the Pennsylvania Assembly to reach a quorum to proceed with any more business. For several days after its June 8 vote granting Pennsylvania's delegates to the Continental Congress permission to vote for independence, the Pennsylvania Assembly failed for reach a quorum of members in attendance. Whether the absence of members was a protest by those against independence or a move by those in favor of independence to prevent the conservative leaning assembly from backtracking is unclear, but whatever the cause, after its vote on June 8, the Pennsylvania Assembly struggled to reach a quorum to conduct further business.

As a result, the Conference of Committees undertook at least one legislative duty, recommending unanimously that Pennsylvania's counties embody 4,500 militia which, when added to the three battalions of 1,500 troops that were already in the field, would allow

Pennsylvania to reach its quota of militia for the Flying Camp created by the Continental Congress.[57]

The Conference then turned to one last pressing issue, independence. On June 24, the Conference of Committees unanimously adopted a resolution declaring that

> We, the Deputies of the people of Pennsylvania . . . unanimously declare our willingness to concur in a vote of the Congress declaring the United Colonies free and independent States . . . .[58]

Although the resolution had no binding force, it was hoped that any of Pennsylvania's delegates to the Continental Congress who were undecided about independence would be persuaded by the action of the Conference of Committees.

DELAWARE

News of the Continental Congress's resolves of May 15 was greeted with a mixed reaction in the three Lower Counties of Delaware. Those inclined toward independence supported the resolution, but a majority of colonists in Delaware either believed the resolution did not apply to them, or outright opposed it.[59]

Patriot leaders in Kent County drafted a petition instructing their representatives in the Delaware Assembly to comply with the recommendation of Congress. If support failed in the assembly, the representatives were to withdraw in protest to force its dissolution.[60]

Colonel John Haslet, the commander of Delaware's sole Continental regiment, was concerned about the sudden rise of Tory sentiment. In late May, he informed Caesar Rodney, a delegate to the Continental Congress, that "A vast Majority in Sussex are against" the May 15 resolve and Kent County's petition of support. "What the fate of our Application here will be, I cannot with certainty yet inform you, but fear Congress must either disarm a large Part of Kent & Sussex, or see their Recommendation treated with contempt."[61]

Captain Thomas Rodney informed his brother Caesar in late May that the Kent County petition in favor of the May 15 resolve was "offered to my company [of militia] yesterday & twenty-six of them signed it, the rest Chose to have it under Consideration Till next muster day."[62] Both men were likely troubled by the tepid response of the militia, but Captain Rodney reported that by the next day "many of them say they are now ready to sign."[63]

A counter-petition, claiming that the May 15 resolution of Congress had been misinterpreted because it only applied to governments in disorder, which Delaware's was not, began to circulate in the Lower Counties. Thomas Robinson, a Tory leader from Sussex County, claimed that the counter-petition garnered 5,000 signatures while the one from Kent County in support of the Continental Congress's resolve of May 15, only received three hundred signatures.[64]

Whatever the numbers, it was clear that strong Tory sentiment existed in Delaware. This was demonstrated at a militia muster in Kent County in early June. Petitions against independence were circulated among those gathered at the muster and according to Colonel Haslet, "a scene of confusion ensued. Some [of the militia] would muster not at all, others, once a fortnight, & they broke up in disorder."[65]

This situation was even more dire for the patriots farther south in Sussex County. Encouraged by the presence of British warships offshore, hundreds of Tories rose up in Sussex County. Enoch Anderson, a lieutenant in Delaware's Continental regiment, was posted in Lewestown, in Sussex County, but received permission to visit his family in New Castle in May. When he passed through the town of Dover on his return to the regiment in late May he received a shock.

> Here all was confusion. The Tories had risen in Sussex, it was said, our troops were surrounded in Lewistown and would be all cut off. That to-morrow a regiment of Tories would be at Dover to destroy the town.[66]

The unrest was sparked when a crowd in Dover seized John Clark and placed him in the pillory to prevent him from delivering the Tory counter-petition to the Continental Congress. Outraged at this abuse and the destruction of the petition, hundreds of Tories formed to march on Dover.[67]

With no Continentals then in Dover, Anderson volunteered to serve as a private with the local militia. When the Tories did not appear, he grew restless and continued on to rejoin his company at

Lewestown. He encountered a regiment of armed men that he took for Tories heading for Dover, but they left him alone. After a brief stop at a tavern to rest, Anderson, who was dressed in his uniform, encountered about thirty armed Tories. He recalled that they exclaimed, "Here is one of d——d Haslet's men. You're a d——d rebel, we have got you now and will take care of you."[68]

The fact that Anderson managed to talk his way out of this confrontation suggests that the Tories were not incited to the point of violence against their fellow colonists, even an apparent patriot dressed in a regimental uniform. In fact, confrontation and bloodshed in Dover was averted when two ministers convinced the Tories to withdraw.[69] Nevertheless, the number of Tories who took up arms to challenge the patriots was alarming.

When Lieutenant Anderson arrived in Lewestown, he found 300 Delaware troops, Continentals and militia, all in alarm. He was told that 1,500 Tories were posted just three miles away, armed with muskets, pitch-forks, and clubs to confront them.[70] Thomas McKean, the President of the Delaware Assembly, learned of the unrest in Sussex County early in the morning of June 13, and immediately informed the Continental Congress.

> There are a thousand Tories under arms in Sussex County . . . assembled . . . about eighteen miles this side of Lewes, and their intention was to proceed there and join the British forces from on board some men-of-war . . . who were to land this night in order to cut off three companies of the Continental troops at that place.[71]

Within twelve hours of this letter, McKean informed Congress that "the insurgents in Sussex County have dispersed, after a conference had by some of their leaders with some of the Council of Safety of this Government."[72] McKean added, "They deny all intercourse with the men-of-war, or disaffection to the American cause; but the real cause of their assembling in such large numbers and in so hostile a manner is as yet unknown." Calling it a "strange affair," McKean informed Congress that the Delaware Assembly had sent a committee to Lewes to "endeavour to quiet the imprudent people, by reason, if practicable, and if not in that way, then by force of arms."[73]

The Continental Congress reacted to the news from Delaware by sending one ton of gunpowder to the colony and requesting Pennsylvania to send a regiment of its provincial riflemen there.[74] Four hundred Pennsylvania riflemen under Colonel Samuel Miles arrived in Lewes on June 20, but there was little for them to do as the Tories had all dispersed.[75]

In Newcastle, the Delaware Assembly, unperturbed by the Tory unrest, voted on June 15 to formally end royal authority in Delaware.

> Whereas it is become absolutely necessary for the safety, protection, and happiness of the good people of this Colony, forthwith to establish some authority adequate to the exigencies of their affairs, until a new Government can be formed . . . all persons holding any office, civil or military, in this Colony, on the 13th day of June . . . may and shall continue to execute the same, in the name of the Government of the Counties of Newcastle, Kent, and Sussex, upon Delaware, as they used legally to exercise it in the name of the King, until a new Government shall be formed, agreeable to the Resolution of Congress on the 15th of May last.[76]

The assembly also approved new instructions for its three delegates to the Continental Congress.

They were to,

> Concur with the other Delegates in Congress, in forming such further compact between the United Colonies, concluding such treaties with foreign Kingdoms and states, and in adopting such other measures as shall be judged necessary for promoting the liberty, safety, and interests of America.[77]

The instructions did not order the delegates to vote for independence, but rather, follow the lead of the other colonies on the question. That was good enough for John Adams, the leading proponent of independence in Congress.

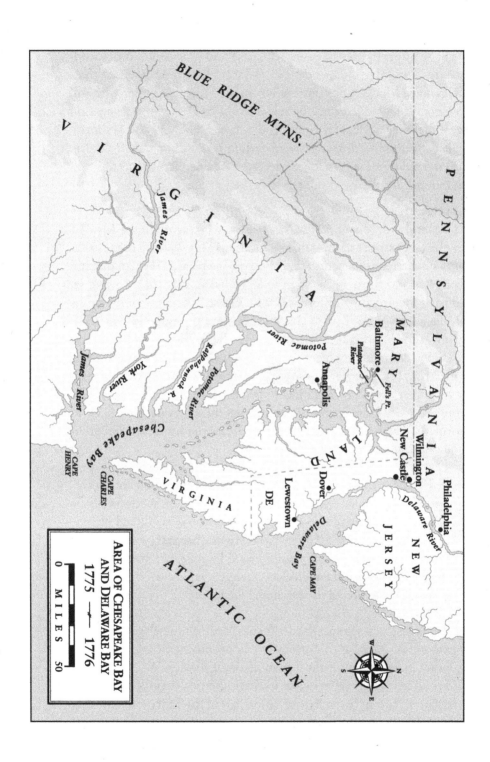

AREA OF CHESAPEAKE BAY
AND DELAWARE BAY
1775 → 1776

0   MILES   50

In an effort to pressure Samuel Chase and Maryland's other leaders to support independence, Adams informed Chase that,
"[Thomas] McKean has returned from the Lower Counties with full
Powers."[78] He added that the instructions to Delaware's delegation
were the same as Pennsylvania's and that he had it on good authority
that New Jersey's delegates were certain to vote for independence.
"Maryland now stands alone," declared Adams, "I presume She will
soon join Company—if not she must be left alone."[79]

MARYLAND
The Maryland Convention was in session when word of the May 15
resolve of Congress arrived in Annapolis on May 20. Five days earlier
the Convention took action that should have pleased the Continental
Congress and those in favor in independence, it voted to dispense,
"during the unhappy differences with Great Britain" with the oaths
of allegiance to the British Crown that were typically administered
to government officials.[80] This seemed to be a rejection of British authority in Maryland, which is what Congress's resolution of May 15
called for. The Maryland resolve, however, was meant to be a temporary measure, to be rescinded when the long hoped for reconciliation between Britain and the colonies returned everything back to
normal. To stress that point further, the Convention passed an additional resolution on May 21.

> That as this Convention is firmly persuaded that a reunion with
> Great Britain on constitutional principles would most effectually
> secure the rights and liberties and increase the strength and pro-
> mote the happiness of the whole empire, objects which this
> Province has ever had in view, the said Deputies are bound and
> directed to govern themselves by the instructions given to them
> by this Convention in its session in December.[81]

These instructions specifically forbid Maryland's delegation to the
Continental Congress to "assent to any proposition to declare these
colonies independent of the crown of Great Britain."[82]
Proponents of independence were disappointed and confused by
Maryland's action. Even before he learned of the Maryland Conven-

tion's resolve, John Adams had expressed his frustration about Maryland. Writing to his friend, James Warren, on May 20, Adams declared,

> [Maryland] is so excentric a Colony—some time so hot, sometimes so cold—now so high, then so low—that I know not what to say about it or to expect from it. I have often wished it could exchange Places with Hallifax. When they get going I expect some wild extravagant Flight or other from it.[83]

Richard Henry Lee, another leader of the independence movement and the man who introduced Virginia's resolution for independence to the Continental Congress, also expressed frustration with the Maryland Convention. Convinced that the Convention's actions did not represent the will of the people of Maryland, Lee chided the Convention in a letter to General Charles Lee.

> Is the Convention of Maryland a Conclave of Popes, a mutilated legislature or an Assembly of wise Men. By the manner in which they dispense with oaths it would seem they conceived themselves as the first of these, for surely a mutilated legislature, an unorganized Government, cannot do what these men by their Resolve of May the 15th have undertaken. Nor is their 2nd resolve of the 21st better founded, unless they can shew, which I believe is not in their power, that the people had in contemplation these things when they chose them and elected them accordingly. What do these folks mean by a "Reunion with G. Britain *on constitutional principles?*" I profess I do not understand them, nor do I believe the best among them have any sensible ideas annexed to these terms.[84]

The Maryland Convention took a similar approach in its dealings with the royal Governor, Robert Eden. Proclaiming that they could find no "unfriendly intent" in the Governor's intercepted correspondence with London, but noting that as governor, he was required to execute the instructions of the King and his ministers, the Convention decreed on May 22 that "the public quiet and safety . . . require that [Governor Eden] leave this province, and that he is at full liberty to depart peacefully with his effects."[85] He departed without incident a month later aboard the HMS *Fowey*, which sailed into Annapolis Harbor on June 23 under a flag of truce.[86] Eden's departure signified the end of any remaining royal authority in Maryland.

Three days after the Convention ordered Governor Eden to leave Maryland, the delegates concluded the convention with an action that likely confirmed their eccentricity to the likes of John Adams and Richard Henry Lee. It ordered that "every prayer and petition for the king's majesty, in the book of common prayer and administration of the sacraments and other rites and ceremonies of the church . . . except the second collect for the king in the communion service, be henceforth omitted in all churches and chapels in this province."[87] One can just envision Mr. Adams and Mr. Lee shaking their heads in disbelief.

The Maryland Committee of Safety undertook the governance of Maryland over the next month. When the Continental Congress's request for 3,400 Maryland militia to serve for the rest of the year in a Flying Camp (reserve) for the defense of the Middle Colonies arrived on June 10, the committee informed Congress that it did not have the authority to act on the request, so it called forth another convention, which would have such authority, to meet on June 20.[88]

The next convention convened in Annapolis on June 21 and took up the matter of the Flying Camp. It authorized the formation of four new militia regiments, totally 3,405 men, to serve until December 1.[89] It took the Convention several more days to properly organize the militia, and then, on June 28, it turned its attention once again to the topic on everyone's mind, independence.

Voting unanimously to recall its previous instructions and restrictions on the issue of independence, the new Convention resolved that Maryland's delegates,

> Be authorized and empowered to concur with the other United Colonies, or a majority of them, in declaring the United Colonies free and independent States.[90]

Four of the five delegations to the Continental Congress from the Middle Colonies were now authorized by their governing bodies at home to vote for independence, if that was the decision of the majority of colonies. Attention now turned to Philadelphia for a final decision.

CONGRESS VOTES FOR INDEPENDENCE

The Continental Congress had but one issue to consider when it reconvened in Philadelphia on July 1, independence. In the days following Virginia's resolution for independence, opponents cited the uncertainty of support in the Middle Colonies as one reason to oppose independence. Thomas Jefferson recorded their arguments in notes that he took on the debate.

> The people of the middle colonies (Maryland, Delaware, Pennsyla., the Jersies, & N. York) were not yet ripe for bidding adieu to British connection but . . . they were fast ripening & in a short time would join in the general voice of America.[91]

This argument proved correct; during Congress's three week postponement on a vote for independence, from June 10 to June 30, support for independence throughout the colonies and particularly in the Middle Colonies strengthened.

When the delegates gathered on July 1 for the final debate and vote, the outcome seemed certain to all. The arrival of Maryland's new instructions to its delegates that morning ended all doubt about Maryland.[92] John Adams predicted that the resolution on independence "will pass by a great Majority, perhaps with almost Unanimity; yet I cannot promise this. Because one or two Gentlemen may possibly be found, who will vote point blank against the known and declared sense of their Constituents."[93] New York's delegation, writing to its Provincial Congress for further guidance on how to proceed after the vote, agreed with Adams.

> Should Independency be declared, and that it will not we have not the least Reason to expect nor do we believe that (if any) more than one Colony (and the Delegates of that divided) will vote against the Question; every Colony (ours only excepted) having withdrawn their former Instructions, and either positively in-

structed their Delegates to vote for Independency; or concur in such Vote if they shall judge it expedient.[94]

The delegates assured the Provincial Congress that they would abide with their instructions, which was not to vote on the issue (New York abstained in the vote), but they wanted guidance on how to proceed in the Congress from there. At question was whether New York was to be bound by the vote on independence. The answer would significantly determine the future conduct of the delegation in Congress. New York's Provincial Congress resolved the dilemma on July 9, by unanimously approving the Continental Congress's vote on independence.[95]

Although the Continental Congress unanimously voted for independence on July 2 (with one abstention from New York), it is the Declaration of Independence, approved two days later on July 4, that most people are familiar with. This document, written largely by Thomas Jefferson, outlined the reasons for the colonies' separation from Great Britain and in doing so, established the basis for American government.

Congress ordered that printed copies of the Declaration be sent to each state as well as to several commanding officers of the Continental Army to be read at the head of the army.[96] The Declaration was first revealed to the public in a Philadelphia newspaper on July 6 and spread quickly after that.[97] It was read before a large crowd gathered at the state house in Philadelphia on July 8 and greeted with "general applause and heartfelt satisfaction."[98] Across the Delaware River in New Jersey, the Declaration was "received with loud acclamations," by a "large concourse of the inhabitants," who gathered in Trenton to hear it read.[99]

General Washington had the Declaration read to the troops in New York, where it was "received with loud huzzas and the utmost demonstrations of joy."[100] In the evening a statue of King George III that had been erected just six years earlier, was torn down and the lead taken from it was used for musket balls.[101] The inhabitants of Baltimore not only received the Declaration with "general applause and heartfelt satisfaction" when it was read to them aloud, but later in the evening "the effigy of our late King was carted through the Town, and committed to the flames, amidst the acclamations of many hundreds."[102] Something similar occurred in Delaware. Lieutenant Enoch Anderson of the Delaware Continentals recalled that he and his troops celebrated the news of the Declaration in New Castle:

> We took out of the Court-House all the insignias of Monarchy, all the baubles of Royalty, and made a pile of them before the Court-House, set fire to them and burnt them to ashes. This was our first jubilee [for] the fourth of July, '76 and a merry day we made of it.[103]

Although support for independence had certainly swelled among the colonists in the weeks leading up to the vote, there remained a significant number of colonists who opposed independence. These Tories looked hopefully toward New York, where an enormous British armada arrived in late June and over 30,000 British and Hessian soldiers were expected. The objective of this massive British force was simple, to crush the rebellious Americans in battle and end the rebellion once and for all.

Eight

The Fall of New York City

ASTHE EXCITEMENT OVER INDEPENDENCE GRADUALLY SUBSIDED, attention shifted to New York. The first British ships of what was expected to be an enormous fleet arrived off Sandy Hook days before the vote on independence.[1] By June 30, General Washington informed Congress that 110 British ships were at the Hook with "more in the offing."[2] He speculated that they belonged to the British fleet from Halifax carrying General Howe and his army.[3]

Declaring in his orders of that day that "To be prepared for an engagement is, under God ... more than one half the battle," Washington ordered his officers to ensure that their men were supplied with twenty-four musket rounds and a good flint.[4]

Washington was correct about the identity of the British fleet. It was indeed the force from Halifax under General William Howe. Four British sailors from the fleet who were captured offshore of Long Island reported that they had left Halifax just a few days earlier with 10,000 troops, but far more were expected when Admiral Howe, the General's brother, arrived with a fleet of 150 ships from Britain.[5] Thousands of Hessian troops from several Germanic states were reportedly part of this force that the captured sailors claimed numbered 20,000.[6]

The British fleet already at New York moved up the Lower Bay in early July and landed British troops on Staten Island on July 3.[7] There was nothing Washington could do to stop them. Across the Arthur Kill Straight, a narrow passage of water separating Staten Island from New Jersey, General Hugh Mercer, who had just arrived from Virginia, scrambled per Washington's orders to organize the New Jersey militia.

Mercer was a veteran officer of the French and Indian War who had commanded Pennsylvania troops in that conflict. He was also a doctor and, until his promotion in June, had been colonel of the 3rd Virginia Regiment. Acquainted with Mercer through his service in the French and Indian War as well as his medical practice in Fredericksburg, Virginia, Washington assured New Jersey's militia commanders that, "in [Mercer's] Experience & Judgement you may repose great Confidence."[8] Washington appointed Mercer commander of the Flying Camp in New Jersey in mid-July.[9] It was to comprise 10,000 militia from Pennsylvania, Delaware, and Maryland, but on July 25, General Mercer recorded that just over 3,000 men, posted opposite Staten Island in several locations, were in the Flying Camp.[10] Like Washington in New York, Mercer eagerly waited for reinforcements to arrive before the British made their move against New York.

Along with leading the massive British military effort to subdue the rebellious Americans once and for all, General Howe and his brother, Admiral Richard Howe, were also charged by the British government with leading one last reconciliation effort. Admiral Howe had arrived off New York ahead of his fleet from Britain in early July. While both British commanders waited for the rest of Howe's fleet to arrive, Admiral Howe carried out his instructions as a peace commissioner. On July 13, he sent a letter under a flag of truce to Washington offering to meet with him in New York. As the letter was addressed to George Washington Esq. instead of General Washington (a clear slight to Washington) the Americans refused to accept it. Ambrose Serle, Admiral Howe's secretary, amusingly described the interaction between the two parties involved in the delivery of the letter.

[Lieutenant Brown] was dispatched with a Flag of Truce to Washington at New York. . . . Upon being told that he had a Letter from Lord Howe to their Commander, [the Americans] ordered him to lay to, while one of the boats went to Shore for Directions. In a short time, three officers came off, and desired to know to whom the Letter was addressed. They would not touch it, but begged the Lieutenant to read it. As the Address was, To George Washington, Esq. they said there was no such Person among them, and therefore would not receive it. Upon being asked what Address they required, it was answered that "all the World knew who Genl. Washington was since the Transactions of last Summer."[11]

The British officer returned to the fleet with the letter. Refusing to concede the point over Washington's title on the letter by simply re-addressing it to General Washington, the Howes tried another tack. They sent General Howe's adjutant, Lieutenant Colonel James Paterson, to meet with Washington. The American commander agreed to a meeting, which by all accounts went courteously with Paterson addressing Washington as, Your Excellency. Paterson assured Washington on behalf of the Howes that no offense was intended in the labeling of the letter and produced it again. Seeing that it was still improperly addressed, Washington refused to accept it.[12]

A discussion on the treatment and exchange of prisoners ensued and then Colonel Paterson conveyed Admiral Howe's message that he wished to reach an accommodation of "the unhappy dispute," on behalf of the King. Washington replied that he had no authority to negotiate on such a topic, but understood that Howe was only authorized to grant pardons. Washington declared that "Those who had committed no Fault wanted no Pardon; that we were only defending what we deemed our indisputable Rights."[13] Paterson changed the subject back to prisoners and the meeting concluded with the American commander offering refreshments to Paterson, who declined citing a late breakfast and impatience to return to General Howe. With the Howe's "peace" overture rebuffed, both sides prepared for battle.

The arrival of Admiral Howe's overdue fleet with thousands of British and Hessian reinforcements was all that General Howe needed to launch his attack on New York. Washington was powerless to strike at the British on Staten Island, so he too waited for the missing fleet. While he did so, he urged Congress and the several states closest to New York to turn out all of the troops they could.

Complaining to his brother in late July that "Harvest and a thousand other excuses are urged" for the low turnout of the militia, Washington wrote that he was unsure what kind of opposition his army might offer.[14] A troop return in late July counted 12,000 officers and men fit for duty to defend New York.[15] This included 1,520 New York Continentals and militia, 1,475 New Jersey militia, and 1,297 Pennsylvania Continentals, as well as thousands of troops from Massachusetts, Connecticut, and Rhode Island.[16]

General Mercer's 3,000 man Flying Camp, which consisted of nearly all Pennsylvanian troops with a handful of New Jersey artillerists in late July, could offer little support to Washington without jeopardizing New Jersey.[17] The Flying Camp was still well short of its authorized strength of 10,000 men and with the transfer of Colonel Smallwood's Maryland Continentals from the Flying Camp to New York in mid-July and the apparent reluctance of much of the militia from Maryland and Delaware to serve outside of their state borders, there seemed little hope the Flying Camp would ever reach full strength.[18]

Congress had authorized the formation of another New York Continental regiment and a combined Continental regiment of German soldiers from Maryland and Pennsylvania in late June to reinforce Washington, but both were a long way from completion.[19] In early July, Washington received authority from Congress to transfer the several Massachusetts Continental regiments still in Boston to New York, which he promptly did.[20] They were replaced by militia.

In mid-July, two regiments of Virginia Continentals were ordered by Congress to join General Mercer's Flying Camp. Congress also requested Pennsylvania to augment its quota of militia for the Flying Camp with four additional militia battalions.[21] New Jersey, which originally was not asked to contribute militia to the Flying Camp because so many of their militia were already in New York, was also asked to raise three new militia battalions for the Flying Camp.[22]

In late July, Congress gave Washington authority to re-deploy the troops at New York, Fort Ticonderoga, and in the Flying Camp as he saw best.[23] With General Burgoyne in Canada making preparations to lead thousands of British troops down Lake Champlain, Washington was reluctant to draw troops from Fort Ticonderoga, and the Flying Camp was still vastly understrength. Even the good news of an American victory in Charleston, South Carolina, in late June was tainted by the fact that the 3,000 British troops involved in the expedition joined General Howe's army on Staten Island in early August.

To make matters worse, the first few of Admiral Howe's overdue ships arrived in New York in early August. His fleet had been scattered and delayed on its voyage across the Atlantic by poor weather, but the arrival of his first ships meant that the rest of Howe's fleet would soon follow. Two British deserters from the HMS *Soleby* reported that "the Attack will soon be made, [when] the other Troops arrive—that they give out they will lay the Jerseys waste with Fire & Sword—the computed Strength of their Army will be 30,000 Men."[24]

Washington's troop woes continued into August. He informed Congress on August 8 that he only had 10,514 men fit for duty. They were posted at several locations including New York City, Long Island, King's Bridge on Manhattan Island, and Governor's Island. He also had 3,000 men present with the army but sick and over six hundred who were absent due to illness.[25]

In desperation, Washington drew from the already depleted Flying Camp for more troops. Two Pennsylvania rifle battalions under Colonel Samuel Miles were sent to New York on August 9, and Colonel Samuel Attlee's Pennsylvania musket battalion followed the next day.[26] General Mercer also sent 1,200 spears and pledged that if more militia did finally turn out for the Flying Camp he would send whatever additional troops he could.[27] The Pennsylvania reinforcements, along with Colonel Smallwood's Maryland Continentals who had been ordered to New York a few weeks earlier, reached the city by August 12.[28]

The bulk of Admiral Richard Howe's overdue fleet appeared off Sandy Hook on the same day.[29] Washington responded to their arrival with an appeal to the troops in his orders of August 13.

> The Enemy's whole reinforcement is now arrived, so that an Attack must, and will soon be made; The General therefore again repeats his earnest request, that every officer, and soldier will have his Arms and Ammunition in good Order; keep within their quarters and encampment, as much as possible; be ready for action at a moments call; and when called to it, remember that Liberty, Property, Life and Honor are all at stake; that upon their Courage and Conduct, rest the hopes of their bleeding and insulted Country; that their Wives, Children and Parents, expect Safety from them only, and that we have every reason to expect Heaven will crown with Success, so just a cause. The enemy will endeavour to intimidate by shew and appearance, but remember how they have been repulsed, on various occasions, by a few brave Americans; Their Cause is bad; their men are conscious of it, and if opposed with firmness and coolness, at their first onset, with our advantage of Works, and Knowledge of the Ground; Victory is most assuredly ours.[30]

Washington included a shorter pep talk the following day in his orders.

> The General flatters himself, that every man's mind and arms, are now prepared for the glorious Contest, upon which so much depends. The time is too precious, nor does the General think it necessary to spend it in exhorting his brave Countrymen and fellow Soldiers to behave like men, fighting for every thing that can be dear to Freemen. We must resolve to conquer, or die; with this resolution and the blessing of Heaven, Victory and Success certainly will attend us. There will then be a glorious Issue to this Campaign, and the General will reward, his brave Fellow Soldiers! With every Indulgence in his power.[31]

Although Washington's addresses to the troops exuded confidence, he was anything but confident inside. On the day of his first address, Washington placed all of his official papers into a large box, nailed it shut, and sent it to Congress. Realizing the poor message such an action might convey if discovered, he informed John Hancock, the President of Congress, that "I have sent off the Box privately that It might raise no disagreeable Ideas."[32]

There was little that Washington could do, however, about the signal an evacuation proclamation for New York would send. He issued such a proclamation on August 17, explaining it in terms of a tactical decision as well as a desire to avoid civilian bloodshed (rather than an assessment of American chances for holding New York).

> Whereas a Bombardment and Attack upon the City of New York, by our cruel, and inveterate Enemy, may be hourly expected. And as there are great Numbers of Women, Children, and infirm Persons, yet remaining in the City, whose Continuance will rather be prejudicial than advantageous to the Army and their Persons exposed to great Danger and Hazard. I do therefore recommend it to all such Persons, as they value their own Safety and Preservation, to remove with all Expedition, out of the said Town, at this critical Period, trusting, that with the Blessing of Heaven, upon the American Arms, they may soon return to it in perfect Security.[33]

Washington did have some reason to be confident; militia from the surrounding states were finally joining his army in large numbers. As a result, General Howe's troop advantage shrank daily. Washington was thus mystified at why Howe did not attack. Two days after his evacuation proclamation, the American commander expressed his befuddlement with Howe to his cousin, Lund Washington.

> Very unexpectedly to me, another revolving Monday is arrived before an Attack upon this City, or a movement of the Enemy. The reason for this is incomprehensible, to me. True it is . . . they expect another arrival of about 5,000 Hessians, but then, they have been stronger than the Army under my Command, which will now, I expect, gain strength faster than theirs, as the Militia

are beginning to come in fast, and have already augmented our numbers in this City and the Posts around about, to about 23,000 Men. The Enemy's numbers now on [Staten] Island and in their Transports which lay off it, are by the lowest Accts 20,000 Men, by the greatest 27,000 to this the expected (5,000) Hessians are to be added.[34]

"Lord Howe takes pains to throw out, upon every occasion, that he is the Messenger of Peace . . . ." added Washington.[35] Washington did not believe, however, that after all the cost and effort to organize this massive invasion force, such peace talk was genuine.

Although Washington was encouraged by the recent arrival of more militia to his army, he was still significantly outnumbered. What was worse was that his troops could not be concentrated in one position or even within easy supporting distance from each other. The troops in New York City and at Kings Bridge, on the opposite ends of Manhattan Island, were fourteen miles apart, while the American troops on Long Island were separated from New York City by the East River. Conversely, General Howe's stronger force was concentrated on Staten Island and aboard British transports and were capable of attacking almost anywhere they chose in overwhelming numbers.

The British Land on Long Island

On August 22, General Howe finally made a move, sending 15,000 British and Hessian soldiers ashore on Long Island at Gravesend Bay.[36] Admiral Howe's secretary, Ambrose Serle, filled with pride at the mighty military display he witnessed, described the landing in his journal.

The Disembarkation of about 15,000 Troops, upon a fine Beach, their forming upon the adjacent Plain, a Fleet of above 300 Ships & Vessels with their Sails spread open to dry . . . exhibited one of the finest & most picturesque Scenes that the Imagination can fancy or the Eye behold.[37]

Serle observed no resistance from the rebels and noted that "The Soldiers & Sailors seemed as merry as on a Holiday, and regaled themselves with the fine apples, which hung every where upon the Trees in great abundance."[38]

The 1st Continental Regiment, a Pennsylvania rifle regiment under Colonel Edward Hand that included a number of veteran riflemen from 1775, was posted in the area and observed the landings. Lieutenant Colonel James Chambers, writing to his wife two weeks after the landing, remembered that when some of the advance troops of the British ventured inland, Hand's riflemen prepared to ambush them, but "an imprudent fellow fired, and [the British] immediately halted and turned to Flatbush."[39] The riflemen followed the British along a parallel track in the woods, but "found it impracticable for so small a force to attack them on the plain." The riflemen settled for burning stacks of grain and killing some cattle to deny them to the enemy before they returned to their camp.[40]

The Pennsylvania riflemen, supported by a regiment of New England troops, advanced toward the enemy again that same afternoon, and spotted a detachment of Hessians near the village of Flatbush. The riflemen attempted to draw the Hessians toward them and into an ambush, but the German troops would not advance, so the riflemen circled around their flank and gave them a severe fire. "We laid a few Hessians low," bragged Colonel Chambers, "and made them retreat out of Flatbush."[41]

Washington in New York City was not convinced that the British landing on Long Island was their main assault. Wrongly informed that only eight or nine thousand British troops had landed at Gravesend, Washington sent only six regiments from New York to reinforce Long Island, informing Congress that they were "all that I can spare at this Time, not knowing but the Fleet may move up with the Remainder of their Army and make an Attack here on the next Flood Tide."[42]

Washington also delivered one last exhortation, along with a threat, to his troops in his August 23 orders.

> The Enemy have now landed on Long Island, and the hour is fast approaching, on which the Honor and Success of this army, and the safety of our bleeding Country depend. Remember officers and Soldiers, that you are Freemen, fighting for the blessing of

Liberty—that slavery will be your portion, and that of your posterity, if you do not acquit yourselves like men. Remember how your Courage and Spirit have been despised, and traduced by your cruel invaders . . . . Be cool, but determined; do not fire at a distance, but wait for orders from your officers. It is the General's express orders that if any man attempts to skulk, lay down, or retreat without Orders he be instantly shot down as an example, he hopes no such Scoundrel will be found in this army; but on the contrary, everyone for himself resolving to conquer, or die, and trusting to the smiles of heaven upon so just a cause, will behave with Bravery and Resolution . . . .[43]

General Nathanael Greene of Rhode Island had commanded a brigade of troops on Long Island all summer, but he fell seriously ill on August 15, and had to leave the field to recover. Washington sent General John Sullivan, who had recently returned from Fort Ticonderoga, to take command of Greene's troops.[44]

The six additional regiments that Washington sent over to Long Island on August 22 totaled 1,800 men and included the Pennsylvania rifle and musket battalions of Colonel Miles and Colonel Atlee that had recently arrived from the Flying Camp, as well as New York and Connecticut militia.[45] They helped defend two American positions on Long Island. The first was a line of forts and earthworks extending one and a half miles along Brooklyn Heights which overlooked, and thus protected, or threatened, New York City, depending on who held the heights. If the Americans were to keep New York City, they had to hold Brooklyn Heights. The other American position was about two miles to the south, along a series of wooded ridges and hills known as Gowanus Heights. This position formed a strong natural defensive barrier that ran somewhat parallel to the Brooklyn lines in a northeast direction and was too strong of a position for General Sullivan to ignore, so he turned it into an advance line of defense.

Four roads cut through gaps in Gowanus Heights; the Martense Lane Pass marked the right flank of the American position. Flatbush Pass and Bedford Pass were in the center of the American line about a mile from each other and Jamaica Pass was far on the left, seemingly not as important because its location was much further from the Brooklyn lines than the other passes.

If the British troops on Long Island intended to attack the American works on Brooklyn Heights, they had to march through one or several of these passes, so Sullivan posted eight hundred men at each of the three main passes, Martense Lane, Flatbush, and Bedford. He also posted another thousand men along the ridges between the passes.[46] Jamaica Pass, deemed an unlikely route for the British, was left unguarded, to be patrolled by Colonel Miles's Pennsylvania riflemen, who were posted on a wooded ridge two miles to the west of it.

Colonel Miles was deeply troubled by the absence of troops to his left and expressed his concern to Sullivan when he visited the lines.

> I told him the situation of the British Army; that Gen'l Howe, with the main body, lay on my left, about a mile and a-half or two miles, and I was convinced when the army moved that Gen'l Howe would fall into the Jamaica road, and I hoped there were troops there to watch them.[47]

Lieutenant Colonel Daniel Brodhead commanded the second battalion of Pennsylvania riflemen under Miles and was also concerned about the Jamaica Pass. In a letter after the battle, Brodhead described a visit from several generals.

> [They could] plainly discover [the enemy] were extending their lines to the left so as to march round us, for our lines to the left, were, for want of Videttes, left open for at least four miles where we constantly scouted by Day, besides mounting a Guard of one hundred men & an advance party . . . [of] thirty to the left of us, was hard Duty for our Reg't.[48]

The lack of available troops, and an assumption that the British would not march so far out of their way to use the Jamaica Pass, meant that only a handful of cavalry were posted there to watch it.

While Washington waited impatiently for more clues of General Howe's intentions, Sullivan's troops on Gowanus Heights skirmished with advance parties of the enemy. Sullivan informed Washington on August 23 that his riflemen gave the enemy, who advanced to probe the American position, a "smart fire," and that when reinforced by musketry and cannon, drove them back.[49]

Washington was still uncertain of Howe's plans on August 24, but when the bulk of the British fleet off Staten Island sailed south through the Narrows and the British were seen striking their tents on Staten Island, he determined that they indeed intended to "make their Grand push" on Long Island.[50] He sent Major-General Israel Putnam of Connecticut, one of the heroes of Bunker Hill, to Long Island to take command.[51] Washington instructed Putnam to use the least experienced and least trained troops in the interior works at Brooklyn Heights, "whilst your best men should at all hazards prevent the enemy's passing the wood [Gowanus Heights] . . . ."[52] General Putnam looked to Sullivan, who retained command of the troops along Gowanus Heights, to fulfill that part of Washington's instructions.[53]

Along with Putnam, Washington sent four more regiments to reinforce Long Island. Colonel Smallwood's Maryland Regiment and Colonel Haslet's Delaware Regiment were two of these four regiments.[54] Neither of the colonels or lieutenant colonels of these two regiments crossed the East River with their men. All four officers were assigned to preside in a court martial that day and Washington refused to delay the proceedings. Majors Mordecai Gist of Maryland and Major Thomas McDonough of Delaware led their troops across the East River to Long Island.[55]

At nightfall of August 26, approximately 21,000 British and Hessian troops were on Long Island. General James Grant commanded two British brigades just south of Martense Lane Pass, facing the right end of the American line at Gowanus Heights. General Leopold de Heister commanded two brigades of Hessians in the village of Flatbush, which lay about a mile south of Flatbush Pass and the center of the American advance line. General Charles Cornwallis was also posted at Flatbush with the British reserve. The main body of British troops were encamped near the village of Flatlands, about two miles south of Flatbush. General Howe, along with Generals Henry Clinton and Hugh Percy, was with these troops.[56]

Standing guard against Howe's army that night were approximately 2,800 Americans posted along a six-mile advance line. General Samuel Parsons of Connecticut was the officer of the day for the advance position on August 26 and thus commanded the troops there. The right flank of the American line was guarded by Pennsylvanians and New Yorkers. Colonel Edward Hand's Pennsylvania riflemen, along with half of Colonel Atlee's Pennsylvania musket battalion (the other half were resting in the earthworks at Brooklyn Heights), part of Colonel Nicholas Lutz's Pennsylvania riflemen and detachments of New York militia were posted at and around the Red Lion Inn upon the coast road, to the north of Martense Lane pass. Troops from the Flying Camp relieved Hand's riflemen at 2 a.m. and they returned to the interior works at Brooklyn Heights for some much needed rest.[57]

Two miles to the left of the Red Lion Inn, at the Flatbush Pass, Colonel Daniel Hitchcock's regiment of Rhode Island Continentals and Colonel Moses Little's Massachusetts Continentals, joined by a battalion of New Jersey militia under Colonel Philip Johnston and a detachment of Connecticut rangers under Lieutenant Colonel Thomas Knowlton, stood watch on the center of the American line. They were supported by an artillery battery of two or three cannon.[58]

A mile farther to the left, two Connecticut Continental regiments under Colonels Samuel Wyllys and John Chester guarded the Bedford Pass and in the woods to their left was Colonel Samuel Miles with two battalions of Pennsylvania riflemen.[59] Several miles farther east was the Jamaica Pass, guarded by just five American horsemen with orders to dash back to Brooklyn Heights to sound the alarm if the enemy approached.

BATTLE OF LONG ISLAND

Aware that the Jamaica Pass was undefended, General Howe resolved to feign a frontal attack upon the defended passes while simultaneously flanking the American advance line through the Jamaica Pass. If all went according to plan, the majority of Howe's troops would be behind the Americans before they noticed, trapping them between two forces. Howe moved the British reserve under

General Cornwallis at Flatbush to Flatlands at sunset and commenced his flanking march to Jamaica Pass at 9 p.m. Approximately 10,000 British troops with nearly 30 cannon marched toward the pass. General Henry Clinton commanded the van of the column, consisting of light dragoons and a brigade of light infantry. Clinton's advance troops managed to get behind the five American horsemen guarding Jamaica Pass undetected around 3 a.m. and captured them without a fight. The British marched through the pass and halted briefly to rest, then continued down the road to cut off the Americans on Gowanus Heights from Brooklyn Heights. [60]

At about the same time Howe reached Jamaica Pass, advance troops of General James Grant's two British brigades made contact with American pickets posted on the western (right) end of the American line near the Red Lion Inn. Word quickly reached the American camp at Brooklyn Heights, prompting General Parsons to ride out to investigate. He found his pickets dispersed and in disarray, but managed to collect twenty men and deploy them upon a hill facing the enemy, who were a half mile away.[61]

Back at Brooklyn Heights, General Putnam ordered General Stirling to take the two nearest regiments in camp, which were Smallwood's Maryland and Haslet's Delaware Continentals, to meet the advancing enemy on the American right flank. Stirling informed Washington after the battle that,

I accordingly Marched, and was on the Road to the Narrows Just as the day light began to appear. We proceeded to within about half a Mile of the Red Lyon and their met Col. Atlee with his Regiment who Informed me, that the Enemy were in Sight, indeed I then Saw their front between us and the Red Lyon, I desired to place his regiment on the left of the Road and to wait their Coming up, while I went to form the two Regiments I had brought with me, along a Ridge from the Road . . . to a piece of wood on the Top of the Hill . . . on very Advantageous ground.[62]

Colonel Atlee, who had been ordered to remain in the open and delay the enemy advance, recounted in his journal that,

This order I immediately obeyed, notwithstanding we must be exposed without any kind of cover, to the great fire of the enemy's musketry and field pieces, charged with round and grape shot, and finely situated upon [an] eminence . . . having the entire command of the ground I was ordered to occupy. My battalion, although new and never before having the opportunity of facing an enemy, sustained their fire until [Stirling's troops] had formed; but finding we could not possibly [halt the enemy advance], I ordered my detachment to file off to the left, and take post in a wood upon the left of [Stirling].[63]

General Stirling remembered that Atlee's men fired two or three rounds before they retreated to the woods and Atlee reported that he lost just one man, who was shot in the neck by grapeshot, in the brief engagement.[64] Colonel Peter Kechlein's battalion of Pennsylvania riflemen and Colonel Jedediah Huntington's regiment of Connecticut Continentals soon joined General Stirling. The Connecticut troops, along with two companies from the Delaware regiment whom Stirling detached, joined Colonel Atlee in the woods upon Stirling's left. General Parsons assumed command of this force.[65] Kechlein's Pennsylvania riflemen were posted along a hedge in the front of the hill and in the nearby woods.[66]

General Grant, who had halted his advance, was likely well pleased by events thus far. The vastly outnumbered Americans to his front stubbornly held their ground, which was exactly what Grant and his commander, Howe, wanted them to do. Grant maintained a steady artillery fire on the Americans for most of the morning and sent detachments forward to skirmish with them, but held his main force back per Howe's orders.

Two miles away at the Flatbush Pass, General Sullivan found a relatively quiet situation when he arrived to investigate around 8:30 a.m.[67] Although some firing had occurred earlier between the two sides, the Hessian brigades to the front of the Americans made no aggressive movement forward. Unbeknownst to Sullivan and the men with him, Howe with the main body of British troops were closing in behind them.

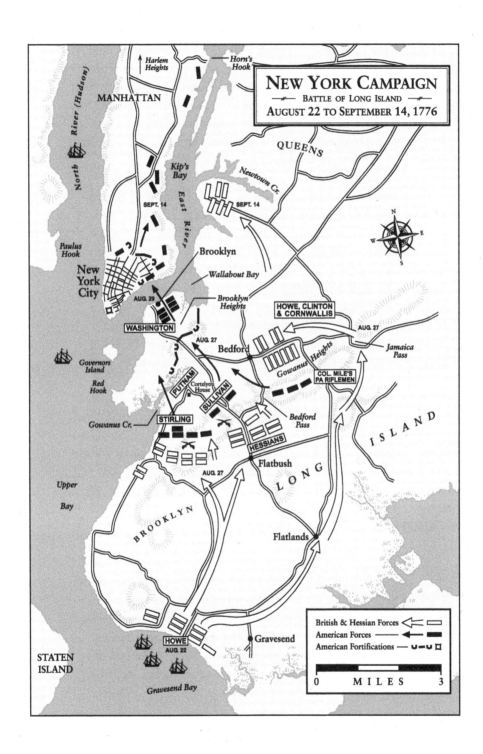

NEW YORK CAMPAIGN
BATTLE OF LONG ISLAND
AUGUST 22 TO SEPTEMBER 14, 1776

MANHATTAN

Harlem Heights

Horn's Hook

North River (Hudson)

QUEENS

Kip's Bay

Newtown Cr.

SEPT. 14

SEPT. 14

East River

Paulus Hook

Brooklyn

Wallabout Bay

New York City

AUG. 29

Brooklyn Heights

HOWE, CLINTON & CORNWALLIS

AUG. 27

WASHINGTON

AUG. 27

Bedford

Jamacia Pass

Governors Island

Gowanus Heights

COL. MILE'S PA RIFLEMEN

Red Hook

PUTNAM

Cortelyou House

SULLIVAN

Bedford Pass

Gowanus Cr.

STIRLING

HESSIANS

ISLAND

Flatbush

AUG. 27

Upper Bay

L O N G

B R O O K L Y N

Flatlands

Flatlands

STATEN ISLAND

HOWE

AUG. 22

Gravesend

British & Hessian Forces

American Forces

American Fortifications

Gravesend Bay

0   M I L E S   3

Although the gunfire at Flatbush Pass around 7 a.m. was light, it attracted the attention of Colonel Miles, who was posted with his Pennsylvania riflemen east of the Bedford Pass, approximately two miles from the Flatbush Pass. Colonel Miles went to investigate but was stopped by Colonel Samuel Wyllys who told Miles they were to stay put and guard the Bedford Pass. Miles recorded in his journal later that,

> I told him I was convinced the main body of the enemy would take the Jamaica road, and that there was no probability of their coming along the road he was guarding, [the Bedford Pass] and if he would not let me proceed to where the firing was, I would return to endeavor to get into the Jamaica road before Gen. Howe. To this he consented, and I immediately made a retrograde march, and after marching nearly two miles . . . I arrived within sight of the Jamaica road, and to my great mortification I saw the main body of the enemy in full march between me and our lines [on Brooklyn Heights] and the baggage guard just coming into the road.[68]

Colonel Miles ordered Colonel Daniel Brodhead, who was farther in the rear with the second battalion of Pennsylvania riflemen, to lead his troops to Brooklyn Heights as best he could. Miles then consulted with the officers of the first battalion, who agreed that to attack the British baggage guard would be futile, and to wait until it passed and then escape would be viewed as cowardly, so they agreed to fight their way through the British flank guards in an effort to reach Brooklyn Heights.[69] Miles recalled that,

> We immediately began our march, but had not proceeded more than half a mile until we fell in with a body of 7 or 800 light infantry, which we attacked without any hesitation, but their superiority of numbers encouraged them to march up with their bayonets, which we could not withstand, having none ourselves. I therefore ordered the Troops to push on toward our lines. I remained on the ground myself until they had all passed me, (the enemy were then within less than 20 yards of us,) . . . . We had

proceeded but a short distance before we were again engaged with a superior body of the enemy, and here we lost a number of men but [briefly captured a British officer].[70]

Realizing that it was impossible to cut their way through the British as a battalion, Miles ordered his men to "make the best of their way as well as they could" back to the lines.[71] Some of his men and many of Lieutenant Colonel Brodhead's men in the second battalion, did make it back to the Brooklyn works, but after evading the British the rest of the day and through the night, Colonel Miles was captured early the next morning.[72]

When the troops guarding the Bedford and Flatbush Passes realized the British had gotten behind them, many panicked. Their fear only intensified when the Hessians to their front began to advance upon them as well. General Sullivan and his men had no choice but to flee. They tried to fight their way through Howe's troops behind them, and many succeeded, but Sullivan was not one of them; he was captured along with scores of his troops.[73]

By the late morning, all that remained of the American defenses on Gowanus Heights were General Stirling's troops standing firm on the right flank. If Sullivan informed Stirling of the disaster on the American center and left flank of their line, and he likely attempted to, the message never reached Stirling. As far as he knew, his brave troops had held the enemy at bay all morning with sheer tenacity. Stirling grew concerned, however, when he noticed the sound of gunfire to the rear. By 11 a.m., aware that the enemy had gained his rear and was now between his troops and the American works on Brooklyn Heights, Stirling acted.

I . . . saw that [the] only Chance of Escaping being all made prisoners, was to pass the Creek near the Yellow Mills, and in order to render this the more practicable I found it Absolutely Necessary to Attack a Body of Troops Commanded by Lord Cornwallis posted at the House near the Upper Mills; this I Instantly did, with about half of Smallwood's, first ordering all the other troops to make the best of their way thro' the Creek . . . .[74]

Stirling had to prevent General Cornwallis from blocking the only escape route for his men. Lieutenant Enoch Anderson with the Delaware Regiment, wounded by a musket ball to the chin, described the race to get across a creek and mill pond to safety in the American lines.

> The Regiment began to move . . . and waded through the mill-dam, neck deep, far below the foot-bridge. For ten minutes . . . our Regiment was surrounded and no escape remained for them but for to wade the mill-dam. Some men were lost.[75]

An unidentified Maryland officer also described the American flight.

> Our battalion has suffered much, a great number of both offi-cers and men are killed and missing. We retreated through a very heavy fire, and escaped by swimming over a river, or creek rather. My height was of use to me, as I touched almost all the way. A number of men got drowned.[76]

A more complete account of the action on the American right flank came from an unidentified American with knowledge of the fight. It was written a day after the battle.

> Our Army, at least the small part that was engaged, behaved most manfully; [the enemy] . . . surrounded our people, and we were obliged to fight our way through them. Colonel Smallwood's battalion has gained immortal honor. He was not with it himself, Lord Stirling commanded it, and the Delaware battalion, as part of his brigade. They fought the enemy treble in number, in open field, several hours, till at last surrounded on the side of a small creek, they were obliged to make the best retreat they could. Most of them swam the creek. Lord Stirling, at the head of three com-panies attempted to force his way through the enemy.[77]

Stirling's attack with the Maryland Continentals was crucial to buy time for the rest of his troops to escape. He described what hap-pened to Washington.

I found it absolutely Necessary to Attack a Body of Troops Commanded by Lord Cornwallis . . . with about half of Small-wood's, first ordering all the other troops to make the best of their way thro' the Creek. We Continued the Attack a Considerable time the Men having been rallied and the Attack renewed five or Six . . . times, and were on the point of driving Lord Cornwallis from his Station, but large [numbers of enemy reinforcements] arriving rendered it impossible to do more.[78]

Major Mordecai Gist commanded the Maryland troops in the battle and was with Stirling for the attack on Cornwallis. He recalled that while the bulk of the American troops were fleeing,

We were left with only five companies of our battalion . . . and after a warm and close engagement for near ten minutes, our little line became so disordered we were under the necessity of retreating to a piece of woods on our right, where we formed and made a second attack, but being overpowered with numbers, and surrounded on all sides . . . we were drove with much precipitation and confusion. General Stirling on this retreat was missing, whose brave example had encouraged and animated our young soldiers with almost invincible resolution. The impracticability of forcing through such a formidable body of troops, rendered it the height of rashness and imprudence to risk the lives or our remaining party in a third attempt, and it became necessary for us to endeavour to effect our escape in the best manner we possibly could. A party immediately retreated to the right through the woods, and Captain Ford and myself, with twenty others, to the left, through a marsh; nine only of whom got safe in.[79]

To the left of Stirling's abandoned position, General Parsons, with Colonel Atlee's Pennsylvanians and Colonel Huntington's Connecticut Continentals, had all but been forgotten. They found themselves completely trapped and could not even reach the marsh to attempt a crossing. Most were forced to surrender, but Parsons managed to hide until nightfall and make his way back through the British lines to Brooklyn Heights by morning.[80]

Despite the bravery of Stirling and the Maryland troops, as well as other Americans that day, the Battle of Long Island was a crushing American defeat. The British had executed their plan almost flawlessly, although the number of captured Americans likely disappointed Howe.

Washington's first report to Congress on the battle was written by one of his aides, who reported that the army "have sustained a pretty considerable loss."[81] It was still too early to determine the losses on either side, but the report suggested that the British had paid a price for their victory.

If they did, it was a small price for what they had accomplished. General Howe reported that he lost less than four hundred British and Hessian officers and men in the battle. Five British officers and fifty-six men were killed, twelve officers and 255 men were wounded, and one officer and thirty men were missing and presumed captured. The Hessians suffered no deaths and had three officers and twenty-three men wounded.[82]

American losses were harder to determine. The capture of Generals Stirling and Sullivan became apparent after two days and the bulk of American losses were men who were captured. Determining an accurate number of captured, killed, and wounded, however, was difficult and it was not until October, after Washington ordered his regimental commanders to list the names of their men killed or captured at Long Island, that an accurate number was even possible.[83] Historian Henry Johnson's analysis of these October troop returns provides perhaps the most accurate estimate of one thousand American officers and men killed, wounded, and missing (captured) at the Battle of Long Island.[84]

The losses were heaviest on the American flanks with the Pennsylvania riflemen under Colonel Miles suffering 176 losses and the troops from Maryland, Delaware, Pennsylvania, and Connecticut under General Stirling on the American right flank suffering 682 losses in officers and men.[85] Try as General Parsons of Connecticut might to besmirch the reputation of New York and Pennsylvania troops in a letter to John Adams, in which he noted, "by way of retaliation" that the troops at the Red Lion Tavern that fled without firing a shot at the initial advance of the British that morning were

from New York and Pennsylvania, the battle accounts and dispro-
portionate losses of Maryland, Delaware, and Pennsylvania troops
at the Battle of Long Island suggested that soldiers from these Middle
Colonies would indeed fight![86]

RETREAT FROM BROOKLYN
Fortunately for the Americans behind the earthworks at Brooklyn
Heights, and perhaps the British and Hessians outside them, Howe
did not press his attack. There was no need to waste the lives of his
men with a frontal assault of the works when it was obvious to Howe
that "the [enemy] lines must have been ours at a very cheap rate by
regular approaches."[87] Howe decided that he would take the American lines by siege.

A heavy rain soaked the troops on both sides the day after the
battle but that did not stop the British from digging a trench line
three hundred yards long, just six hundred yards from the American
lines.[88] Washington convened a war council the next day and it was
unanimously agreed to abandon the Brooklyn works and withdraw
across the East River to New York.[89] It was crucial that they do so
before the British navy cut them off from retreat.

Washington's army commenced its withdrawal under cover of
darkness on August 29. Tense hours passed before the last of the
troops, under cover of a heavy fog that rose just before sunrise,
crossed the river to New York. Exhausted from three days of endless
duty, Washington finally rested and informed Congress of his retreat
the following day.

> Our Retreat was made without any Loss of Men or Ammuni-
> tion and in better order than I expected from Troops in the situa-
> tion ours were—We brought off all our Cannon & Stores, except
> a few heavy pieces.[90]

Washington updated Congress on the results of the battle and was
informed in a letter from General Sullivan that Admiral Howe is
"extremely desirous of seeing some of the Members of Congress."[91]
This was to no doubt present Britain's peace terms. Washington
wrote that he would send Sullivan, who was released on parole by
the British, to Philadelphia with a letter from Lord Howe. In the

meantime, wrote Washington, "I am hurried & Engaged in Arranging and making new Dispositions of our Forces . . . ."[92] Washington, for one, intended to fight on.

Congress reacted to the disappointing news from New York by calling on Virginia, North Carolina, and Rhode Island to send additional regiments of Continental troops to New York. Congress also instructed Washington not to burn the city should he be compelled to abandon it.[93]

The New York Convention, which had been meeting in the village of Harlem on upper Manhattan for several weeks, voted to move sixty miles upriver to the village of Fishkill to place themselves out of the reach of the British navy.[94] The New York Committee of Safety, which assumed authority while the Convention was adjourned, also moved to Fishkill.[95]

In New York, Washington struggled to reorganize the army. He informed Congress on September 2 that,

> Our Situation is truly distressing. The check our Detachment sustained [on Long Island] has dispirited too great a proportion of our Troops and filled their minds with apprehension and despair. The Militia, instead of calling forth their utmost efforts to a brave & manly opposition in order to repair our Losses, are dismayed, Intractable, and Impatient to return. Great numbers of them have gone off.[96]

A week later Washington, after a war council with his officers, seemed to acknowledge that New York City could not be held, at least not without unacceptable risk to the army. Washington recognized the significance of holding the city, especially for morale, but explained to Congress that with the enormous naval and land forces arrayed against him, it was doubtful he could do so. He simply refused to keep the army in a position where it would likely be trapped and destroyed and instead, began shifting troops out of the city.

Although Washington's actions suggested that he knew that New York City would soon be lost, he did not intend to give up the city, or the rest of Manhattan Island, without a fight. Washington believed that the terrain on the northern end of Manhattan was well suited for defense and if held, which he was confident it could be, the communication link between New England and the other states that was now threatened by the British might be secured. With this in mind, Washington divided the army into three divisions. Nine thousand troops were posted on strong ground in the vicinity of Kings Bridge, near the northern end of Manhattan. Five thousand troops were left in the city to defend it from assault, while the remainder of the army, which was really anyone's guess at that point, was posted at several spots in the middle of Manhattan where they could respond in either direction if needed.[97] Washington ordered the removal of all of the military stores in the city except those which were necessary to maintain the troops still posted there. This was yet another signal that he knew the Americans could not hold it.

THE FALL OF NEW YORK CITY

The British were undoubtedly aware of Washington's movements, yet did nothing to interfere. Admiral Howe was determined to meet with representatives from Congress for one last ditch peace effort, and until this was done, General Howe held off his next attack. On September 6, John Adams, Benjamin Franklin, and Edmund Rutledge met with Admiral Howe on Staten Island. The negotiations were cordial but fruitless. The dispute between Great Britain and America would have to be settled by force.

A week after this meeting, the British moved into position to attack Manhattan. General Howe had resolved to land troops a few miles above New York City and then march across the mile wide island to trap the Americans still posted in the city. A heavy naval bombardment of the landing area at Kip's Bay announced their intention early in the morning of September 15. Joseph Plumb Martin, a teenage soldier in the Connecticut militia who was posted at Kip's Bay, recounted the attack years later.

> All of a sudden there came such a peal of thunder from the British shipping that I thought my head would go with the sound. I made a frog's leap for the ditch and lay as still as I possibly

could and began to consider which part of my carcass was to go first. . . . We kept the lines until [the British were almost ashore] when our officers, seeing that we could make no resistance and no orders coming from any superior officer and that we must soon be entirely exposed to the rake of their guns, gave the orders to leave the lines. In retreating we had to cross a level clear spot of ground forty or fifty rods wide, exposed to the whole of the enemy's fire and they gave it to us in prime order. The grapeshot and [lead] flew merrily, which served to quicken our motions.[98]

Washington was dismayed and furious at what he observed when he arrived on the scene.

Parson's & Fellow's Brigades [were] flying in every direction and in the greatest confusion, notwithstanding the exertions of their Generals to form them. I used every means in my power to rally and get them into some order but my attempts were fruitless and ineffectual, and on the appearance of a small party of the Enemy, not more than Sixty or Seventy, their disorder increased and they ran away in the greatest confusion without firing a Single Shot.[99]

Washington left the scene in disgust and raced to organize a defense at Harlem Heights. Behind him marched thousands of frightened and demoralized American troops, including most of those posted in New York who managed to escape before the British cut them off. British troops marched into New York City unopposed later that day.

The first phase of Britain's plan to reconquer its rebelling American colonies was now complete; New York City had fallen to the British at very little cost. Seven more years of bloody conflict lay ahead and much like they did in the first seventeen months of the war, the inhabitants of the mid-Atlantic states of New York, New Jersey, Pennsylvania, Delaware, and Maryland would play a crucial role in the remainder of it.

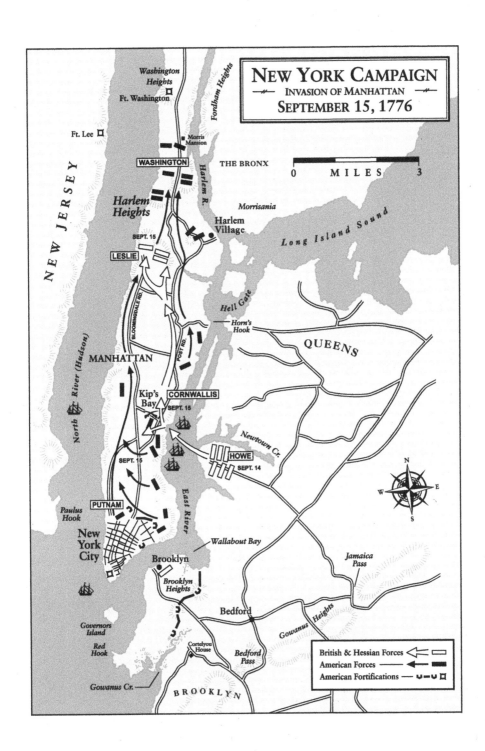

Washington
Heights

Ft. Washington

Fordham Heights

Ft. Lee

Morris
Mansion

WASHINGTON   THE BRONX

NEW YORK CAMPAIGN
— INVASION OF MANHATTAN —
SEPTEMBER 15, 1776

0   MILES   3

Harlem
Heights

Harlem R.

Morrisania

NEW JERSEY

SEPT. 15

LESLIE

Harlem
Village

Long Island Sound

BLOOMINGDALE RD.

POST RD.

Hell Gate

Horn's
Hook

QUEENS

MANHATTAN

North River (Hudson)

Kip's
Bay

CORNWALLIS

SEPT. 15

Newtown Cr.

SEPT. 15

HOWE
SEPT. 14

East River

PUTNAM

Paulus
Hook

New
York
City

Wallabout Bay

Jamaica
Pass

Brooklyn

Brooklyn
Heights

Bedford

Gowanus Heights

Governors
Island

Red
Hook

Cortelyou
House

Bedford
Pass

British & Hessian Forces
American Forces
American Fortifications

Gowanus Cr.

BROOKLYN

NOTES

INTRODUCTION

1. "Estimated Population of American Colonies: 1610 to 1780," *Historical Statistics of the United States: Colonial Times to 1970*, Part 2 (U.S. Census Bureau), 1168.
2. Ibid.
3. Hugh Gaine, "May 23, 1774," *New York Gazette and Weekly Mercury*, 3.
4. Gaine, "July 11, 1774," *New York Gazette and Weekly Mercury*, 4.
5. Ibid.
6. Peter Force, ed., "Proceedings of the New York Assembly, January 26, 1775," *American Archives, Fourth Series*, Vol. 1 (Washington, DC: M. St. Clair Clark and Peter Force, 1837), 1286-1287.
7. K.G. Davies, ed., "Lieut.-Governor Cadwallader Colden to Vice-Admiral Samuel Graves, February 20, 1775," *Documents of the American Revolution*, Vol. 9 (Shannon: Irish University Press, 1975), 53.
8. Davies, ed., "Lieut.-Governor Cadwallader Colden to Earl of Dartmouth, March 1, 1775," *Documents of the American Revolution*, Vol. 9, 59.
9. Ibid.
10. Davies, ed., "Lieut.-Governor Cadwallader Colden to Vice-Admiral Samuel Graves, February 20, 1775," *Documents of the American Revolution*, Vol. 9, 53.
11. Ibid.
12. Ibid.
13. Richard B. Morris, ed., "The New York Committee of Sixty to the New Haven Committee, April 17, 1775," *John Jay: The Making of a Revolutionary, Unpublished Papers, 1745-1780*, Vol. 1 (New York: Harper & Row, 1975), 143.
14. Peter Force, ed., "Minutes of the Provincial Convention of New York, April 21, 1775," *American Archives, Fourth Series*, Vol. 2 (Washington, DC: M. St. Clair Clark and Peter Force, 1839), 357.
15. "Estimated Population of American Colonies: 1610 to 1780," *Historical Statistics of the United States: Colonial Times to 1970*, Part 2 (U.S. Census Bureau), 1168.
16. Davies, ed., "Governor William Franklin to Earl of Dartmouth, May 31, 1774," *Documents of the American Revolution*, Vol. 8 (Shannon: Irish University Press, 1975), 118-119.

17. Gaine, "August 8, 1774," *New York Gazette and Weekly Mercury*, 2.

18. Davies, ed., "Governor William Franklin to James Galloway, March 12, 1775," *Documents of the American Revolution*, Vol. 9 (Shannon: Irish University Press, 1975), 76-77.

19. "Estimated Population of American Colonies: 1610 to 1780," *Historical Statistics of the United States: Colonial Times to 1970*, Part 2 (U.S. Census Bureau), 1168.

20. Davies, ed., "Governor John Penn to Earl of Dartmouth, May 31, 1774," *Documents of the American Revolution*, Vol. 8, 119.

21. John Dunlap, "June 27, 1774," *Pennsylvania Packet*, 3.

22. Dunlap, "August 1, 1774, Supplement," *Pennsylvania Packet*, 2.

23. "Estimated Population of American Colonies: 1610 to 1780," *Historical Statistics of the United States: Colonial Times to 1970*, Part 2 (U.S. Census Bureau), 1168.

24. Claudia Bushman, Harold Hancock, and Elizabeth Homsey, eds., "Proceedings of the Delaware Assembly, March 15-16, 1775," *Proceedings of the Assembly of the Lower Counties on Delaware, 1770-1776* (Newark: University of Delaware Press, 1986), 167-169.

25. "Estimated Population of American Colonies: 1610 to 1780," *Historical Statistics of the United States: Colonial Times to 1970*, Part 2 (U.S. Census Bureau), 1168.

26. Ibid.

27. Alexander Purdie and John Dixon, "July 21, 1774," *Virginia Gazette*, 2.

28. Purdie and Dixon, "October 27, 1774," *Virginia Gazette*, 2.

29. Ibid.

30. Ibid.

CHAPTER ONE: SPRING 1775

1. William Wirt, *Sketches in the Life and Character of Patrick Henry* (Philadelphia, 1817), 136.

2. Ibid.

3. Force, ed., *American Archives, Fourth Series*, Vol. 2, 364.

4. Force, ed., "Extract of a Letter from New York to a Gentleman in Philadelphia, April 24, 1775," *American Archives, Fourth Series*, Vol. 2, 364.

5. Edward Floyd De Lancey, ed., *History of New York During the Revolutionary War . . . by Thomas Jones*, Vol. 1 (New York: New York Historical Society, 1879), 39.

6. Benjamin Towne, "Extract of a letter from New York, April 25, 1775," *Pennsylvania Evening Post*, 4.

7. William Willett, ed., *A Narrative of the Military Actions of Colonel Marinus Willett* (New York: G. & C. & H. Carvill, 1831), 27, and William Bell Clark, ed., "Memoirs of William Smith, Member of the Governor's Council of New York, April 24, 1775," *Naval Documents of the American Revolution*, Vol. 1 (Washington, DC, 1964), 214.

8. De Lancey, ed., *History of New York During the Revolutionary War . . . by Thomas Jones,* Vol. 1, 40.

9. Clark, ed., "Captain James Montagu, R.N. to Vice Admiral Samuel Graves, April 26, 1775," *Naval Documents of the American Revolution*, Vol. 1, 228.

10. Clark, ed., "Peter Vandervoort to Nathaniel Shaw Jr., April 28, 1775," *Naval Documents of the American Revolution*, Vol. 1, 240.

11. Ibid.

12. Margaret Wheeler Willard, ed., "Extract of a letter from a Gentleman at New York, to his friend in England, May 1, 1775," *Letters on the American Revolution, 1774-1776* (Boston & New York: Houghton Mifflin, 1925), 97.

13. Clark, ed., "Vice-Admiral Samuel Graves to Captain George Vandeput, H.M.S *Asia*, May 1, 1775," *Naval Documents of the American Revolution*, Vol. 1, 255.

14. I.N. Phelps Stokes, ed., "April 26, 1775," *The Iconography of Manhattan, 1498-1909* (New York: Robert H. Dodd, 1922), 883.

15. Stokes, ed., "April 29, 1775," *The Iconography of Manhattan, 1498-1909*, 883.

16. Stokes, ed., "April 30, 1775," *The Iconography of Manhattan, 1498-1909*, 884.

17. Davies, ed., "Lieutenant-Governor Cadwallader Colden to the Earl of Dartmouth, May 3, 1775," *Documents of the American Revolution*, Vol. 9, 117-118.

18. Barnet Schecter, *The Battle for New York: The City at the Heart of the American Revolution* (New York: Walker & Co., 2002), 53.

19. Force, ed., "Veritas, June 25, 1775," *American Archives, Fourth Series*, Vol. 2, 1086-1087. Note: Likely Benedict Arnold's account of the attack.

20. Force, ed., "Benedict Arnold to the Massachusetts Committee of Safety, May 19, 1775," *American Archives, Fourth Series*, Vol. 2, 646.

21. Ibid.

22. Worthington Chauncey Ford, ed., "Proceedings of the Continental Congress, May 18, 1775," *Journals of the Continental Congress, 1774-1789*, Vol. 2 (Washington, DC: Government Printing Office, 1905), 55-56.

23. Ford, ed., "Proceedings of the Continental Congress, May 15, 1775." *Journals of the Continental Congress, 1774-1789*, Vol. 2, 52.

24. Ibid.

25. Ford, ed., "Proceedings of the Continental Congress, May 31, 1775." *Journals of the Continental Congress, 1774-1789*, Vol. 2, 73-74.

26 Stokes, ed., "New York Mercury," *The Iconography of Manhattan, 1498-1909*, 887.

27. Ford, ed., "Proceedings of the Continental Congress, May 25, 1775." *Journals of the Continental Congress, 1774-1789*, Vol. 2, 59-61.

28. "Newark Committee April 24, 1775," *Minutes of the Provincial Congress and the Council of Safety of the State of New Jersey* (Trenton: Naar, Day & Naar, 1879), 101.

29. "Morris Committee and Woodbridge Committee, May 1, 1775," *Minutes of the Provincial Congress and the Council of Safety of the State of New Jersey*, 105, 107.

30. "Monmouth County, May 4, 1775," *Minutes of the Provincial Congress and the Council of Safety of the State of New Jersey*, 111.

31. Davies, ed., "Governor William Franklin to Earl of Dartmouth, May 6, 1775," *Documents of the American Revolution*, Vol. 9, 125-126.

32. "New Jersey Committee of Correspondence, May 2," *Minutes of the Provincial Congress and the Council of Safety of the State of New Jersey*, 108-109.

33. "Proceedings of the New Jersey Assembly, May 20, 1775," *Minutes of the Provincial Congress and the Council of Safety of the State of New Jersey*, 148.

34. "Proceedings of the New Jersey Provincial Congress, May 25, 1775," *Minutes of the Provincial Congress and the Council of Safety of the State of New Jersey*, 173.

35. "Proceedings of the New Jersey Provincial Congress, June 3, 1775," *Minutes of the Provincial Congress and the Council of Safety of the State of New Jersey*, 179.

36. Ibid., 179-180.

37. Ibid., 180.

38. Ibid., 181-182.

39. Margaret W. Willard, ed., "Extract of a letter from Philadelphia, April 28, 1775," *Letters on the American Revolution: 1774-1776* (Boston & New York, Houghton Mifflin., 1925), 94.

40. Hall & Sellers, *Pennsylvania Gazette*, May 3, 1775, 3.

41. Ibid.

42. M.K. Goddard, "May 17, 1775," *Maryland Journal*, 3.

43. Thomas Verenna, "Explaining Pennsylvania's Militia," *Journal of the American Revolution*, June 17, 2014.

44. Ibid.

45. Force, ed., "Extract of a Letter from Reading, Pennsylvania, April 26, 1775," *American Archives, Fourth Series*, Vol. 2, 400.

46. Force, ed., "Proceedings of the Pennsylvania Assembly, May 4, 1775," *American Archives, Fourth Series*, Vol. 2, 454-455.

47. Ibid.

48. Ibid.

49. Force, ed., "Proceedings of the Pennsylvania Assembly, May 12, 1775," *American Archives, Fourth Series*, Vol. 2, 456-457.

50. Smith, ed., "Richard Caswell to William Caswell, May 11, 1775," *Letters of Delegates to Congress*, Vol. 2, 339-340.

51. Smith, ed., "Joseph Hewes to Samuel Johnston, May 11, 1775," *Letters of Delegates to Congress*, Vol. 2, 342.

52. Ibid.

53. Smith, ed., "Silas Deane to Elizabeth Deane, May 12, 1775,"; *Letters of Delegates to Congress*, Vol. 2, 345-346.

54. Harold B. Hancock, "County Committees and the Growth of Independence in the Three Lower Counties on the Delaware, 1765-1776," *Delaware History*, Vol. 15, October 1973 (Historical Society of Delaware), 284.

55. George H. Ryden, ed., "Thomas Rodney to Caesar Rodney, May 10, 1775,"

Letters to and from Caesar Rodney, 1756-1784 (Philadelphia, University of Pennsylvania Press, 1933), 57-58.

56. Ryden, ed., "Caesar Rodney to Thomas Rodney, May 8, 1775," *Letters to and from Caesar Rodney, 1756-1784*, 57.

57. Ford, ed., "Newcastle Committee Proceedings, May 18, 1775," *American Archives, Fourth Series*, Vol. 2, 633.

58. *Pennsylvania Journal*, "December 28, 1774," 3.

59. Hancock, "County Committees and the Growth of Independence in the Three Lower Counties on the Delaware, 1765-1776," *Delaware History*, Vol. 15, 285.

60. Clark, ed., "Governor Robert Eden to his Brother, William Eden, April 28, 1775," *Naval Documents of the American Revolution*, Vol. 1, 242.

61. Ibid., 243.

62. Smith, ed., "Richard Caswell to William Caswell, May 11, 1775," *Letters of Delegates to Congress*, Vol. 2, 440.

63. J. Thomas Scharf, *History of Maryland*, Vol. 2 (Hatboro, PA: Tradition Press, 1967), 178.

64. "Proceedings of the Convention of the Province of Maryland, April 29, 1775," *Proceedings of the Conventions of the Province of Maryland . . . 1774-1776* (Baltimore: James Lucas & E.K. Deaver, 1836), 12.

65. Ibid., 12-13.

66. Ibid., 13.

67. Ibid.

68. Davies, ed., "Deputy Governor Robert Eden to Earl of Dartmouth, May 5, 1775," *Documents of the American Revolution*, Vol. 9, 124.

69. Ford, ed., "Proceedings of the Continental Congress, May 15, 1775," *Journals of the Continental Congress, 1774-1789*, Vol. 2, 52.

70. Ibid.

71. Ford, ed., "Proceedings of the Continental Congress, May 17, 1775," *Journals of the Continental Congress, 1774-1789*, Vol. 2, 54.

72. Ford, ed., "Proceedings of the Continental Congress, May 18, 1775," *Journals of the Continental Congress, 1774-1789*, Vol. 2, 55-56.

73. Ibid., 56.

74. Ford, ed., "Proceedings of the Continental Congress, May 25, 1775," *Journals of the Continental Congress, 1774-1789*, Vol. 2, 59-60.

75., Ibid. 60-61.

76. Ford, ed., "Proceedings of the Continental Congress, May 26, 1775," *Journals of the Continental Congress, 1774-1789*, Vol. 2, 64-65.

77. Ford, ed., "Proceedings of the Continental Congress, May 29 and May 31, 1775," *Journals of the Continental Congress, 1774-1789*, Vol. 2, 68-70, 73-74.

78. Ford, ed., "Proceedings of the Continental Congress, June 1, 1775," *Journals of the Continental Congress, 1774-1789*, Vol. 2, 75.

CHAPTER TWO: SUMMER 1775

1. Ford, ed., "Proceedings of the Continental Congress, June 2, 1775," *Journals of the Continental Congress, 1774-1789*, Vol. 2, 76-78.

2. Ford, ed., "Proceedings of the Continental Congress, June 14-15, 1775," *Journals of the Continental Congress, 1774-1789,* Vol. 2, 89-92.

3. Davies, ed., "Lieut.-Governor Cadwallader Colden to Earl of Dartmouth, June 7, 1775," *Documents of the American Revolution, 1770-1783,* Vol. 9, 162-163, and William M. Willett, ed., *The Military Actions of Colonel Marinus Willett, Taken Chiefly from his Own Manuscript* (New York: G & H Carvill, 1831), 30.

4. Willett, ed., *The Military Actions of Colonel Marinus Willett, Taken Chiefly from his Own Manuscript,* 30.

5. Ibid., 30-31.

6. Ibid., 31.

7. Clark, ed., "Major Isaac Hamilton to Lieutenant Governor Cadwallader Colden, June 8, 1775," *Naval Documents of the American Revolution,* Vol. 1, 632.

8. Ford, ed., "Proceedings of the Continental Congress, June 14-15, 1775," *Journals of the Continental Congress, 1774-1789,* Vol. 2, 99.

9. Michael P. Gabriel, *Major General Richard Montgomery: The Making of an American Hero* (Madison: Fairleigh Dickinson University Press, 2002), 20, 28, 32-34.

10. Ibid., 56, 59, 72, and Berthold Fernow, ed., "Proceedings of the New York Provincial Congress, June 7, 1775," *New York in the Revolution* (1972), 7-8.

11. Gaine, "June 26, 1775," *New York Gazette and Weekly Mercury,* 3.

12. Davies, ed. "Governor William Tryon to Earl of Dartmouth, July 4, 1775," *Documents of the American Revolution,* Vol. 11 (Shannon: Irish University Press, 1975), 35.

13. Ford, ed., "Proceedings of the Continental Congress, June 14-15, 1775," *Journals of the Continental Congress, 1774-1789,* Vol. 2, 109-110.

14. Davies, ed., "Governor William Tryon to Earl of Dartmouth, July 4, 1775," *Documents of the American Revolution, 1770-1783,* Vol. 11, 35.

15. Ibid.

16. Gaine, "July 3, 1775," *New York Gazette & Weekly Mercury,* 3.

17. Berthold Fernow, ed., "Proceedings of the New York Provincial Congress, June 30, 1775," *New York in the Revolution* (Cottonport, LA: Polyanthos, Inc., 1972), 13.

18. Fernow, ed., "Proceedings of the New York Provincial Congress, July 4, 1775," *New York in the Revolution,* 16.

19. Davies, ed., "Governor William Tryon to Earl of Dartmouth, August 7, 1775," *Documents of the American Revolution, 1770-1783,* Vol. 11, 69.

20. Fernow, ed., "Proceedings of the New York Provincial Congress, August 11, 1775," *New York in the Revolution,* 25.

21. Ibid.

22. Fernow, ed., "The Militia Bill . . . , August 22, 1775," *New York in the Revolution,* 31.

23. Ibid., 30, 33.

24. Gaine, "August 28, 1775," *New York Gazette and Weekly Mercury,* 3.

25. Ibid.

26. Ibid.

27. Gaine, "Captain Vandeput to the Mayor and Magistrates of New York," August 28, 1775," *New York Gazette and Weekly Mercury*, 3.

28. Davies, ed., "Daniel Coxe to Cortland Skinner, July 4, 1774," *Documents of the American Revolution, 1770-1783*, Vol. 11, 37-38.

29. Davies, ed., "Governor William Franklin to Earl of Dartmouth, August 2, 1774," *Documents of the American Revolution, 1770-1783*, Vol. 11, 65-66.

30. Ibid.

31. "Proceedings of the New Jersey Provincial Congress, August 12, 1775," *Minutes of the Provincial Congress and the Committee of Safety of the State of New Jersey*, 185-186.

32. Ibid., 186.

33. "Proceedings of the New Jersey Provincial Congress, August 16, 1775," *Minutes of the Provincial Congress and the Committee of Safety of the State of New Jersey*, 189.

34. Ibid., 188.

35. Ibid., 190.

36. Ibid., 190-191.

37. "Proceedings of the New Jersey Provincial Congress, August 17, 1775," *Minutes of the Provincial Congress and the Committee of Safety of the State of New Jersey*, 194.

38. James C. Ballagh, ed., "Richard Henry Lee to Arthur Lee, February 14, 1775," *Letters of Richard Henry Lee*, Vol. 1 (New York: Macmillan Co., 1911), 130-131.

39. Smith, "John Adams to James Warren, July 6, 1775," *Letters of Delegates to Congress*, Vol. 1, 590.

40. Ford, ed., "Proceedings of the Continental Congress, June 14, 1775," *Journals of the Continental Congress, 1774-1789*, Vol. 2, 89-90.

41. Ford, ed., "Proceedings of the Continental Congress, June 22, 1775," *Journals of the Continental Congress, 1774-1789*, Vol. 2, 103-104.

42. Ford, ed., "Proceedings of the Continental Congress, July 11, 1775," *Journals of the Continental Congress, 1774-1789*, Vol. 2, 173.

43. Robert J. Gray, "William Thompson and the Pennsylvania Riflemen," in *Pennsylvania's Revolution*, ed., William Pencak (University Park: Pennsylvania State University Press, 2010), 212.

44. Ibid., 217-218.

45. Hall & Sellers, "June 21, 1775," *Pennsylvania Gazette*, 3.

46. Force, ed., "Proceedings of the Pennsylvania Assembly, June 30, 1775," *American Archives, Fourth Series*, Vol. 2, 1173-1174.

47. Ibid., 1174.

48. Ibid., 1173.

49. "Minutes of the Pennsylvania Committee of Safety, July 5, 1775," *Minutes of the Provincial Council of Pennsylvania*, Vol. 10 (Harrisburg: Theo. Fem & Co., 1852), 282.

50. "Minutes of the Pennsylvania Committee of Safety, July 6, 1775," *Minutes of the Provincial Council of Pennsylvania*, Vol. 10, 283.

51. Ibid.

52. "Minutes of the Pennsylvania Committee of Safety, August 3, 1775," *Minutes of the Provincial Council of Pennsylvania*, Vol. 10, 298.

53. "Minutes of the Pennsylvania Committee of Safety, August 17, 1775," *Minutes of the Provincial Council of Pennsylvania*, Vol. 10, 308-312.

54. "Minutes of the Pennsylvania Committee of Safety, August 28, 1775," *Minutes of the Provincial Council of Pennsylvania*, Vol. 10, 322.

55. B. Floyd Flickinger, "Captain Morgan and His Riflemen," *Winchester-Frederick County Historical Society Journal*, Vol. 14 (2002), 58-59.

56. James Thacher, M.D., *Military Journal of the American Revolution* (Gansevoort, New York: Corner House Historical Publications, 1998), 31.

57. Philander D. Chase, ed., "General Washington to General Philip Schuyler, July 28, 1775," *The Papers of George Washington, Revolutionary War Series*, Vol. 1 (Charlottesville: University Press of Virginia, 1985), 189.

58. Thomas L. Montgomery, ed., "Col. William Thompson's Battalion of Riflemen, June 25, 1775—July 1, 1776," *Pennsylvania Archives, Fifth Series*, Vol. 2 (Harrisburg, PA: Harrisburg Publishing Co., State Printer, 1906), 6.

59. Chase, ed., "General Washington to John Hancock, August 4, 1775," *The Papers of George Washington, Revolutionary War Series*, Vol. 1, 226.

60. Robert J. Taylor, ed., "James Warren to John Adams, August 9, 1775," *The Papers of John Adams*, Vol. 3 (Cambridge, MA: Belknap Press, 1979), 114-155.

61.Claudia L. Bushman, Harold B. Hancock, and Elizabeth Moyne Homsey, eds., "Proceedings of the Assembly of the Lower Counties of Delaware, June 5, 1775," *Proceedings of the Assembly of the Lower Counties on Delaware 1770-1776, of the Constitutional Convention of 1776, and of the House of Assembly of the Delaware State 1776-1781* (Newark: University of Delaware Press, 1986), 186.

62. Ibid.

63. Clark, ed., "Vice Admiral Samuel Graves to Captain John Collins, June 11, 1775," *Naval Documents of the American Revolution*, Vol. 1, 657.

64. Ibid.

65. Clark, ed., "Captain John Collins to Vice Admiral Samuel Graves, September 5, 1775," *Naval Documents of the American Revolution*, Vol. 2, 19.

66. Ibid., 21.

67. Bushman, Hancock, and Homsey, eds., "Proceedings of the Assembly of the Lower Counties of Delaware, August 30, 1775," *Proceedings of the Assembly of the Lower Counties on Delaware 1770-1776, of the Constitutional Convention of 1776, and of the House of Assembly of the Delaware State 1776-1781*, 191.

68. Bushman, Hancock, and Homsey, eds., "Proceedings of the Assembly of the Lower Counties of Delaware, September 2, 1775," *Proceedings of the Assembly of the Lower Counties on Delaware 1770-1776, of the Constitutional Convention of 1776, and of the House of Assembly of the Delaware State 1776-1781*, 197.

69. *Archives of Maryland, Biographical Series*, "Thomas Price," Online.

70. Scharf, *History of Maryland*, 181.

71. Goddard, "Extract of a Letter to a Gentleman in Philadelphia, Frederick Town to his Friend in this Town [Baltimore] August 2, 1775," *Maryland Journal*, 4.

72. Ibid.

73. Ibid.

74. Scarf, 182.

75. William H. Browne, ed., "Proceedings of the Fifth Maryland Convention, July 31, 1775," *Archives of Maryland, Journal of the Maryland Convention, July 26-August 14, 1774* . . . . (Baltimore: Maryland Historical Society, 1892), 6.

76. Browne, ed., "Proceedings of the Fifth Maryland Convention, August 7, 1775," *Archives of Maryland, Journal of the Maryland Convention, July 26-August 14, 1774* . . . ., 12.

77. Ibid.

78. Browne, ed., "Proceedings of the Fifth Maryland Convention, August 14, 1775," *Archives of Maryland, Journal of the Maryland Convention, July 26-August 14, 1774* . . . ., 15-16.

79. Ibid., 16-18.

80. Ibid., 19

81. Ibid., 19-20.

82. Ibid. 24.

83. Ibid. 27.

84. Ibid., 23.

CHAPTER THREE: FALL 1775

1. Ford, ed., "Proceedings of the Continental Congress, June 27, 1775," *Journals of the Continental Congress, 1774-1779*, Vol. 2, 109-110.

2. Chase, ed., "General Schuyler to General Washington, July 31, 1775," *The Papers of George Washington, Revolutionary War Series*, Vol. 1, 202.

3. Chase, ed., "General Schuyler to General Washington, August 5, 1775," *The Papers of George Washington, Revolutionary War Series*, Vol. 1, 256-257.

4. Chase, ed., "General Schuyler to General Washington, August 20, 1775," *The Papers of George Washington, Revolutionary War Series*, Vol. 1, 331-333.

5. Ibid., 331.

6. Chase, ed., "General Schuyler to General Washington, August 31, 1775," *The Papers of George Washington, Revolutionary War Series*, Vol. 1, 393-394.

7. William Clark, ed., "General Schuyler to John Hancock, September 8, 1775," *Naval Documents of the American Revolution*, Vol. 2 (Washington, DC: 1966), 43-44.

8. Clark, ed., "General Schuyler to John Hancock, September 8, 1775," *Naval Documents of the American Revolution*, Vol. 2, 43-44.

9. Ibid.

10. Ibid.

11. Ibid.

12. Ibid., 44-45.

13. Philander D. Chase, ed., "General Schuyler to General Washington, September 20, 1775," *The Papers of George Washington, Revolutionary War Series*, Vol. 2 (Charlottesville: University Press of Virginia, 1987), 17-21.

14. Ibid.

15. Mark R. Anderson, *The Battle for the Fourteenth Colony: America's War of Liberation in Canada, 1774-1776* (Hanover and London: University Press of New England, 2013), 111.

16. Ibid., 112.

17. Chase, ed., "General Schuyler to General Washington, September 20, 1775," *The Papers of George Washington, Revolutionary War Series*, Vol. 2, 21.

18. Clark, ed., "General Richard Montgomery to Major General Philip Schuyler, September 19, 1775, *Naval Documents of the American Revolution*, Vol. 2, 145.

19. Anderson, *The Battle for the Fourteenth Colony: America's War of Liberation in Canada, 1774-1776*, 113.

20. Ibid., 116-117.

21. Ibid., 118.

22. Ibid., 122.

23. Clark, ed., "General Montgomery to General Schuyler, October 13, 1775," *Naval Documents of the American Revolution*, Vol. 2, 430.

24. Ibid.

25. Ibid.

26. Ibid., 431.

27. Clark, ed., "General Montgomery to General Schuyler, October 20, 1775," *Naval Documents of the American Revolution*, Vol. 2, 531.

28. Anderson, *The Battle for the Fourteenth Colony: America's War of Liberation in Canada, 1774-1776*, 130.

29. Ibid.

30. Clark, ed., "General Montgomery to General Schuyler, October 20, 1775," *Naval Documents of the American Revolution*, Vol. 2, 533.

31. Anderson, *The Battle for the Fourteenth Colony: America's War of Liberation in Canada, 1774-1776*, 133.

32. Ibid., 155-161.

33. Ibid., 160.

34. Clark, ed., "Governor William Tryon to Lord Dartmouth, September 5, 1775," *Naval Documents of the American Revolution*, Vol. 2, 23-24.

35. Clark, ed., "Vice Admiral Samuel Graves to Captain Vandeput, September 10, 1775," *Naval Documents of the American Revolution*, Vol. 2, 70-71.

36. Clark, ed., "Vice Admiral Samuel Graves to Captain Vandeput, September 13, 1775," *Naval Documents of the American Revolution*, Vol. 2, 87.

37. Clark, ed., "Governor William Tryon to Lord Dartmouth, September 5, 1775," and "Vice-Admiral Samuel Graves to Philip Stephens, September 22, 1775," *Naval Documents of the American Revolution*, Vol. 2, 23-24 and 178.

38. Clark, ed., "Minutes of the New York Committee of Safety, September 19, 1775," *Naval Documents of the American Revolution*, Vol. 2, 153.

39. Clark, ed., "Governor William Tryon to Whitehead Hicks, October 13, 1775," *Naval Documents of the American Revolution*, Vol. 2, 440-441.

40. Clark, ed., "Governor William Tryon to Whitehead Hicks, October 19, 1775," *Naval Documents of the American Revolution*, Vol. 2, 526.

41. Frederick W. Ricord and William Nelson, eds., "Governor Franklin to Earl of Dartmouth, September 5, 1775," *Archives of the State of New Jersey, First Series*, Vol. 10 (Newark, NJ: Daily Advertiser Printing House, 1886), 657.

42. Ibid.

43. Ford, "Proceedings of the Continental Congress, October 9, 1775," *Journals of the Continental Congress, 1774-1789*, Vol. 3, 285.

44. Ricord and Nelson, eds., "Proceedings of the New Jersey Provincial Congress, October 26, 1775," *Archives of the State of New Jersey, First Series*, Vol. 10, 233-234.

45. Ricord and Nelson, eds., "Proceedings of the New Jersey Provincial Congress, October 18, 1775," *Archives of the State of New Jersey, First Series*, Vol. 10, 218.

46. Clark, ed., "Minutes of the Pennsylvania Committee of Safety, October 21, 1775," *Naval Documents of the American Revolution*, Vol. 2, 558.

47. Clark, ed., "Pennsylvania Evening Post, October 24, 1775," *Naval Documents of the American Revolution*, Vol. 2, 597.

48. Clark, ed., "Minutes of the Pennsylvania Committee of Safety, October 21, 1775," *Naval Documents of the American Revolution*, Vol. 2, 558.

49. Ricord and Nelson, eds., "Proceedings of the New Jersey Provincial Congress, October 24, 1775," *Archives of the State of New Jersey, First Series*, Vol. 10, 229.

50. Ibid.

51. Ricord and Nelson, eds., "Proceedings of the New Jersey Provincial Congress, October 28, 1775," *Archives of the State of New Jersey, First Series*, Vol. 10, 245-246.

52. Peter Force, ed., "Governour Franklin to the Earl of Dartmouth, January 5, 1776," *American Archives, Fourth Series*, Vol. 3 (Washington, 1837), 1872.

53. Thomas Thorleifur Sobol, "William Maxwell, New Jersey's Hard Fighting General," *Journal of the American Revolution* (Online, August 15, 2016).

54. Ricord and Nelson, eds., "Governor Franklin's Address to the New Jersey Assembly, November 16, 1775," *Archives of the State of New Jersey, First Series*, Vol. 10, 283-284.

55. Ibid., 284.

56. Ibid.

57. Ricord and Nelson, eds., "Proceedings of the New Jersey Assembly, November 21-30, 1775," *Archives of the State of New Jersey, First Series*, Vol. 10, 288-308.

58. Ricord and Nelson, eds., "Address of the New Jersey Assembly to Governor Franklin, November 30, 1775," *Archives of the State of New Jersey, First Series*, Vol. 10, 309-310.

59. Chase, ed., "General Washington to Lund Washington, August 20, 1775," *The Papers of George Washington, Revolutionary War Series*, Vol. 1, 336.

60. Ibid., 335-336.
61. Ibid., and "General Washington to Richard Henry Lee, August 29, 1775," *The Papers of George Washington, Revolutionary War Series,* Vol. 1, 375.
62. Chase, ed., "General Washington to Richard Henry Lee, August 29, 1775," *The Papers of George Washington, Revolutionary War Series,* Vol. 1, 375.
63. Henry S. Commager and Richard B. Morris, *The Spirit of Seventy-Six: The Story of the American Revolution as Told by Its Participants* (New York: Harper Collins, 1967), 156-157.
64. Ibid
65. Ibid.
66. Ibid.
67. Kenneth Roberts, ed., "George Morison Journal, September 28, 1775," *March to Quebec: Journals of the Members of Arnold's Expedition* (New York: Country Life Press, 1938), 511.
68. Roberts, ed., "Simon Thayer Journal, September 30, 1775, *March to Quebec: Journals of the Members of Arnold's Expedition,* 250.
69. Roberts, ed., "George Morrison Journal, October 9, 1775," *March to Quebec: Journals of the Members of Arnold's Expedition,* 513-514.
70. Roberts, ed., "John Joseph Henry Journal, October 22-23, 1775," *March to Quebec: Journals of the Members of Arnold's Expedition,* 330.
71. Roberts, ed., "Isaac Senter Journal, October 5, 1775," *March to Quebec: Journals of the Members of Arnold's Expedition,* 203.
72. Roberts, ed., "George Morison Journal, October 25, 1775," *March to Quebec: Journals of the Members of Arnold's Expedition,* 517-518.
73. Roberts, ed., "John Joseph Henry Journal, October 28, 1775," *March to Quebec: Journals of the Members of Arnold's Expedition,* 335-336.
74. Roberts, ed., "George Morrison Journal, October 23, 1775," *March to Quebec: Journals of the Members of Arnold's Expedition,* 515-516.
75. Roberts, ed., "George Morison Journal, October 30, 1775," *March to Quebec: Journals of the Members of Arnold's Expedition,* 524.
76. Roberts, ed., "Isaac Senter Journal, November 1, 1775," *March to Quebec: Journals of the Members of Arnold's Expedition,* 218-219.
77. Roberts, ed., "George Morison Journal, November 2, 1775," *March to Quebec: Journals of the Members of Arnold's Expedition,* 524.
78. Clark, ed., "Samuel Morris to Cadwalader Morris, September 7, 1775," *Naval Documents of the American Revolution,* Vol. 2, 41.
79. "Proceedings of the Pennsylvania Committee of Safety, September 28, 1775," *Minutes of the Provincial Council of Pennsylvania,* Vol. 10, 349.
80. Ibid.
81. Ibid., 350.
82. Ibid.
83. "Proceedings of the Pennsylvania Committee of Safety, October 16, 1775," *Minutes of the Provincial Council of Pennsylvania,* Vol. 10, 370-371.
84. Charles F. Hoban, ed., "Proceedings of the Pennsylvania Assembly, October 24, 26, 1775," *Pennsylvania Archives, Eighth Series,* Vol. 8 (1935), 7314, 7324-7325.

85. Ford, ed., "Proceedings of the Continental Congress, November 25, 1775," *Journals of the Continental Congress*, Vol. 3, 370.

86. Ford, ed., "Proceedings of the Continental Congress, January 22, 1776," *Journals of the Continental Congress*, Vol. 4, 78.

87. Clark, ed., "Minutes of the Pennsylvania Committee of Safety, September 16, 1775," *Naval Documents of the American Revolution*, Vol. 2, 122.

88. Clark, ed., "Vice Admiral Samuel Graves's Order to Captain John Collins, September 17, 1775," *Naval Documents of the American Revolution*, Vol. 2, 130.

89. William & Thomas Bradford, "November 8, 1775," *Pennsylvania Journal*, 2.

90. Clark, ed., "Governor Robert Eden to Lord Dartmouth, October 1, 1775," *Naval Documents of the American Revolution*, Vol. 2, 266.

91. Eric Sterner, "The Connolly Plot," *Journal of the American Revolution* (Online, October 28, 2020).

92. Ibid.

93. Ibid.

94. Purdie, "March 29, 1776," *Virginia Gazette*, 1.

CHAPTER FOUR: WINTER 1775–1776

1. Clark, ed., "Colonel Benedict Arnold to General Richard Montgomery, November 20, 1775," *Naval Documents of the American Revolution*, Vol. 2, 1078-1079.

2. Anderson, *The Battle for the Fourteenth Colony*, 159-160.

3. Ibid.

4. Ibid.

5. Ibid., 167.

6. Clark, ed., "General Richard Montgomery to General David Wooster, December 16, 1775," *Naval Documents of the American Revolution*, Vol. 3, 120.

7. Ford, ed., "Proceedings of the Continental Congress, January 24, 1776," *Journals of the Continental Congress*, Vol. 4, 82-83.

8. Ibid.

9. Lt. Col. Strange, "Historical Notes on the Defence of Quebec in 1775," *The Centenary Fete of the Literary and Historical Society of Quebec*, 1876, 23-24.

10. "Diary of Colonel Charles Porterfield," *Magazine of American History*, Vol. 21 (April 1889), 318-319.

11. Roberts, ed., "John Joseph Henry's Journal, January 1, 1775," *March to Quebec: Journals of the Members of Arnold's Expedition*, 375-376.

12. "Diary of Colonel Charles Porterfield," *Magazine of American History*, Vol. 21, 319.

13. Dawson, "General Daniel Morgan: An Autobiography," *The Historical Magazine and Notes and Queries Concerning the Antiquities, History and Biography of America, 2nd Series*, Vol. 9, 379-380.

14. Ibid., 380.

15. Ibid., and "Diary of Colonel Charles Porterfield," *Magazine of American History*, Vol. 21, 319.

16. Dawson, "General Daniel Morgan: An Autobiography," *The Historical Magazine and Notes and Queries Concerning the Antiquities, History and Biography of America, 2nd Series,* Vol. 9, 380.
17. "Diary of Colonel Charles Porterfield," *Magazine of American History,* Vol. 21, 319.
18. J.M. LeMoine, "Col. Caldwell to Gen. James Murray, Spring, 1776," *The Centenary Fete of the Literary and Historical Society of Quebec* (1876), 62.
19. Ibid., and Roberts, ed., "John Joseph Henry's Diary, January 1, 1775," 378.
20. Roberts, ed., "John Joseph Henry's Diary, January 1, 1775," *March to Quebec: Journals of the Members of Arnold's Expedition,* 377.
21. Roberts, ed., "Abner Stocking's Journal," *March to Quebec: Journals of the Members of Arnold's Expedition,* 565.
22. "Diary of Colonel Charles Porterfield," *Magazine of American History,* Vol. 21, 319.
23. Roberts, ed., "George Morison's Journal," *March to Quebec: Journals of the Members of Arnold's Expedition,* 537.
24. Roberts, ed., "John Joseph Henry's Diary, January 1, 1775," *March to Quebec: Journals of the Members of Arnold's Expedition,* 378.
25. Ibid.
26. "Diary of Colonel Charles Porterfield," *Magazine of American History,* Vol. 21, 319.
27. LeMoine, "Col. Caldwell to Gen. James Murray, Spring, 1776," *The Centenary Fete of the Literary and Historical Society of Quebec,* 62.
28. Ford, ed., "Proceedings of the Continental Congress, January 24, 1776," *Journals of the Continental Congress,* Vol. 4, 84.
29. Davies, ed., "Governor William Tryon to Lord Dartmouth, December 6, 1775," *Documents of the American Revolution,* Vol. 11, 206.
30. Ibid.
31. Ford, ed., "Proceedings of the Continental Congress, December 30, 1775," *Journals of the Continental Congress,* Vol. 3, 466-467.
32. Philander D. Chase, ed., "General Schuyler to General Washington, January 22, 1776," *The Papers of George Washington, Revolutionary War Series,* Vol. 3 (Charlottesville: University Press of Virginia, 1988), 167.
33. Chase, ed., "General Washington to General Lee, January 8, 1776," *The Papers of George Washington, Revolutionary War Series,* Vol. 3, 53-54.
34. Ford, ed., "Proceedings of the Continental Congress, January 19, 1776," *Journals of the Continental Congress,* Vol. 4, 69.
35. Chase, ed., "General Washington to General Lee, February 5-6, 1776," *The Papers of George Washington, Revolutionary War Series,* Vol. 3, 250.
36. Chase, ed., "General Washington to General Lee, February 5-6, February 10, and February 19, 1776," *The Papers of George Washington, Revolutionary War Series,* Vol. 3, 250-251, 310-311, 339-340.
37. Chase, ed., "Colonel Henry Knox to General Washington, January 5, 1776," *The Papers of George Washington, Revolutionary War Series,* Vol. 3, 29.
38. Ibid., 29-30.

39. Ford, ed., "Proceedings of the Continental Congress, December 8, 1775," *Journals of the Continental Congress*, Vol. 3, 416.

40. Ford, ed., "Proceedings of the Continental Congress, January 8, 1776," *Journals of the Continental Congress*, Vol. 4, 39.

41.Ford, ed., "Proceedings of the Continental Congress, January 10, 1776," *Journals of the Continental Congress*, Vol. 4, 47.

42. John Holt, "December 28, 1775," *New York Journal*, 3.

43. Ford, ed., "Proceedings of the Continental Congress, January 3, 1776," *Journals of the Continental Congress*, Vol. 4, 27.

44. Ford, ed., "Proceedings of the Continental Congress, January 2, 1776," *Journals of the Continental Congress*, Vol. 4, 19-20.

45. Ibid.

46. K. G. Davies, ed., "Governor William Franklin to Lord George Germain, March 28, 1776," *Documents of the American Revolution*, Vol. 12 (Shannon: Irish University Press, 1976), 96-98.

47. "Proceedings of the New Jersey Provincial Congress, February 13-14, 1776," and "An Ordinance for . . . the election of Deputies to Serve in Provincial Congress," *Minutes of the Provincial Congress and the Council of Safety of the State of New Jersey*, 366-367, 429-432.

48. Clark, ed., "Captain Hyde Parker to Lord Sandwich, January 6, 1776," *Naval Documents of the American Revolution*, Vol. 3, 653-654.

49. Ford, ed., "Proceedings of the Continental Congress, October 13, 1775," *Journals of the Continental Congress*, Vol. 3, 293.

50. Ford, ed., "Proceedings of the Continental Congress, October 30, 1775," *Journals of the Continental Congress*, Vol. 3, 311.

51. Clark, ed., "Intelligence of Continental Navy, January 4, 1776," *Naval Documents of the American Revolution*, Vol. 3, 616.

52. Ibid.

53. Ford, ed., "Proceedings of the Continental Congress, December 9, 1775," *Journals of the Continental Congress*, Vol. 3, 418.

54. "Proceedings of the Pennsylvania Council of Safety, January 2-3, 1776," *Minutes of the Provincial Council of Pennsylvania*, Vol. 10, 442-443.

55. Ford, ed., "Proceedings of the Continental Congress, January 4, 1776," *Journals of the Continental Congress*, Vol. 4, 29.

56. Ibid.

57. "Proceedings of the Pennsylvania Council of Safety, January 4, 1776," *Minutes of the Provincial Council of Pennsylvania*, Vol. 10, 450.

58. Ford, ed., "Proceedings of the Continental Congress, January 8, 1776," *Journals of the Continental Congress*, Vol. 4, 39.

59. Ford, ed., "Proceedings of the Continental Congress, February 20, 1776," *Journals of the Continental Congress*, Vol. 4, 163.

60. Ford, ed., "Proceedings of the Continental Congress, February 12, 1776," *Journals of the Continental Congress*, Vol. 4, 128.

61. Ford, ed., "Proceedings of the Continental Congress, December 9, 1775," *Journals of the Continental Congress*, Vol. 3, 418.

62. Ford, ed., "Proceedings of the Continental Congress, January 19, 1776," *Journals of the Continental Congress,* Vol. 4, 69.

63. "Proceedings of the Maryland Convention, January 12, 1776," *Proceedings of the Conventions of the Province of Maryland . . . 1774-1776,* 82-83.

64. Clark, ed., "Proceedings of the Continental Congress, December 13, 1775," and "Autobiography of Joshua Barney," *Naval Documents of the American Revolution,* Vol. 3, 90, 1263-1264.

65. "Proceedings of the Maryland Convention, January 1-2, 1776," *Proceedings of the Conventions of the Province of Maryland . . . 1774-1776,* 66-67.

66. Ibid.

67. "Proceedings of the Maryland Convention, January 14, 1776," *Proceedings of the Conventions of the Province of Maryland . . . 1774-1776,* 96.

68. Ford, ed., "Proceedings of the Continental Congress, January 8, 1776," *Journals of the Continental Congress,* Vol. 4, 40-41.

69. Robert Scribner and Brent Tarter, eds., "Northampton County Committee to Captains William Henry and James Kent, February 15, 1776," *Revolutionary Virginia, The Road to Independence,* Vol. 6 (Charlottesville: University Press of Virginia, 1981), 100.

70. Clark, ed., "Naval Committee to Captain William Stone, January 10, 1776," *Naval Documents of the American Revolution,* Vol. 3, 719.

71. Ibid., 720.

72. Clark, ed., "*Andrew Doria* Journal, February 11-18, 1776," *Naval Documents of the American Revolution,* Vol. 3, 1219.

CHAPTER FIVE: SPRING 1776

1. Chase, ed., "Council of War, February 22, 1776," *The Papers of George Washington, Revolutionary War Series,* Vol. 3, 321-322.

2. Chase, ed., "General Washington to Lt. Col. Joseph Reed, February 26-March 9, 1776," *The Papers of George Washington, Revolutionary War Series,* Vol. 3, 370-371.

3. Chase, ed., "Boston Selectmen to General Washington, March 8, 1776," *The Papers of George Washington, Revolutionary War Series,* Vol. 3, 434.

4. Fernow, ed., "Lord Stirling to the New York Committee of Safety, March 18, 1776," *New York in the Revolution,* 88.

5. Ibid.

6. Fernow, ed., "Journal of the New York Provincial Congress, March 14, 1776," *New York in the Revolution,* 84.

7. William Clark, ed., "Colonel Gold Selleck Silliman to Rev. Joseph Fisk, April 2, 1776, *Naval Documents of the American Revolution,* Vol. 4 (Washington, 1969), 626.

8. Clark, ed., "Charles Carroll of Carrollton to Charles Carroll Sr., March 29, 1776," *Naval Documents of the American Revolution,* Vol. 4, 565.

9. Ibid.

10. Clark, ed., "Colonel Gold Selleck Silliman to his Wife, March 29, 1776," *Naval Documents of the American Revolution,* Vol. 4, 564.

11. Clark, ed., "Charles Carroll of Carrollton to Charles Carroll Sr., March 29, 1776," *Naval Documents of the American Revolution*, Vol. 4, 565.

12. Clark, ed., "Minutes of the New York Committee of Safety, March 30, 1776," *Naval Documents of the American Revolution*, Vol. 4, 577.

13. Clark, ed., "Captain Otho Holland Williams to Elie Williams, April 11, 1776," *Naval Documents of the American Revolution*, Vol. 4, 770.

14. Clark, ed., "Major-General Israel Putnam to John Hancock, April 7, 1776," *Naval Documents of the American Revolution*, Vol. 4, 698.

15. Chase, ed., "General Washington to John Hancock, April 15, 1776," *The Papers of George Washington, Revolutionary War Series*, Vol. 4 (Charlottesville, University Press of Virginia, 1991), 69.

16. Chase, ed., "General Orders, April 27, 1776," *The Papers of George Washington, Revolutionary War Series*, Vol. 4, 140-141.

17. Chase, ed., "General Washington to John Hancock, April 25-26, 1776, *The Papers of George Washington, Revolutionary War Series*, Vol. 4, 128-129.

18. Chase, ed., "General Washington to the New York Committee of Safety, April 17, 1776," *The Papers of George Washington, Revolutionary War Series*, Vol. 4, 77.

19. Clark, ed., "New York Provincial Congress to General Lee, February 20, 1776, *Naval Documents of the American Revolution*, Vol. 4, 20.

20. Ibid.

21. Chase, ed., "General Lee to General Washington, February 29, 1776," *The Papers of George Washington, Revolutionary War Series*, Vol. 4, 391.

22. Clark, ed., "Journal of the New York Provincial Congress, March 8, 1776," *Naval Documents of the American Revolution*, Vol. 4, 234-235.

23. Chase, ed., "General Washington to the New York Committee of Safety, April 17, 1776," *The Papers of George Washington, Revolutionary War Series*, Vol. 4, 77.

24. Chase, ed., "New York Committee of Safety to General Washington, April 18, 1776," *The Papers of George Washington, Revolutionary War Series*, Vol. 4, 81.

25. Chase, ed., "General Washington to New York Committee of Safety, April 20, 1776," *The Papers of George Washington, Revolutionary War Series*, Vol. 4, 98-99.

26. Chase, ed., "New York Committee of Safety to General Washington, April 25, 1776," *The Papers of George Washington, Revolutionary War Series*, Vol. 4, 134-135.

27. Chase, ed., "General Washington to the New York Committee of Safety, April 27, 1776," *The Papers of George Washington, Revolutionary War Series*, Vol. 4, 144-145.

28. Ibid.

29. Chase, ed., "New York Committee of Safety to General Washington, April 29, 1776," *The Papers of George Washington, Revolutionary War Series*, Vol. 4, 168.

30. Ibid.

31. Chase, ed., "General Washington to John Augustine Washington, April 29, 1776," *The Papers of George Washington, Revolutionary War Series*, Vol. 4, 172-173.

32. "Proceedings of the New Jersey Provincial Congress, February 28, 1776," *Minutes of the Provincial Congress and the Council of Safety of the State of New Jersey*, 381.

33. "Proceedings of the New Jersey Provincial Congress, February 28, 1776," *Minutes of the Provincial Congress and the Council of Safety of the State of New Jersey*, 392.

34. "Proceedings of the New Jersey Provincial Congress, March 1, 1776," *Minutes of the Provincial Congress and the Council of Safety of the State of New Jersey*, 404.

35. "Proceedings of the New Jersey Provincial Congress, March 2, 1776," *Minutes of the Provincial Congress and the Council of Safety of the State of New Jersey*, 402.

36. "An Ordinance for . . . Incorporating the Minute men lately raised in this Colony into the Body of Militia," *Minutes of the Provincial Congress and the Council of Safety of the State of New Jersey*, 436-437.

37. Force, ed., "New Jersey Committee of Safety, March 26, 1776," *American Archives, Series 4*, Vol. 5, 508.

38. "Directing the Manner of Signing the General Association," *Minutes of the Provincial Congress and the Council of Safety of the State of New Jersey*, 407.

39. Davies, "Governor William Franklin to Lord George Germain, March 28, 1776," *Documents of the American Revolution*, Vol. 12, 96-100.

40. Ford, ed., "Proceedings of the Continental Congress, March 14, 1776," *Journals of the Continental Congress*, Vol. 4, 204.

41. William S. Stryker, ed., "Extract of a letter from an officer in Cumberland County, West-New Jersey, May 6, 1776," *Documents Relating to the Revolutionary History of the State of New Jersey* Vol. 1 (Trenton, NJ: John L. Murphy Publishers, 1901), 97-98.

42. Force, ed., "Proceedings of the Pennsylvania Assembly, March 5, 1776," *American Archives, Fourth Series*, Vol. 5, 676.

43. Clark, ed., "Intelligence of Continental Navy, January 4, 1776," *Naval Documents of the American Revolution*, Vol. 3, 616, and "Commodore Esek Hopkins to John Hancock, April 9, 1776," *Naval Documents of the American Revolution*, Vol. 4, 735.

44. Clark, ed., "Commodore Esek Hopkins to John Hancock, April 9, 1776," *Naval Documents of the American Revolution*, Vol. 4, 735.

45. Ibid.

46. Clark, ed., "Lieutenant John Paul Jones to Joseph Hewes, April 14, 1776," *Naval Documents of the American Revolution*, Vol. 4, 817.

47. Clark, ed., "Journal of H.M.S. *Glasgow*, April 6, 1776," *Naval Documents of the American Revolution*, Vol. 4, 680.

48. Clark, ed., "*Newport Mercury*, April 8, 1776," *Naval Documents of the American Revolution*, Vol. 4, 708.

49. Clark, ed., "Journal of H.M.S. *Roebuck*, May 7, 1776," *Naval Documents of the American Revolution*, Vol. 4, 1447.

50. William J. Morgan, ed., "Narrative of Captain Andrew Hamond, May 8, 1776," *Naval Documents of the American Revolution*, Vol. 5 (Washington, 1970), 15.

51. Clark, ed., "Colonel Samuel Miles to the Pennsylvania Committee of Safety, May 8, 1776," *Naval Documents of the American Revolution*, Vol. 4, 1466.

52. Morgan, ed., "Extract of a Letter from Philadelphia dated . . . May 9, 1776," *Naval Documents of the American Revolution*, Vol. 5, 14.

53. Morgan, ed., "Journal of the H.M.S. *Roebuck*, May 9, 1776," *Naval Documents of the American Revolution*, Vol. 5, 18.

54. Morgan, ed., "Journal of the H.M.S. *Roebuck*, May 9-10, 1776," *Naval Documents of the American Revolution*, Vol. 5, 18, 37.

55. Morgan, ed., "*Pennsylvania Event Post*, May 11, 1776," *Naval Documents of the American Revolution*, Vol. 5, 53, and "Extract of a Letter from Philadelphia, May 12, 1776," *New York Packet*, May 16, 1776.

56. Clark, ed., "Minutes of the Pennsylvania Committee of Safety, September 16, 1775," *Naval Documents of the American Revolution*, Vol. 2, 121.

57. Clark, ed., "Henry Fisher to the Pennsylvania Committee of Safety, March 25, 1776, 7 o'clock," *Naval Documents of the American Revolution*, Vol. 4, 510-512.

58. Clark, ed., "Henry Fisher to the Pennsylvania Committee of Safety, April 1, 1776," *Naval Documents of the American Revolution*, Vol. 4, 618-619.

59. Clark, ed., "Henry Fisher to the Pennsylvania Committee of Safety, April 1, 1776," and "Colonel John Haslet to John Hancock, April 7, 1776," *Naval Documents of the American Revolution*, Vol. 4, 619, 700-701.

60. Clark, ed., "Henry Fisher to the Pennsylvania Committee of Safety, April 1, 1776," *Naval Documents of the American Revolution*, Vol. 4, 618.

61. Force, ed., "Extract of a Letter from the Commanding Officer at Lewes, April 9, 1776," *American Archives, Fourth Series*, Vol. 5, 838-839.

62. "Extract of a Letter from Lewestown dated April 17, 1776," *Pennsylvania Evening Post*, April 20, 1776.

63. Clark, ed., "Henry Fisher to the Pennsylvania Committee of Safety, May 1, 1776," *Naval Documents of the American Revolution*, Vol. 4, 1367.

64. Ibid.

65. Morgan, ed., "Colonel John Haslet to Caesar Rodney, May 13, 1776," *Naval Documents of the American Revolution*, Vol. 5, 79.

66. Ibid.

67. Morgan, ed., "Henry Fisher to the Pennsylvania Committee of Safety, May 15, 1776," *Naval Documents of the American Revolution*, Vol. 5, 108.

68. Clark, ed., "Captain Andrew Snape Hamond to Captain Mathew Squire, February 26, 1776," *Naval Documents of the American Revolution*, Vol. 4, 92-93.

69. Ibid.

70. William Hand Browne, ed., "Council of Safety to Colonel John Hall, March 5, 1776," *Archives of Maryland: Journal and Correspondence of the Maryland Council of Safety . . .* , Vol. 11 (Baltimore: Maryland Historical Society, 1892), 201.

71. Clark, ed., "Extract of a Letter from Annapolis, March 15, 1776," *Naval Documents of the American Revolution*, Vol. 4, 356.

72. Browne, ed., "Proceedings of the Council of Safety, March 6, 1776," *Archives of Maryland: Journal and Correspondence of the Maryland Council of Safety*, Vol. 11, 202-203.

73. Clark, ed., "Captain Mathew Squire to Governor Robert Eden, March 8, 1776," *Naval Documents of the American Revolution*, Vol. 4, 244.

74. Clark, ed., "Baltimore Committee to the Maryland Council of Safety, March 8, 1776," *Naval Documents of the American Revolution*, Vol. 4, 240.

75. Clark, ed., "Samuel Purviance Jr. to Daniel of St. Thomas Jenifer, March 8, 1776," *Naval Documents of the American Revolution*, Vol. 4, 241.

76. Ibid.

77. Clark, ed., "Joseph Smith to Elnathan Smith, March 20, 1776," *Naval Documents of the American Revolution*, Vol. 4, 422-424.

78. Browne, ed., "Maryland Council of Safety to the Virginia Committee of Safety, March 13, 1776," *Archives of Maryland: Journal and Correspondence of the Maryland Council of Safety*, Vol. 11, 242-243.

79. Browne, ed., "Proceedings of the Maryland Council of Safety, April 16, 1776," *Archives of Maryland: Journal and Correspondence of the Maryland Council of Safety*, Vol. 11, 333-334.

80. Browne, ed., "Governor Eden to Carroll, Hall and Paca, April 17, 1776," *Archives of Maryland: Journal and Correspondence of the Maryland Council of Safety*, Vol. 11, 337-338.

81. Browne, ed., "Maryland Council of Safety to Governor Eden, April 18, 1776," *Archives of Maryland: Journal and Correspondence of the Maryland Council of Safety*, Vol. 11, 338-339.

82. Ibid., 339.

83. "General Charles Lee to Samuel Purviance, April 6, 1776," *The Lee Papers*, Vol. 1, 381-382.

84. Clark, ed., "Captain Samuel Smith Narrative of his Conduct, April 26, 1776," *Naval Documents of the American Revolution*, Vol. 4, 1270-1272.

85. Ford, ed., "Proceedings of the Continental Congress, April 16, 1776," *Journals of the Continental Congress*, Vol. 4, 285-286.

86. Browne, ed., "Maryland Council of Safety to the Deputies of Maryland in Congress, April 18, 1776," *Archives of Maryland: Journal and Correspondence of the Maryland Council of Safety*, Vol. 11, 354-355.

87. Browne, ed., "Samuel Purviance Jr. to the Maryland Council of Safety, April 22, 1776," *Archives of Maryland: Journal and Correspondence of the Maryland Council of Safety*, Vol. 11, 363-364.

88. "Proceedings of the Convention of the Province of Maryland . . . May 22, 1776," *Maryland Archives*, Vol. 78, 143-144.

CHAPTER SIX: CANADA

1. Force, ed., "A Return of the Forces of the United Colonies in Camp before Quebec, fit for duty, February 18, 1776," *American Archives, Fourth Series*, Vol. 5, 104.

2. Chase, ed., "General Schuyler to General Washington, January 13, 1776," *The Papers of George Washington, Revolutionary War Series*, Vol. 3, 78-79.
3. Ford, ed., "Proceedings of the Continental Congress, January 8, 1776," *Journals of the Continental Congress*, Vol. 4, 39.
4. Ibid., 39-40.
5. Ibid.
6. Ibid., 40.
7. Ford, ed., "Proceedings of the Continental Congress, January 19, 1776," *The Journals of the Continental Congress*, Vol. 4, 70-71.
8. Ford, ed., "Proceedings of the Continental Congress, February 17, 1776," *The Journals of the Continental Congress*, Vol. 4, 157.
9. Ford, ed., "Proceedings of the Continental Congress, March 6, 1776," *The Journals of the Continental Congress*, Vol. 4, 186.
10. Chase, ed., "General Washington to John Hancock, March 7-9, 1776," *The Papers of George Washington, Revolutionary War Series*, Vol. 3, 423.
11. Chase, ed., "General Schuyler to General Washington, February 14, 1776," *The Papers of George Washington, Revolutionary War Series*, Vol. 3, 313.
12. Chase, ed., "General Benedict Arnold to General Washington, February 27, 1776," *The Papers of George Washington, Revolutionary War Series*, Vol. 3, 381.
13. Ibid.
14. Chase, ed., "General Schuyler to General Washington, March 9-10, 1776," *The Papers of George Washington, Revolutionary War Series*, Vol. 3, 441.
15. Ibid., 442.
16. Ford, ed., "Proceedings of the Continental Congress, March 25, 1776," *Journals of the Continental Congress*, Vol. 4, 236.
17. Chase, ed., "General Orders, April 15, 1776," *The Papers of George Washington, Revolutionary War Series*, Vol. 4, 65.
18. Ford, ed., "Proceedings of the Continental Congress, April 23, 1776," *Journals of the Continental Congress*, Vol. 4, 302.
19. Chase, ed., "General Orders, April 27, 1776," *The Papers of George Washington, Revolutionary War Series*, Vol. 4, 140-141.
20. Force, ed., "Return of the Regiments going on command to Canada, April 28, 1776," *American Archives, Fourth Series,* Vol. 1153-1154.
21. Force, ed., "A Return of the Troops before Quebec . . . March 30, 1776," *American Archives, Fourth Series,* Vol. 5, 1100.
22. Mark R. Anderson, *The Battle for the Fourteenth Colony: America's War of Liberation in Canada, 1774-1776* (Hanover and London: University Press of New England, 2013), 285.
23. Ibid., and Chase, ed., "General Schuyler to General Washington, April 27, 1776, Note 4," *The Papers of George Washington, Revolutionary War Series*, Vol. 4, 150.
24. Chase, ed., "General Thomas to General Washington, April 27, 1776," *The Papers of George Washington, Revolutionary War Series*, Vol. 4, 151.
25. Ford, ed., "Proceedings of the Continental Congress, March 20, 1776," *Journals of the Continental Congress*, Vol. 4, 215-28.

26. Paul H. Smith, ed., "Commissioners to Canada to John Hancock, May 1, 1776," *Letters to Delegates to Congress: 1774-1789*, Vol. 3 (Washington, DC: Library of Congress, 1978), 611.

27. Ibid.

28. Chase, ed., "General Sullivan to General Washington, May 10, 1776," *The Papers of George Washington, Revolutionary War Series*, Vol. 4, 270-271.

29. Chase, ed., "General Thomas to General Washington, May 8, 1776," *The Papers of George Washington, Revolutionary War Series*, Vol. 4, 231.

30. Ibid.

31. Ibid., 232.

32. Ibid.

33. Force, ed., "General Thomas to the Commissioners in Canada, May 20, 1776," *American Archives, Fourth Series,* Volume 6, 592.

34. Force, ed., "Extract of a Letter Dated Montreal, May 17, 1776," *American Archives, Fourth Series*, Vol. 6, 493.

35. Force, ed., "General Thomas to the Commissioners in Canada, May 20, 1776," *American Archives, Fourth Series*, Volume 6, 592.

36. Davies, ed., "General Guy Carleton to Lord George Germain, June 2, 1776," *Documents of the American Revolution*, Vol. 12, 144-145.

37. Smith, ed., "Samuel Chase to Richard Henry Lee, May 17, 1776," *Letters to Delegates to Congress: 1774-1789*, Vol. 4, 21-22.

38. Anderson, 320.

39. Ibid.

40. Robert M. Hatch, *Thrust for Canada: The American Attempt on Quebec in 1775-76* (Boston: Houghton Mifflin Co., 1979), 198.

41. Anderson, 320-321.

42. Smith, ed., "Commissioners to Canada to John Hancock, May 27, 1776," *Letters to Delegates to Congress: 1774-1789*, Vol. 4, 82-83.

43. Anderson, 321-322.

44. Chase, ed., "General Thompson to General Washington, June 2, 1776," *The Papers of George Washington, Revolutionary War Series*, Vol. 4, 428.

45. Ibid.

46. Chase, ed., "General Sullivan to General Washington, June 3, 1776," *The Papers of George Washington, Revolutionary War Series*, Vol. 4, 433.

47. Chase, ed., "General Thompson to Congress, June 3, 1776, Footnote 2," *The Papers of George Washington, Revolutionary War Series*, Vol. 4, 433.

48. Chase, ed., "General Sullivan to General Washington, June 3, 1776," *The Papers of George Washington, Revolutionary War Series*, Vol. 4, 433.

49. Chase, ed., "General Sullivan to General Washington, June 6, 1776," *The Papers of George Washington, Revolutionary War Series*, Vol. 4, 440-441.

50. Chase, ed., "General Sullivan to General Washington, June 6, 1776, Footnote 3" *The Papers of George Washington, Revolutionary War Series*, Vol. 4, 444.

51. Morgan, ed., "General Thompson to General Sullivan, June 7, 1776," *Naval Documents of the American Revolution*, Vol. 5, 408.

52. Anderson, 327.

53. Charles J. Stille, "Colonel Wayne to Dr. Franklin and Others," *Major-General Anthony Wayne and the Pennsylvania Line in the Continental Army* (Port Washington, NY: Kennikat Press, 1968), 29, and Force, ed., "Extract of a Letter from the Camp at the Mouth of the Sorel, June 12, 1776," *American Archives, Series 4*, Vol. 6, 826.

54. Chase, ed., "General Sullivan to General Washington, June 12," *The Papers of George Washington, Revolutionary War Series*, Vol. 4, 466.

55. Morgan, ed., "Captain Henry Harvey to Captain Charles Douglas, June 11, 1776," *Naval Documents of the American Revolution*, Vol. 5, 467.

56. Stille, "Colonel Wayne to Dr. Franklin and Others," *Major-General Anthony Wayne and the Pennsylvania Line in the Continental Army*, 29.

57. Ibid.

58. Morgan, ed., "Captain Henry Harvey to Captain Charles Douglas, June 11, 1776," *Naval Documents of the American Revolution*, Vol. 5, 467.

59. Stille, "Colonel Wayne to Dr. Franklin and Others," *Major-General Anthony Wayne and the Pennsylvania Line in the Continental Army*, 30.

60. Force, ed., "Extract of a Letter from the Camp at the Mouth of the Sorel, dated June 12, 1776," *American Archives, Fourth Series*, Vol. 6, 826-827.

61. Ibid., 827.

62. Anderson, 329.

63. Force, ed., "Extract of a Letter from the Camp at the Mouth of the Sorel, dated June 12, 1776," *American Archives, Fourth Series*, Vol. 6, 827.

64. Ibid.

65. Ibid.

66. Ibid.

67. Davies, ed., "General Guy Carleton to Lord George Germain, June 20, 1776," *Documents of the American Revolution*, Vol. 12, 152.

68. Morgan, ed., "General Arnold to General Sullivan, June 10, 1776," *Naval Documents of the American Revolution*, Vol. 5, 443-444.

69. Force, ed., "A Return of the Continental Forces in Canada, June 12, 1776," *American Archives, Fourth Series*, Vol. 6, 915-916.

70. Chase, ed., "General Sullivan to General Washington, June 8-12, 1776," *The Papers of George Washington, Revolutionary War Series*, Vol. 4, 466.

71. Force, ed., "General Schuyler to General Sullivan, June 20, 1776," *American Archives, Fourth Series*, Vol. 6, 997.

72. Ibid.

73. Philander D. Chase, ed., "General Sullivan to General Washington, July 2, 1776," *The Papers of George Washington, Revolutionary War Series*, Vol. 5 (Charlottesville: University Press of Virginia, 1993), 186-187.

CHAPTER SEVEN: SUMMER 1776

1. Ford, ed., "Proceedings of the Continental Congress, May 15, 1776," *Journals of the Continental Congress*, Vol. 4, 357-358.

2. Ibid.

3. Ford, ed., "Proceedings of the Continental Congress, May 10, 1776," *Journals of the Continental Congress*, Vol. 4, 342.

4. Smith, ed., "John Adams to Horatio Gates, March 23, 1776," *Letters of Delegates to Congress*, Vol. 3, 431.

5. Ibid.

6. Brent Tarter, ed., "Proceedings of the 5th Virginia Convention, May 15, 1776," *Revolutionary Virginia: The Road to Independence*, Vol. 7, Part 1 (Charlottesville: University Press of Virginia, 1983), 143.

7. Force, ed., "Proceedings of the New York Provincial Congress, May 27, 1776," *American Archives, Fourth Series*, Vol. 5, 1337-1338.

8. Smith, ed., "James Duane to John Jay, May 18, 1776," *Letters of Delegates to Congress*, Vol. 4, 34-35.

9. Smith, ed., "New York Delegates to the New York Convention, June 8, 1776," *Letters of Delegates to Congress*, Vol. 4, 171.

10. Force, ed., "Proceedings of the New York Provincial Congress, June 11, 1776," *American Archives, Fourth Series*, Vol. 6, 1395.

11. Smith, ed., "John Adams to Cotton Tufts, June 23, 1776," *Letters of Delegates to Congress*, Vol. 4, 298.

12. Smith, ed., "John Adams to William Tudor, June 24, 1776," *Letters of Delegates to Congress*, Vol. 4, 306.

13. Ford, ed., "Proceedings of the Continental Congress, June 3, 1776," *Journals of the Continental Congress*, Vol. 4, 412, and Lesser, "General Return of the Army . . . Commanded by his Excellency George Washington, May 19, 1776," *Sinews of Independence*, 22.

14. Ford, ed., "Proceedings of the Continental Congress, June 3, 1776," *Journals of the Continental Congress*, Vol. 4, 412-413.

15. Force, ed., "Proceedings of the New York Provincial Congress, June 7, 1776," *American Archives, Fourth Series*, Vol. 6, 1382.

16. Force, ed., "Proceedings of the New York Provincial Congress, June 9, 1776," *American Archives, Fourth Series*, Vol. 6, 1387.

17. Smith, ed., "John Hancock to Certain Colonies, June 11, 1776," *Letters of the Continental Congress*, Vol. 5, 189.

18. Ibid.

19. Ford, ed., "Proceedings of the Continental Congress, June 11, 1776," *Journals of the Continental Congress*, Vol. 5, 431.

20. Chase, ed., "General Washington to John Hancock, June 10, 1776," *The Papers of George Washington, Revolutionary War Series*, Vol. 4, 487-488.

21. Ibid.

22. Chase, ed., "General Washington to John Hancock, June 28, 1776," *The Papers of George Washington, Revolutionary War Series*, Vol. 5, 134-135.

23. Bradford, "New York, June 26, 1776," *Pennsylvania Journal and Weekly Advertiser*, 2.

24. Chase, ed., "General Washington to John Hancock, June 30, 1776," *The Papers of George Washington, Revolutionary War Series*, Vol. 5, 160.

25. Lesser, ed., "General Return of the Army in the Service of . . . His Excellency George Washington, June 29, 1776," *Sinews of Independence*, 25.

26. Ibid.

27. "Proceedings of the New Jersey Congress, June 14, 1776," *Provincial Congress and the Council of Safety of the State of New Jersey*, 454-456.

28. Ibid., 457-458.

29. "Proceedings of the New Jersey Congress, June 18, 1776," *Provincial Congress and the Council of Safety of the State of New Jersey*, 461.

30. Ibid., 462.

31. "Proceedings of the New Jersey Congress, June 21, 1776," *Provincial Congress and the Council of Safety of the State of New Jersey*, 470.

32. Ford, ed., "Proceedings of the Continental Congress, June 24, 1776," *Journals of the Continental Congress*, Vol. 5, 473.

33. "Proceedings of the New Jersey Congress, June 21, 1776," *Provincial Congress and the Council of Safety of the State of New Jersey*, 471.

34. Ibid., 473.

35. Smith, ed., "John Adams to Samuel Chase, June 14, 1776," *Letters of Delegates to Congress*, Vol. 4, 210.

36. Morgan, ed., "Captain Lambert Wickes to Samuel Wickes, July 2, 1776," *Naval Documents of the American Revolution*, Vol. 5, 882-883.

37. Ibid., 883.

38. Gaine, "Extract of a Letter from Philadelphia, July 15, 1776," *The New York Gazette and Weekly Mercury*, 3.

39. Morgan, ed., "Captain Lambert Wickes to Samuel Wickes, July 2, 1776," *Naval Documents of the American Revolution*, Vol. 5, 88-883.

40. Gaine, "Extract of a Letter from Philadelphia, July 15, 1776," *The New York Gazette and Weekly Mercury*, 3.

41. Ibid.

42. Morgan, ed., "Journals of the HMS *Kingfisher* and HMS *Orpheus*, June 29, 1776," *Naval Documents of the American Revolution*, Vol. 5, 817-818, and Morgan, ed., "Captain Lambert Wickes to Samuel Wickes, July 2, 1776," *Naval Documents of the American Revolution*, Vol. 5, 883.

43. "Proceedings of the New Jersey Congress, June 29, 1776," *Provincial Congress and the Council of Safety of the State of New Jersey*, 484.

44. Lesser, ed., "Return of the Army . . . Commanded by his Excellency George Washington, July 27, 1776," *Sinews of Independence*, 26.

45. Force, ed., "To the Honourable the Continental Congress: The Memorial of the Committee of Safety of the Province of Pennsylvania, May 21, 1776," *American Archives, Fourth Series*, Vol. 6, 660-661.

46. Ibid.

47. Ford, ed., "Proceedings of the Continental Congress, June 14, 1776," *Journals of the Continental Congress*, Vol. 5, 443.

48. Gaine, "Philadelphia, May 22, 1776," *The New York Gazette and Weekly Mercury*, 2.

49. Charles F. Hoban, ed., "Proceedings of the Pennsylvania Assembly, April 6, 1776," *Pennsylvania State Archives, Series 8*, Vol. 8 (Department of Property and Supplies, 1935), 7513.

50. Hoban, ed., "Proceedings of the Pennsylvania Assembly, May 22, 1776," *Pennsylvania State Archives, Series 8*, 7516.

51. Hoban, ed., "Proceedings of the Pennsylvania Assembly, June 5, 1776," *Pennsylvania State Archives, Series 8*, 7535.
52. Hoban, ed., "Proceedings of the Pennsylvania Assembly, June 7-8, 1776," *Pennsylvania State Archives, Series 8*, 7539.
53. Hoban, ed., "Instructions to the Delegates of this Province in Congress, June 13, 1776," *Pennsylvania State Archives, Series 8*, 7542-43.
54. Ibid.
55. Force, ed., "Proceedings of the Provincial Conference of Committees of the Province of Pennsylvania, June 18-19, 1776," *American Archives, Fourth Series*, Vol. 6, 951-953.
56. Force, ed., "Proceedings of the Provincial Conference of Committees of the Province of Pennsylvania, June 21, 1776," *American Archives, Fourth Series*, Vol. 6, 954.
57. Force, ed., "Proceedings of the Provincial Conference of Committees of the Province of Pennsylvania, June 23, 1776," *American Archives, Fourth Series*, Vol. 6, 961.
58. Force, ed., "Proceedings of the Provincial Conference of Committees of the Province of Pennsylvania, June 24 1776," *American Archives, Fourth Series*, Vol. 6, 962-963.
59. Hancock, *The Delaware Loyalists*, 11.
60. Ryden, ed., "John Haslett to Caesar Rodney, May, 1776," *Letters to and from Caesar Rodney, 1765-1784*, 87.
61. Ibid.
62. Ryden, ed., "Thomas Rodney to Caesar Rodney, May 26, 1776," *Letters to and from Caesar Rodney, 1765-1784*, 84.
63. Ibid.
64. Hancock, *The Delaware Loyalists*, 13.
65. Ryden, ed., "John Haslett to Caesar Rodney, June 5, 1776," *Letters to and from Caesar Rodney, 1765-1784*, 88.
66. Henry Hobart Bellas, ed., *Personal Recollections of Captain Enoch Anderson, an Officer of the Delaware Regiments in the Revolutionary War* (Wilmington: The Historical Society of Delaware, 1896), 9-10.
67. Hancock, *The Delaware Loyalists*, 13.
68. Bellas, ed., *Personal Recollections of Captain Enoch Anderson, an Officer of the Delaware Regiments in the Revolutionary War*, 10.
69. Hancock, *The Delaware Loyalists*, 13.
70. Bellas, ed., *Personal Recollections of Captain Enoch Anderson, an Officer of the Delaware Regiments in the Revolutionary War*, 13-14.
71. Force, ed., "Thomas McKean to President of Congress, June 13, 1776, half past 2 o'clock A.M.," *American Archives, Fourth Series*, Vol. 6, 833.
72. Force, ed., "Thomas McKean to President of Congress, June 13, 1776, 7 o'clock P.M.," *American Archives, Fourth Series*, Vol. 6, 833.
73. Ibid.
74. Ford, ed., "Proceedings of the Continental Congress, June 13, 1776," *Journals of the Continental Congress*, Vol. 5, 436.

75. Bellas, ed., *Personal Recollections of Captain Enoch Anderson, an Officer of the Delaware Regiments in the Revolutionary War*, 16.
76. Force, ed., "Proceedings of the Delaware Assembly, June 15, 1776," *American Archives, Fourth Series*, Vol. 6, 884.
77. Ryden, ed., "Instructions to the Deputies . . . ., June 15, 1776," *Letters to and from Caesar Rodney, 1765-1784*, 92.
78. Smith, ed., "John Adams to Samuel Chase, June 14, 1776," *Letters of Delegates to Congress*, Vol 4., 210.
79. Ibid.
80. "Proceedings of the Convention of the Province of Maryland . . . May 15, 1776," *Maryland Archives*, Vol. 78, 134.
81. "Proceedings of the Convention of the Province of Maryland . . . May 21, 1776," *Maryland Archives*, Vol. 78, 141-142.
82. "Proceedings of the Maryland Convention, January 12, 1776," *Maryland Archives*, Vol. 78, 82-83.
83. Smith, ed., "John Adams to James Warren, May 20, 1776," *Letters of Delegates to Congress*, Vol. 4, 40.
84. Smith, ed., "Richard Henry Lee to Charles Lee, May 27, 1776," *Letters of Delegates to Congress*, Vol. 4, 86.
85. "Proceedings of the Convention of the Province of Maryland . . . May 22, 1776," *Maryland Archives*, Vol. 78, 151-152.
86. Morgan, ed., "Journal of HMS *Fowey*, June 23, 1776," *Naval Documents of the American Revolution*, Vol. 5, 699.
87. "Proceedings of the Convention of the Province of Maryland . . . May 25, 1776," *Maryland Archives*, Vol. 78, 156.
88. Browne, ed., "Council to Hancock, June 10, 1776," *Archives of Maryland: Journal and Correspondence of the Maryland Council of Safety*, Vol. 11, 475.
89. "Proceedings of the Convention of the Province of Maryland . . . June 25, 1776," *Maryland Archives*, Vol. 78, 170.
90. "Proceedings of the Convention of the Province of Maryland . . . June 28, 1776," *Maryland Archives*, Vol. 78, 176.
91. Smith, ed., "Thomas Jefferson's Notes of Proceedings in Congress, June 7-28, 1776," *Letters of Delegates to Congress*, Vol. 4, 160.
92. Smith, ed., "John Adams to Samuel Chase, July 1, 1776," *Letters of Delegates to Congress*, Vol. 4, 347.
93. Ibid.
94. Smith, ed., "New York Delegates to the New York Provincial Congress, July 2, 1776," *Letters of Delegates to Congress*, Vol. 4, 371-372.
95. Peter Force, ed., "Proceedings of the New York Provincial Congress, July 9, 1776," *American Archives, Fifth Series*, Vol. 1 (Washington, DC: M. St. Clair Clark and Peter Force, 1843), 1391.
96. Ford, ed., "Proceedings of the Continental Congress, July 4, 1776," *Journals of the Continental Congress*, Vol. 5, 516.
97. Ibid., Footnote 1, 516.
98. Force, ed., *American Archives, Fifth Series*, Vol. 1, 119.

99. Alexander Purdie, "Trenton, July 26, 1776," *Virginia Gazette*, 2.
100. Ibid.
101. Ibid.
102. Force, ed., *American Archives, Fifth Series*, Vol. 1, 633.
103. Bellas, ed., *Personal Recollections of Captain Enoch Anderson, an Officer of the Delaware Regiments in the Revolutionary War*, 20.

CHAPTER EIGHT: THE FALL OF NEW YORK CITY
1. Chase, ed., "General Washington to John Hancock, June 29, 1776," *The Papers of George Washington: Revolutionary War Series*, Vol. 5, 148.
2. Chase, ed., "General Washington to John Hancock, June 30, 1776," *The Papers of George Washington: Revolutionary War Series*, Vol. 5, 160.
3. Ibid.
4. Chase, ed., "General Orders, June 30, 1776," *The Papers of George Washington: Revolutionary War Series,* Vol. 5, 155.
5. Chase, ed., "General Nathanael Greene, July 5, 1776," *The Papers of George Washington: Revolutionary War Series,* Vol. 5, 212.
6. Ibid.
7. Morgan, ed., "Journal of HMS *Phoenix*, July 3, 1776," *Naval Documents of the American Revolution*, Vol. 5, 895.
8. Chase, ed., "General Washington to General William Livingston, July 6, 1776," *The Papers of George Washington: Revolutionary War Series,* Vol. 5, 224.
9. Chase, ed., "General Washington to the Commanding Officer of the Pennsylvania Troops, July 14, 1776," *The Papers of George Washington: Revolutionary War Series,* Vol. 5, 315.
10. Force, ed., "A General Return of the Troops in New-Jersey, under . . . Brig. Gen. Mercer, July 25, 1776," *American Archives, Fifth Series*, Vol. 1, 574.
11. Edward Tatum, Jr., "July 14, 1776," *The American Journal of Ambrose Serle* (New York: New York Times & Arno Press, 1969), 32-33.
12. Chase, ed., "Memorandum of an Interview with Lieutenant Colonel James Paterson, July 20, 1776," *The Papers of George Washington: Revolutionary War Series,* Vol. 5, 398.
13. Ibid., 400-401.
14. Chase, ed., "General Washington to John Augustine Washington, July 22, 1776," *The Papers of George Washington: Revolutionary War Series,* Vol. 5, 428.
15. Lesser, ed., "Return of the Army in the Service of the United Colonies . . . Commanded by His Excellency George Washington, July 27, 1776," *Sinews of Independence*, 26.
16. Ibid.
17. Ibid.
18. Ford, ed., "Proceedings of the Continental Congress, July 17, 1776," *Journals of the Continental Congress*, Vol. 5, 571.
19. Ford, ed., "Proceedings of the Continental Congress, June 21 and June 27, 1776," *Journals of the Continental Congress*, Vol. 5, 471, 487-488.

20. Ford, ed., "Proceedings of the Continental Congress, July 8, 1776," *Journals of the Continental Congress*, Vol. 5, 527.

21. Ford, ed., "Proceedings of the Continental Congress, July 20, 1776," *Journals of the Continental Congress*, Vol. 5, 597.

22. Ibid.

23. Ford, ed., "Proceedings of the Continental Congress, July, 23, 1776," *Journals of the Continental Congress*, Vol. 5, 602.

24. Chase, ed., "General Washington to John Hancock, August 7, 1776," *The Papers of George Washington: Revolutionary War Series*, Vol. 5, 606.

25. Chase, ed., "General Washington to John Hancock, August 8-9, 1776," *The Papers of George Washington: Revolutionary War Series*, Vol. 5, 627.

26. Chase, ed., "General Mercer to General Washington, August 9-10, 1776," *The Papers of George Washington: Revolutionary War Series*, Vol. 5, 651, 659.

27. Chase ed., "General Mercer to General Washington, August 11, 1776," *The Papers of George Washington: Revolutionary War Series*, Vol. 5, 666.

28. Chase, ed., "General Washington to John Hancock, August 12, 1776," *The Papers of George Washington: Revolutionary War Series*, Vol. 5, 677.

29. Tatum, Jr., "August 12, 1776," *The American Journal of Ambrose Serle*, 62.

30. Philander D. Chase and Frank E. Grizzard Jr., eds., "General Orders, August 13, 1776," *The Papers of George Washington, Revolutionary War Series*, Vol. 6 (Charlottesville: University Press of Virginia, 1994), 2.

31. Chase and Grizzard Jr., ed., "General Orders, August 14, 1776," *The Papers of George Washington, Revolutionary War Series*, Vol. 6, 18.

32. Chase and Grizzard Jr., ed., "General Washington to John Hancock, August 13, 1776," *The Papers of George Washington, Revolutionary War Series*, Vol. 6, 4-5.

33. Chase and Grizzard Jr., ed., "Proclamation for the Evacuation of New York, August 17, 1776," *The Papers of George Washington, Revolutionary War Series*, Vol. 6, 45-46.

34. Chase and Grizzard Jr., ed., "General Washington to Lund Washington, August 19, 1776," *The Papers of George Washington, Revolutionary War Series*, Vol. 6, 82-83.

35. Ibid.

36. Morgan, ed., "Journal of HMS *Preston*, August 22, 1776," *Naval Documents of the American Revolution*, Vol. 6, 268.

37. Tatum, Jr., "August 22, 1776," *The American Journal of Ambrose Serle*, 71.

38. Ibid.

39. Lewis H. Garrard, "James Chambers to his Wife, September 3, 1776," *Chambersburg in the Colony and the Revolution: A Sketch* (T.K. & P.G. Collins, 1856), 46.

40. Ibid.

41. Ibid., 47.

42. Chase and Grizzard Jr., ed., "General Washington to John Hancock, August 23, 1776," *The Papers of George Washington, Revolutionary War Series*, Vol. 6, 111.

43. Chase and Grizzard Jr., ed., "General Orders, August 23, 1776," *The Papers of George Washington, Revolutionary War Series*, Vol. 6, 109-110.

44. Chase and Grizzard Jr., ed., "General Orders, August 20, 1776," *The Papers of George Washington, Revolutionary War Series*, Vol. 6, 89.

45. Henry Johnston, *The Campaign of 1776 Around New York and Brooklyn* (Brooklyn, NY: Long Island Historical Society, 1878), 142.

46. Johnston, "Major General Sullivan's Orders, August 25, 1776," *The Campaign of 1776 Around New York and Brooklyn, Part II, Documents*, 30.

47. Johnston, "Journal of Col. Samuel Miles," *The Campaign of 1776 Around New York and Brooklyn, Part II, Documents*, 61.

48. Johnston, "Lieut.-Col. Daniel Brodhead to ——— Sep'r 5, 1776," *The Campaign of 1776 Around New York and Brooklyn, Part II, Documents*, 64.

49. Chase and Grizzard Jr., ed., "General Sullivan to General Washington, August 23, 1776," *The Papers of George Washington, Revolutionary War Series*, Vol. 6, 115.

50. Chase and Grizzard Jr., ed., "General Washington to John Hancock, August 26, 1776," *The Papers of George Washington, Revolutionary War Series*, Vol. 6, 129.

51. William Reed, "Joseph Reed to his Wife, August 24, 1776," *The Life and Correspondence of Joseph Reed* (Philadelphia: Lindsay and Blakiston, 1847), 220.

52. Twohig, ed., "General Washington to Major General Putnam, August 25, 1776," *The Papers of George Washington, Revolutionary War Series*, Vol. 6, 128.

53. Johnston, *The Campaign of 1776 Around New York and Brooklyn*, 150.

54. Force, ed., "Colonel Smallwood to Maryland Convention, October 12, 1776," *American Archives, Fifth Series*, Vol. 2, 1011-1012.

55. Ibid., 1012.

56. Johnston, *The Campaign of 1776 Around New York and Brooklyn*, 160.

57. Ibid., 156, 159-160.

58. Ibid., 155-156.

59. Ibid., 156.

60. Ibid., 176-177.

61. Johnston, "Brig. Gen. Parsons to John Adams, Oct. 8, 1776," *The Campaign of 1776 Around New York and Brooklyn, Part II, Documents*, 35.

62. Chase and Grizzard Jr., ed., "General Stirling to General Washington, August 29, 1776," *The Papers of George Washington, Revolutionary War Series*, Vol. 6, 159-160.

63. Force, ed., "Journal of the Transactions of August 27, 1776, upon Long-Island; by Colonel Samuel Atlee," *American Archives, Fifth Series*, Vol. 1, 1251-1252.

64. Chase and Grizzard Jr., ed., "General Stirling to General Washington, August 29, 1776," *The Papers of George Washington, Revolutionary War Series*, Vol. 6, 159-160, and Force, ed., "Journal of the Transactions of August 27, 1776, upon Long-Island; by Colonel Samuel Atlee," *American Archives, Series 5*, Vol. 1, 1252.

65. Johnston, "Brig. Gen. Parsons to John Adams, August 29, 1776," *The Campaign of 1776 Around New York and Brooklyn, Part II, Documents*, 33.

66. Chase and Grizzard Jr., ed., "General Stirling to General Washington, August 29, 1776," *The Papers of George Washington, Revolutionary War Series*, Vol. 6, 160.

67. Johnston, *The Campaign of 1776 Around New York and Brooklyn*, 175.

68. Johnston, "Journal of Samuel Miles," *The Campaign of 1776 Around New York and Brooklyn, Part II, Documents*, 62.

69. Ibid.

70. Ibid.

71. Ibid.

72. Ibid.

73. Johnston, *The Campaign of 1776 Around New York and Brooklyn*, 186.

74. Chase and Grizzard Jr., ed., "General Stirling to General Washington, August 29, 1776," *The Papers of George Washington, Revolutionary War Series*, Vol. 6, 160.

75. Bellas, ed., *Personal Recollections of Captain Enoch Anderson*, 22.

76. Force, ed., "Extract of a Letter from a Marylander, Dated New York, August 28, 1776," *American Archives, Fifth Series*, Vol. 1, 1195.

77. Force, ed., "Extract of a Letter from New York Dated August 28, 1776," *American Archives, Fifth Series*, Vol. 1, 1194.

78. Chase and Grizzard Jr., ed., "General Stirling to General Washington, August 29, 1776," *The Papers of George Washington, Revolutionary War Series*, Vol. 6, 160.

79. Force, ed., "Extract of a Letter from a Marylander, Dated New York, August 30, 1776," *American Archives, Fifth Series*, Vol. 1, 1232.

80. Johnston, *The Campaign of 1776 Around New York and Brooklyn*, 190.

81. Chase and Grizzard Jr., ed., "Lieutenant Colonel Robert Harrison to John Hancock, August 29, 1776, Eight OClock, p.m.," *The Papers of George Washington, Revolutionary War Series*, Vol. 6, 141-142.

82. Johnston, *The Campaign of 1776 Around New York and Brooklyn*, 202-203.

83. Chase and Grizzard Jr., ed., "General Orders, October 8, 1776," *The Papers of George Washington, Revolutionary War Series*, Vol. 6, 503.

84. Johnston, *The Campaign of 1776 Around New York and Brooklyn*, 203.

85. Ibid., 203-204.

86. Johnston, "Brig. Gen. Parsons to John Adams, October 8, 1776," *The Campaign of 1776 Around New York and Brooklyn, Part II, Documents*, 35.

87. Davies, "General Howe to Lord Germain, September 3, 1776, *Documents of the American Revolution*, Vol. 12, 216-218.

88. Schecter, *The Battle of New York: The City at the Heart of the American Revolution*, 158.

89. Chase and Grizzard Jr., ed., "Council of War, August 29, 1776," *The Papers of George Washington, Revolutionary War Series*, Vol. 6, 153-154.

90. Chase and Grizzard Jr., ed., "General Washington to John Hancock, August 31, 1776," *The Papers of George Washington, Revolutionary War Series*, Vol. 6, 177.

91. Ibid., 178.

92. Ibid.

93. Ford., ed., "Proceedings of the Continental Congress, September 3, 1776," *Journals of the Continental Congress*, Vol. 5, 733-734.

94. Force, ed., "Proceedings of the New York Convention, August 28-29, 1776," *American Archives, Fifth Series*, Vol. 1, 1555-1556.

95. Force, ed., "Proceedings of the New York Committee of Safety, September 2, 1776," *American Archives, Fifth Series*, Vol. 1, 1562.

96. Chase and Grizzard Jr., ed., "General Washington to John Hancock, September 2, 1776," *The Papers of George Washington, Revolutionary War Series*, Vol. 6, 199.

97. Chase and Grizzard Jr., ed., "General Washington to John Hancock, September 8, 1776," *The Papers of George Washington, Revolutionary War Series*, Vol. 6, 248-251.

98. Joseph Plum Martin, *Private Yankee Doodle: Being a Narrative of Some of the Adventures, Dangers and Sufferings of a Revolutionary Soldiers* (Eastern Acorn Press, 1962), 34-35.

99. Chase and Grizzard Jr., ed., "General Washington to John Hancock, September 16, 1776," *The Papers of George Washington, Revolutionary War Series*, Vol. 6, 313-314.

BIBLIOGRAPHY

PRIMARY SOURCES

Archives of Maryland, Biographical Series. "Thomas Price." Online.

Ballagh, James C. ed., *Letters of Richard Henry Lee*, Vol. 1. New York: Macmillan, 1911.

Bellas, Henry Hobart, ed. *Personal Recollections of Captain Enoch Anderson, an Officer of the Delaware Regiments in the Revolutionary War*. Wilmington: The Historical Society of Delaware, 1896.

Browne, William Hand, ed. *Archives of Maryland: Journal and Correspondence of the Maryland Council of Safety* . . . , Vol. 11. Baltimore: Maryland Historical Society, 1892.

Bushman, Claudia L., Harold B. Hancock, and Elizabeth Moyne Homsey, eds. *Proceedings of the Assembly of the Lower Counties on Delaware 1770-1776, of the Constitutional Convention of 1776, and of the House of Assembly of the Delaware State 1776-1781*. Newark: University of Delaware Press, 1986.

Chase, Philander D., ed. *The Papers of George Washington, Revolutionary War Series*, Vol. 1-5. Charlottesville: University Press of Virginia, 1985-1993.

Chase, Philander D. and Frank Grizzard Jr., eds. *The Papers of George Washington, Revolutionary War Series*, Vol. 6. Charlottesville: University Press of Virginia, 1994.

Clark, William, ed. *Naval Documents of the American Revolution*, Vol. 1-4. Washington, DC: 1964-1969.

Davies, K.G. ed. *Documents of the American Revolution, 1770-1783*, Vol. 8-12. Shannon: Irish University Press, 1975-1976.

Dawson, Henry B. "General Daniel Morgan: An Autobiography," *The Historical Magazine and Notes and Queries Concerning the Antiquities, History and Biography of America, 2nd Series*, Vol. 9, 1871.

Fernow, Berthold, ed. *New York in the Revolution*, Cottonport. LA: Polyanthos, 1972.

Force, Peter, ed. *American Archives, Fourth Series*, Vol. 1-6. Washington, DC: M. St. Clair and Peter Force, 1839-1843.

Force, Peter, ed. *American Archives, Fifth Series*, Vol. 1-3. Washington, DC: M. St. Clair and Peter Force, 1848-1853.

Ford, Worthington C., ed. *Journals of the Continental Congress, 1774-1789*, Vol. 2-9. Washington DC: U.S. Government Printing Office, 1905-1907.

Garrard, Lewis H. *Chambersburg in the Colony and the Revolution: A Sketch*. T.K. & P.G. Collins, 1856.

Hoban, Charles F. ed. *Pennsylvania Archives, Eighth Series*, Vol. 8. Department of Property and Supplies 1935.

The Lee Papers, Vol. 1-2. New York: New-York Historical Society, 1872.

LeMoine, J.M. *The Centenary Fete of the Literary and Historical Society of Quebec*, 1876.

Lesser, Charles H., ed. *The Sinews of Independence: Monthly Strength Reports of the Continental Army*. Chicago: University of Chicago Press, 1976.

Martin, Joseph Plum. *Private Yankee Doodle: Being a Narrative of Some of the Adventures, Dangers and Sufferings of a Revolutionary Soldiers*. Eastern Acorn Press, 1962.

Minutes of the Provincial Congress and the Council of Safety of the State of New Jersey. Trenton: Naar, Day & Naar, 1879.

Minutes of the Provincial Council of Pennsylvania, Vol. 10. Harrisburg: Theo. Fem & Co., 1852.

Morris Richard B. *The Making of a Revolutionary, Unpublished Papers, 1745-1780*, Vol. 1. New York: Harper & Row, 1975.

Porterfield, Charles. "Diary of Colonel Charles Porterfield," *Magazine of American History*, Vol. 21, April 1889.

Proceedings of the Conventions of the Province of Maryland . . . 1774-1776. Baltimore: James Lucas & E.K. Deaver, 1836.

Reed, William. *The Life and Correspondence of Joseph Reed.* Philadelphia: Lindsay and Blakiston, 1847.

Ricord, Frederick W. and William Nelson, eds. *Archives of the State of New Jersey, First Series,* Vol. 10. Newark, NJ: Daily Advertiser Printing House, 1886.

Roberts, Kenneth, ed. *March to Quebec: Journals of the Members of Arnold's Expedition.* New York: Country Life Press, 1938.

Ryden, George H., ed. *Letters to and from Caesar Rodney, 1756-1784.* Philadelphia: University of Pennsylvania Press, 1933.

Scott, Kenneth, ed. *Rivington's New York Newspaper: Excerpts from a Loyalist Press, 1773-1783.* New York: New-York Historical Society, 1973.

Scribner, Robert, and Brent Tarter, eds. *Revolutionary Virginia, The Road to Independence,* Vol. 6. Charlottesville: University Press of Virginia, 1981.

Smith, Paul H., ed. *Letters of Delegates to Congress: 1774-1789,* Vol. 1-4. Washington, DC: Library of Congress, 1976.

Stryker, William S., ed. *Documents Relating to the Revolutionary History of the State of New Jersey,* Vol. 1. Trenton, NJ: John L. Murphy Publishers, 1901.

Tarter, Brent, ed. *Virginia: The Road to Independence,* Vol. 7, Part 1. Charlottesville: University Press of Virginia, 1983.

Tatum, Jr., Edward. *The American Journal of Ambrose Serle.* New York: New York Times & Arno Press, 1969.

Taylor, Robert J. ed. *The Papers of John Adams,* Vol. 3. Cambridge, MA: Belknap Press, 1979.

Thacher, James, M.D. *Military Journal of the American Revolution.* Gansevoort, NY: Corner House Historical Publications, 1998.

Willard, Margaret Wheeler, ed. *Letters on the American Revolution, 1774-1776.* Boston & New York: Houghton Mifflin, 1925.

U.S. Census Bureau. "Estimated Population of American Colonies: 1610 to 1780," *Historical Statistics of the United States: Colonial Times to 1970,* Part 2. U.S. Census Bureau.

SECONDARY SOURCES

Abbott, Wilbur C. *New York in the American Revolution.* New York & London: Charles Scribner's Sons, 1929.

Anderson, Mark R. *The Battle for the Fourteenth Colony: America's War of Liberation in Canada, 1774-1776.* Hanover and London: University Press of New England, 2013.

Andrews, Matthew Page. *History of Maryland: Province and State.* Hatboro, PA: Tradition Press, 1965.

Commager, Henry S. and Richard B. Morris. *The Spirit of Seventy-Six: The Story of the American Revolution as Told by Its Participants.* New York: Harper Collins, 1967.

De Lancey, Edward Floyd ed., *History of New York During the Revolutionary War . . . by Thomas Jones,* Vol. 1, New York: New York Historical Society, 1879.

Flickinger, B. Floyd. "Captain Morgan and His Riflemen," *Winchester-Frederick County Historical Society Journal,* Vol. 14, 2002.

Gabriel, Michael P. *Major General Richard Montgomery: The Making of an American Hero.* Madison, NJ: Fairleigh Dickinson University Press, 2002.

Gray, Robert J. "William Thompson and the Pennsylvania Riflemen," in *Pennsylvania's Revolution,* ed., William Pencak. University Park: Pennsylvania State University Press, 2010.

Hancock, Harold B. "County Committees and the Growth of Independence in the Three Lower Counties on the Delaware, 1765-1776," *Delaware History,* Vol. 15, October 1973. Historical Society of Delaware.

Hatch, Robert M. *Thrust for Canada: The American Attempt on Quebec in 1775-76.* Boston: Houghton Mifflin, 1979.

Illick, Joseph E. *Colonial Pennsylvania: A History.* New York: Charles Scribner's Sons, 1976.

Johnston, Henry. *The Campaign of 1776 Around New York and Brooklyn.* Brooklyn, NY: Long Island Historical Society, 1878.

Kammen, Michael. *Colonial New York: A History.* New York: Charles Scribner's Sons, 1975.

Kelly Jr., Joseph J. *Pennsylvania: The Colonial Years, 1681-1776.* Garden City, NY: Doubleday, 1980.

Land, Aubrey C. *Colonial Maryland: A History*. Millwood, NY: KTO Press, 1981.

McSherry, James. *History of Maryland*. Baltimore: Baltimore Book Co., 1904.

Montgomery Thomas L., ed. "Col. William Thompson's Battalion of Riflemen, June 25, 1775—July 1, 1776," *Pennsylvania Archives, Fifth Series*, Vol. 2. Harrisburg, PA: Harrisburg Publishing Co., State Printer, 1906.

Munroe, John A. *Colonial Delaware: A History*. Millwood, NY: KTO Press, 1978.

_____. *Federalist Delaware, 1775-1815*. New Brunswick, NJ: Rutgers University Press, 1954.

_____. *History of Delaware*. Newark, NJ: University of Delaware Press, 1979.

Phillips, Kevin. *1775: A Good Year for Revolution*. New York: Viking, 2012.

Pomfret, John E. *Colonial New Jersey: A History*. New York: Charles Scribner's Sons, 1973.

Rossman, Kenneth R. *Thomas Mifflin and the Politics of the American Revolution*. Chapel Hill: University of North Carolina Press, 1952.

Ryerson, Richard Alan. *The Revolution is Now Begun: The Radical Committees of Philadelphia, 1765-1776*. Philadelphia: University of Pennsylvania Press, 1978.

Scharf, J. Thomas, *History of Maryland*, Vol. 2. Hatboro, PA: Tradition Press, 1967.

Schecter, Barnet. *The Battle for New York: The City at the Heart of the American Revolution*. New York: Walker & Co., 2002.

Skemp, Sheila L. *William Franklin: Son of a Patriot, Servant of a King*. New York & Oxford: Oxford University Press, 1990.

Sobol, Thomas Thorleifu. "William Maxwell, New Jersey's Hard Fighting General." *Journal of the American Revolution*, Online, August 15, 2016.

Sterner, Eric. "The Connolly Plot." *Journal of the American Revolution*, Online, October 28, 2020.

Stille, Charles J. *Major-General Anthony Wayne and the Pennsylvania Line in the Continental Army*. Port Washington, NY: Kennikat Press, 1968.

Stokes, I.N. Phelps, ed. *The Iconography of Manhattan, 1498-1909*. New York: Robert H. Dodd, 1922.

Strange, Lt. Col. "Historical Notes on the Defence of Quebec in 1775." *The Centenary Fete of the Literary and Historical Society of Quebec*, 1876.

Tiedemann, Joseph S. *Reluctant Revolutionaries: New York City and the Road to Independence, 1763-1776*. Ithaca and London: Cornell University Press, 1997.

Valentine, Alan. *Lord Stirling*. New York: Oxford University Press, 1969.

Verenna, Thomas. "Explaining Pennsylvania's Militia." *Journal of the American Revolution*, June 17, 2014.

Ward, Harry M. *General William Maxwell and the New Jersey Continentals*. Westport, CT: Greenwood Press, 1997.

Wildes, Harry E. *Anthony Wayne: Trouble Shooter of the American Revolution*. Westport, CT: Greenwood Press, 1969.

Willett, William M., ed. *The Military Actions of Colonel Marinus Willett, Taken Chiefly from his Own Manuscript*. New York: G. & H. Carvill, 1831.

Wirt, William. *Sketches in the Life and Character of Patrick Henry*. Philadelphia, 1817.

NEWSPAPERS

Bradford, *Pennsylvania Journal*, December 28, 1774.

Bradford, *Pennsylvania Journal*, November 8, 1775.

Bradford, *Pennsylvania Journal*, June 26, 1776.

Dunlap, *Pennsylvania Packet*, June 27, 1774.

Dunlap, *Pennsylvania Packet* August 1, 1774, Supplement.

Gaine, *New York Gazette and Weekly Mercury*, July 11, 1774.

Gaine, *New York Gazette and Weekly Mercury*, August 8, 1774.

Gaine, *New York Gazette and Weekly Mercury*, June 26, 1775.

Gaine, *New York Gazette and Weekly Mercury*, July 3, 1775.

Gaine, *New York Gazette and Weekly Mercury*, August 28, 1775.

Gaine, *New York Gazette and Weekly Mercury*, May 22, 1776.

Gaine, *New York Gazette and Weekly Mercury*, July 15, 1776.

Goddard, *Maryland Journal*, May 17, 1775.

Goddard, *Maryland Journal*, August 2, 1775.

Hall and Sellers, *Pennsylvania Gazette*, May 3, 1775.

Hall and Sellers, *Pennsylvania Gazette*, June 21, 1775.

Loudon, *New York Packet*, May 16, 1776.

Purdie, *Virginia Gazette*, March 29, 1776.

Purdie, *Virginia Gazette*, July 26, 1776.

Purdie and Dixon, *Virginia Gazette*, July 21, 1774.

Purdie and Dixon, *Virginia Gazette*, October 27, 1774.

Towne, *Pennsylvania Evening Post*, April 25, 1775.

Towne, *Pennsylvania Evening Post*, April 20, 1776.

ACKNOWLEDGMENTS

I LEARNED LONG AGO THAT WRITING IS A TEAM EFFORT AND I AM, as always, very grateful to the wonderful staff at the *Journal of the American Revolution* and Westholme Publishing for all their assistance with this book. As editor of JAR, Don N. Hagist oversees the publication of numerous articles and books on the American Revolution and we should all be thankful, as am I, for his dedication and hard work. Thanks, too, to my copy editor Allison Schaeffer, Trudi Gershenov for producing another outstanding book design, and proofreader Mike Kopf. Tracy Dugan created all the great maps in the book, and publisher Bruce H. Franklin guided the entire process and offered helpful suggestions.

The resources of the Rockefeller Library at Colonial Williamsburg were the wellspring for my research for the book and the staff there, as always, very welcoming and helpful. I continue to be thankful that such an oasis of historical research as the "Rock" exists so close to where I live in Williamsburg.

Lastly, the talented and wonderful people at Colonial Williamsburg and my friends in the Revolutionary War reenacting community continue to inspire me to learn more about this amazing time in American history and I remain ever grateful for their help and support.

INDEX

Third Provincial Congress, 80
3rd Virginia Regiment, 151
Thomas, John, 111-118
Thompson, William, 13, 30-33, 56,
    82, 90, 112, 118, 120-123
Three Rivers, 115-116, 118, 120-
    125
Tories, 26-27, 37, 64-65, 76-77, 80,
    84, 91, 103, 128, 131-132,
    140-142, 149
Tryall, 35
Tryon, William, xii, 22-23, 48-50,
    76, 78, 120, 131

Vandeput, George, 24, 26, 48-49
Vandervoort, Peter, 4-5
van Schaick, Goose, 23
Viper, 51
Virginia, 83
Virginia State Navy, 107

Warner, Seth, 7, 24, 44, 47
Warren, James, 34, 145
Washington, George
  appeal to the troops in his orders
    of August 13 and, 155
  appointed to command the army
    and, 19-22
  arrest of John Connolly and, 66
  British evacuation from Boston
    and, 87-88
  British fleet arrives in Sandy Hook
    and, 150-151
  determined to strike at Canada
    and, 41
  dissatisfaction with independent
    rifle companies and, 53-54
  effect of Pennsylvania riflemen
    and, 33-34
  fall of New York City and, 173-
    174
  General Thomas bleak report and,
    113-114
  letters to New York Committee of
    Safety and, 90-91

  orders to disarm the numerous
    loyalists in Tryon County
    and, 76
  peace offerings from General
    Howe and, 151-152
  planning expedition through the
    Maine wilderness to Quebec
    and, 56-57
  plot against and, 131-132
  reinforcing General Schuyler's
    troops in Canada and, 90
  reports of large scale Tory support
    on Long Island and, 77
  report to Congress on the Battle
    of Long Island and, 170
  retreat from Brooklyn and, 171-
    172
  reviewing of troops and, 31
  sending regiments in Canada and,
    112-113
Washington, Lund, 54, 156
Wasp, 83-84, 96, 98
Wayne, Anthony, 13, 31, 81-82,
    112, 118, 120-124
Westchester County, 76
West Point, 49, 78
Whigs, 26
Winds, William, 112, 118
Wolf's Cove, 68
Wooster, David, 76, 110, 113
Wyllys, Samuel, 162, 166